UNDOING SEX STEREOTYPES

UNDOING SEX STEREOTYPES

RESEARCH AND RESOURCES FOR EDUCATORS

Marcia Guttentag
and
Helen Bray

with
Jane Amsler
Virginia Donovan
Gordon Legge
Wendy Willson Legge
Ronnie Littenberg
Sandra Stotsky

McGraw-Hill Book Company
New York St. Louis San Francisco Auckland
Bogotá Düsseldorf Johannesburg London
Madrid Mexico Montreal New Delhi Panama
Paris São Paulo Singapore Sydney Tokyo Toronto

Library of Congress Cataloging in Publication Data

Guttentag, Marcia.
Undoing sex stereotypes.

Bibliography: p.
Includes index.
I.   Sex discrimination in education.   I.   Bray,
Helen, joint author.   II.   Title.
LC212.G87   301.41   76-49036
ISBN 0-07-025380-3
ISBN 0-07-025381-1 pbk.

123456789   BPBP   75432109876

The editors for this book were Thomas H. Quinn and
Janine Parson, the designer was Elaine Gongora, and the
production supervisor was Milton Heiberg. The book was
set in Times Roman by University Graphics, Inc.

Printed and bound by Book Press.

To Caroline Weichlein
in gratitude and affection
for her unfailing warmth and wisdom

Epigraph

Once upon a time there was a man, and his wife cooked. One day his wife said, "I'm tired of cooking," so they switched jobs. She went out to his field to pick corn, and he cooked. He cooked some dough. The dough began to rise and rise and rise. It got on the babies. The babies cried so much that the china rattled. It broke. And when she came back it was a big mess.

Cindy is the only lady mechanic in her city. She works at her husband's gas station. One Saturday Cindy was just sitting down relaxing when this man drove up. He told Cindy he needed a new muffler. After he left, she ran to a pay phone and called her husband. She didn't even know how to fix mufflers. Nobody answered the phone. "What am I going to do?" she thought. For about ten minutes she was worried stiff. When she was about to have a nervous breakdown, her husband pulled in the gas station.

Once there was a boy who all his life was very gentle. He never hit anyone or started a fight and when some of his friends weren't feeling well, he was loving and kind to them. When he got older he never changed. People started not liking him because he was weak, petite, and he wasn't like any of the other men—not strong or tough. Most of his life he sat around thinking about why no one liked him. Then one day he went out and tried to act like the other men. He joined a baseball team but he was no good, he always got out. Then he decided to join the hockey team. He couldn't play good. He kept on breaking all the rules, so he quit the team and joined the soccer team. There men were understanding to him. He was really good at soccer, and was the best on the team. That year they won the championship and the rest of his life he was happy.

O nce there was a lady. She couldn't find anyone to marry so she just had to work alone. She couldn't work at a woman's job to be a secretary and things like that 'cause she just didn't want to. She decided to become a mechanic. She did very well at the job and became president of that working firm and lived happily ever after.

T here once was a woman who thought of herself as a gentleman. But other people didn't think that because she was really bossy. She thought that she was very strong because she could lift heavy things. One day she met a man and said, "I'll have a weightlifting contest with you." So they did. This man happened to be strong, and he won. She said, "Go away." She was disappointed, so she went up to a gentleman and said, "I bet I can be more of a gentleman than you." So they both got a woman and acted like a gentleman, but she liked the gentleman better. So the man won. So she went to find a bossy person to be better than him at that. So all day long they bossed people around. And the woman finally got pretty tired of doing all this, so she decided just to be a woman, and not be strong, or like a gentleman, or bossy.

M aybe she's an enlisted woman in the army trying to play the role of an officer. She's strong physically and in thought she's overconfident in what she's doing because she's one rank over the other men who are soldiers. She's conceited because she made it up to the rank men have and feels she can do just as good a job. She'll work to prove herself. She considers herself masculine in the sense that she's reached a masculine status but she still feels herself feminine.

Contents

Acknowledgments

The entire project was possible only because of the dedicated efforts and informed understanding of Dr. Terry Saario of the Ford Foundation. The research and curriculum development reported were supported by the Ford Foundation. The authors thank the three school systems for cooperating so completely with this project. Many teachers and school administrators contributed in multiple ways to the development of the ideas and methods presented in this volume.

The work reported in this book is the product of the work of many people. Ginna Donovan, Ronnie Littenberg, Jane Amsler, and Marcia Guttentag developed the original conceptualization and research design. Wendy Willson Legge and Helen Bray played important roles in the conceptualization, planning, and carrying out of the research and in the data analysis and writing. Sandy Stotsky was in charge of the entire curriculum development and implementation. Gordon Legge helped to design and carry out the data analyses. There was a working group of Harvard and Radcliffe students who assisted in classroom interviews and observations: Lisa Citron, Stewart Crocker, Dale Lupur, and Kim Hayes deserve particular thanks. Dora Ullian's work on a cognitive developmental view of sex roles stimulated the conceptualization of the age and curricula rationale. Betty Bonatti made an important contribution in her work with teachers and school administrators. Cindy Lanners and Kate Burleigh typed assiduously and contributed their thoughts as well to the project.

The entire project would not have been possible without the dedicated cooperation and commitment of the three school systems, their parent boards, the school administrators, and most especially the teachers who participated in the study.

Marcia Guttentag
Helen Bray

UNDOING SEX STEREOTYPES

Introduction

The educational system is increasingly aware of its responsibility to uphold nonsexist standards for the children it teaches. Sexism in the classroom has become an old-fashioned and unpopular characteristic of the educational process. Administrators, school boards, teachers, and concerned parents are attempting to break out of patterns of differential treatment for boys and girls, which were perpetuated under the guise of preparing boys and girls for different adult roles in society. Recent concern has resulted in the overturning of many obviously sex-biased policies and attitudes. Many school boards have set up committees to examine curriculum, budget, and facilities for overlooked inequities. These are commendable efforts. But will these efforts reach the most sex-role-stereotyped participant in the educational process—the child?

What can be done to make a classroom nonsexist? What works in helping students adopt nonstereotyped views? With the aim of answering these questions, a research team headed by the authors and funded by the Ford Foundation conducted the first major field survey and intervention program for changing sex-role stereotyping in children. In several school systems, at three different age levels, in cooperation with teachers and administrators, using many diverse types of materials, we first measured children's attitudes about sex roles and then attempted to change them toward nonstereotyped perspectives. During the course of the project, much was learned about children's views, about stereotyping in the schools, and about effective ways to change sex-role stereotyping in the classroom. This book is a report of what we did and what the effects were on the children, teachers, and classrooms which participated in the sex-role stereotyping intervention program.

Sex-Role Stereotypes

Many people ardently believe that girls should be frilly and boys should be tough. Why is such sex-role typing wrong? After all, boys will be boys and girls will be girls. Perhaps boys *should* do boy things and girls *should* do girl things. After all, boys *want* to do boy things and girls *want* to do girl things. Why complicate matters? This is the query of more than one parent or teacher concerned that a child may become confused and anxious in the midst of rapidly changing social norms and values. In the past in our society sex differentiation has been the criterion for dividing up tasks and maintaining social order and control. Rituals, myths, and expectations have developed concerning the "woman's role" or the "man's role" which ignore the abilities and capacities of the individual person.

Stereotypes of the content of sex-role standards continue to be quite traditional. In Broverman et al. (1972) an extensive questionnaire survey found evidence of persistent and pervasive stereotypes in our culture, stereotypes which were consistent across groups varying in age, sex, marital status, and education. Commonly shared male stereotypes included such descriptions as independent, objective, active, competitive, logical, skilled in business, worldly, adventurous, able to make decisions easily, self-confident, and always acting as a leader. The stereotypic perception of women was defined by a relative absence of these traits. Women were perceived to be dependent, subjective, passive, noncompetitive, illogical. The positively valued feminine traits formed a cluster which reflected warmth and expressiveness. Attributes such as gentle, sensitive to the feelings of others, tactful, religious, neat, and quiet were included in the cluster. When women define themselves according to society's sex-role expectations, they automatically include many negative aspects of femininity which may lower their own self-esteem (Spence, Helmreich, & Stapp, 1974).

These stereotypic differences are widely accepted. College students portray the ideal woman as less competent than the ideal man, and mental health professionals tend to see mature healthy women as more submissive, less independent, etc., than either healthy mature men or adults, sex unspecified. Women are put in a double bind by the fact that different standards exist for women and adults.

The present study and survey of over 400 children revealed that a surprising number of the children were familiar with the ideal of equality of opportunity for men and women. Yet in many subtle ways they were still bound by the stereotypical image of the strong man and the silly woman. The story below, told to us during the study by a fifth grade boy, began in a liberated spirit. In it a woman functioned admirably in a nontraditional job. But her work turned out to be inadequate, and she was promptly fired:

> This woman works at a gas station and she is now working on the boss's car. She's working on the transmission. She fixes the car good and she's been asking for a raise for a long time. Since she did a good job on the car, he is going to give her a big raise. She thought that was great. Then he gave her an extra bonus and she got to go home and cook a meal because her father was at work where he was a chef in a pizza place.
>
> But when she went home, the boss found a mistake. There was a hole in a gasoline part and it cost him a whole lot of money. But he decided that he wouldn't take off the raise because she did a good job on all the other parts. When he shut the trunk the whole car fell apart. And then he got ferocious and called her up and said, "You are fired." The end.

This story illustrates some of the important issues in sex-role stereotyping among today's children. In the survey of children's attitudes which was the initial part of the study, we gathered information about several of the major concerns which children believe are related to sex roles.

Achievement

With equal rights legislation, jobs can no longer be automatically withheld from women. Children now can see women who work in many occupations traditionally closed to them, like bus driver, doctor, and mail deliverer. The children in our study had little resistance to such occupational roles and quite readily saw hypothetical female characters in nontraditional jobs. Their stereotyping surfaced in the socioemotional roles, opportunities, and attitudes which they believed hypothetical women possessed in nonstereotypical occupations. Usually they told stories in which women had low-status roles (working in a gas station rather than being head mechanic), had little opportunity for advancement or pay raises (unless they fought for it), and were seldom in supervisory positions. Men, on the other hand, were presented as quite successful, and as encountering few obstacles of any sort. Children, however, believed that there was great pressure on men. They believed that men *must* work and *must* earn money, and that men had little flexibility in their family and socioemotional roles.

Competency

Women may have jobs, but they are not very good at them. This myth was prevalent in children's attitudes. They emphasized that a woman doing a "man's job" must be rechecked and evaluated by males who know what they are doing. According to children's beliefs, women also doubt that they can accomplish difficult tasks, fear challenges, and remain reluctant to try new options.

Socioemotional Abilities

The children believe that women are best at being friendly and caring for people. Men, they believe, are not good at doing tasks around the home or taking care of children. The female gas station worker, after diligently working on a car, is delighted, they believe, to go home and prepare dinner for everyone. Women are always viewed in relation to the men in their lives. Children in the study believed that as long as a woman continued to do the "womanly" activities of cooking, hostessing, and child care, she could also work at any job. Men's first priority was work. Their extra time was spent in traditional male leisure-time activities like sports.

The Nonsexist Intervention

The purpose of the nonsexist intervention program was to modify the rigidity of children's sex-role stereotypes. The aim of the intervention was to encourage individual openness and flexibility as boys and girls considered adult occupational, family, and socioemotional possibilities for both men and women. Flexible, non-sex-stereotyped attitudes give children of both sexes an advantage in problem solving, and make it possible for them to take advantage of a variety of learning experiences. For example, curriculum materials were used which demonstrated that women could be competent and skilled at occupations which they had chosen in accordance with their abilities and training, despite stereotyped definitions of such jobs. The enrichment of men's lives, which occurs with an increase in traditionally "feminine" qualities, like sensitivity, gentleness, and nurturance, was depicted in materials about relationships with spouse, children, friends, and peers.

The nonsexist intervention study had the following parts: first, children's sex-role beliefs and attitudes about occupational, familial, and socioemotional roles for men and women were surveyed. Kindergarten, fifth grade, and ninth grade boys and girls were chosen to obtain a wide range of age-related differences in sex-role concepts. With the results of this survey in hand, a survey which showed considerable evidence of sex-role stereotyping, the staff designed nonsexist curriculum materials and nonsexist teacher-pupil interaction methods for use with young children, middle-school children, and adolescents. A six-week intervention project was then instituted in three quite different school systems. It was preceded by teacher training sessions. Experimental and control groups were used to determine the effects of the intervention, and any measurement effects. Following the intervention, children at the three age levels were reassessed for changes in their concepts of occupational, familial, and socioemotional role possibilities for men and women.

Results from the study were intriguing and provided important information about stability and change in children's sex-role stereotyping useful for educators. The findings supported the following generalizations:

- Sex-role attitudes are hard to change in children of all ages.

- Children are generally nonsexist about themselves.

- Children are somewhat sexist about same-sexed peers.

- Children are very sexist about opposite-sexed peers.

- Kindergartners can learn to be occupationally nonsexist.

- Girls are trying to create life-styles that integrate home and career.

- Boys generally disregard or squelch nonsexist values.

- As perceived by children, the male's role is tight, while the female's role is more flexible.

- A little intervention is/may be dangerous; a strong intervention has/can have powerful positive effects.

Findings from the study indicated important age distinctions, critical teacher behaviors, and a number of social variables which influenced the presence or absence of sex-role stereotypy. These are discussed in this volume. The findings of the intervention study point to a sociopsychological model for the explanation of sex-role stereotypy. The findings provide strong support for the potential effectiveness of nonsexist intervention within the schools for children at any age.

The book contains nonsexist curriculum packets which have been evaluated for practicality and effectiveness by use in actual classrooms. Background materials, resource agencies, and bibliographies are provided to help administrators and teachers achieve nonsexism in their classrooms.

ONE

Sex-Role Stereotyping: How, What, Why

Stereotypes about men and women abound in our society. The recent controversy and publicity over the rights of women have caused the blatant myths about the inadequacy of women for jobs and careers to disappear. But the subtle stereotypes have not vanished; they have gone underground. People may not admit that a woman cannot be a mechanic, but they hint that she wouldn't enjoy it. People may not malign a man who works in a nursery school, but they may feel snobbish toward him. These attitudes are misperceptions of the realities of both personality and society.

Androgyny and Male and Female Roles

Many current thinkers believe that traditional prescriptions for male and female roles are dysfunctional in today's fast-paced society. Technology has eliminated many of the tasks which used to require muscularity or extended time. Mechanized tools like vacuums and irons make household activities less tedious, but also limit the sense of fulfillment and skill that a housewife can feel. The barriers surrounding "men's jobs" are eroding. Women, anxious to contribute economically to the family, are taking nontraditional jobs. Women with special skills and intellectual abilities are being called on more often to

9

participate in professional, research, and advisory roles in all fields.

Not only may stereotypical male and female role distinctions be useless for societal reasons, they may also be dysfunctional to the individual. Although the stereotype of the Southern belle may be a bit farfetched, it is just an exaggeration of the view that a woman, hemmed in by the need to be elegant, graceful, and beautiful all the time, can do little to develop her talents and abilities in any useful direction. In the same way, one is mildly surprised when a champion prizefighter is powerfully triumphant in the ring and on the next day can be seen on television feeding his daughter soggy cereal. Yet women are not helpless feminine wisps, nor men hardhearted tough guys. Rather, people are individual blends of capabilities considered both masculine and feminine according to the traditional stereotypes. This is the concept of androgyny: that an adult of either sex can have both "masculine" and "feminine" characteristics.

Sandra Bem of Stanford University has developed a sex-role inventory (Bem, 1974) which allows a person to label him or herself as both cautious and adventurous, both assertive and yielding, i.e., with both masculine and feminine adjectives. People who use both sets of terms are "androgynous." Androgynous subjects were tested by Bem in comparison with strongly feminine and masculine subjects (of both sexes) for their skill in solving a variety of problems.

Bem's hypothesis was that sex-typed males and females place limits on their behavior when they are required to perform sex-reversed activities, and such limits impede their problem solving. For example, females might not think of fixing the plumbing, or a male might not consider squeezing fresh orange juice for breakfast. An androgynous person could adapt more easily to different situational demands by producing the most reasonable behaviors which are required, regardless of whether the behaviors required fall within the usual sex-role stereotypes.

Androgynous people can be situationally relevant in their problem solving. That is, androgynous men can fix a baby bottle, handle a kitten, or iron a shirt, while "masculine" men could not do so, or prefer not to do so even with monetary rewards. Androgynous women can give independent evaluations, use a hammer, and solve an abstract problem, while feminine women are usually too paralyzed to perform any task adequately. Among researchers who study sex-role socialization there is little disagreement that arbitrary decisions about what sex role is appropriate tend to limit the development of any person to his or her fullest potential.

Are Sex-Role Differences Learned or Inherent?

Does being born a boy or girl predetermine certain capacities or predispose the child toward certain abilities? Is the masculinity-femininity issue largely settled at birth by genes and hormones? Or is the boyness or girlness of the individual determined almost completely by input from the environment? Currently, an interactionist view of the nature-nurture controversy is favored. For example, a girl becomes a fine seamstress only if she has an ability for fine motor coordination and also is encouraged by someone to spend time and effort in learning how to sew. This widely held hypothesis suggests that hormones may interact with learning to produce a few sex differences, but very few differences can be found. For example, Maccoby and Jacklin (1974), after reviewing hundreds of studies of sex differences in children, could find only a few behaviors which were different: males were more aggressive and better at spatial and mathematical tasks; girls showed earlier verbal facility.

The study of actual sex differences is important not only for the sake of the curious, detached researcher, but also for people who are involved on a day-to-day basis as socializers of the child. Understanding what actual sex differences are and what sex stereotypes are imposed can help both teacher and parent adjust to children and meet their needs at any age level. In our modern society, geared to materialistic and reputational achievement, it is not strange that major sex differences in attitudes and behaviors occur on the level of achievement/competency. The major arena for this is the school.

What factors in a child's physical, social, and mental development cause boys to be troublemakers in school, high school girls to be incompetent at mathematics, and boys to enter professions and trades while girls with similar abilities and training become housewives?

There are data which show that the brightest women often fail to live up to their intellectual potential and that even those women who do go into the sciences and professions rarely achieve eminence (Rossi, 1964). Horner (1969) has suggested that bright women fear intellectual success because their anticipation of success is accompanied by anticipation of negative consequences in the form of social rejection or loss of femininity. Many girls in high school believe the social myth that boys think "brainy" girls are not fun to be with. Girls purposefully present themselves as bouncy and beautiful, rather than smart. In high school most intelligent girls from elementary school blend into the background category of "good student" rather than "brilliant student." Despite the fact that girls get better grades throughout school, girls' expectations of success are less than their actual achievement behavior, girls are not as accurate or realistic as boys in their self-concept judgments, and both sexes judge boys to do better on achievement tasks (Torrance, 1963).

Cognitively, males and females of all ages are extremely similar. No general difference between the sexes in intelligence has been found (Maccoby & Jacklin, 1974) as measured by tests of ability on motor skills, perceptual performance, and reasoning patterns. Yet, as measured by tests of achievement, girls are distinctively "verbal" in their orientation and behavior at all ages. Girls are verbal earlier than boys; they speak and are more articulate sooner. Boys appear to catch up by age four, but have greater reading problems until about age ten. From ten onward, girls outscore boys on a variety of verbal skills, such as reading comprehension, writing, vocabulary, and relational terms. Verbal skills seem to be more important in the eventual intellectual functioning of women.

Mathematics and science have been the academic areas of male excellence. Girls learn to count at an earlier age, but throughout the elementary years there are no consistent sex differences in skill at arithmetic computation. Boys begin to excel at higher-level mathematics early in high school, and the difference between boys and girls continues to accelerate.

Sex Preferences and Achievement

Children know their gender label by age three (Kagan, 1969; Levy, 1972). By the preschool years they know not only which sex they are but also the behavior patterns, play preferences, and psychological characteristics expected of them (Brown, 1956; Kohlberg, 1966). By age six or seven children can present a clear bifurcation of sex-role definitions. The interests, activities, and attitudes of boys and girls diverge dramatically. In our pilot work, when asked about differences between boys and girls, boys complained that girls didn't play sports or rough games but preferred jump rope or playing with dolls. Girls who do prefer active, strenuous muscular activities are usually considered loners or tomboys with little group support for their preference, even at such young ages.

Children tested at second, sixth, and twelfth grades (Stein & Smithells, 1969) show an increase in sex differences when asked "Do you think this is a more boyish or girlish thing to do?" Younger children agreed with older subjects in areas considered appropriate to their sex, but younger children's views of areas appropriate to the opposite sex were deviant and changed gradually toward sex-role stereotyping with age. Young girls, for example, rated arithmetic and athletic skills as feminine while older girls did not.

Sex-typed preferences affect the achievement patterns on sex-typed tasks. Stein et al. (1969) demonstrated that boys expected and desired less on tasks defined as feminine and their achievement scores dropped, while on tasks defined as masculine achievement scores improved. For girls, the label of "feminine" on tasks did not lead to higher achievement scores, and their expectations of success were low on masculine tasks. Girls are generally found to underestimate their ability, while boys overestimate theirs (Brandt, 1958; Crandall, 1969). If girls underestimate their chances of success and are unrealistic in assessing their abilities, they may fear failure more, or at least derive less pleasure from the knowledge of competence. These ambivalent feelings would be intensified by defining tasks as masculine and therefore inappropriate. How do children learn what is proper and improper, what is expected and refused, what is desirable and undesirable about the masculine and feminine roles?

Theories of Sex-Role Learning

Psychologists have proposed some theories to account for how a child perceives and learns appropriate sex roles. Some of these theories differ critically in the assumptions they make about children and their socializers, i.e., parents and teachers. These theoretical aspects of sex-role learning are important to consider, since believing the tenets of any one system prescribes the types of interactions with children that could encourage or inhibit sex-role stereotypy. Three influential models of sex-role learning are the psychoanalytic, social-learning, and cognitive-developmental models. They are summarized below.

For a long time, the contribution of Freudian and

psychoanalytic concepts forcefully and at times uncritically held sway over concepts of emotional development. In relation to sex-role identity such concepts hypothesize that the young child initially identifies with the mother. This identification is cemented for the girl by an anaclitic dependency and comradeship with the supposedly "castrated" mother. The boy, however, gives up his love and desire for possession of the mother in fear of the father's powerful wrath. The boy chooses to identify with the father and to reject the values of the mother. The major process of learning one's sex role, given these pressing motivations, occurs through direct imitation of the appropriate parent. Although the psychoanalytic explanation seems conceptually unfeasible, there is evidence that children are more likely to incorporate into their behavior actions selected from available adult role models. These actions, however, are not selected only from same-sex parents. Children of either sex are as apt to copy nurturant qualities from the mother's role as powerful qualities from the father's role. Whatever characteristics are shown to be valuable and liked by others will be imitated by the child.

The social-learning model holds that socializing agents differentially reward and punish certain behaviors for boys and girls. Parents positively reinforce those behaviors they appreciate in their children, and negatively reinforce those behaviors they do not value. The concept of masculine and feminine characteristics is fixed in the parents' mind, and actual child behaviors are compared with those ideal sex-role models. Social-learning theorists attempt to locate the exact contingencies, like what behaviors are reinforced, discipline techniques, father absence, etc., which predict children's sex-role attitudes and behaviors.

The cognitive-development theories, on the other hand, suggest that sex-role identity is as much a part of the internal cognitive development as is gender identity.

When a child can label him- or herself as male or female the child will choose to do those things which emphasize maleness or femaleness according to this theory. The development of the concept of sex role that a child considers appropriate remains under the control of internal, cognitive factors. Sex-typed behavior and sex-role concepts parallel the child's conceptual growth and can be predicted by it.

While none of these models alone can account for sex-role stereotypy, the mechanisms they employ (i.e., imitation, learning through reinforcements, and cognitive development) all play a part in the process of learning and accepting sex-typed roles. Children *do* imitate role models, parents *do* intervene and influence children about sex-role-related behaviors, and children *do* believe differently about sex roles for themselves at different ages. The sociopsychological situation of the child, with its social influences, peer pressures, and cultural views, needs to be examined more closely in order to isolate important environmental pressures on children's sex-role attitudes.

Sex Differences in the Socialization Practices of Parents

What are the socialization practices that pull boys toward achievement and girls toward ambivalence about achievement? What actions and attitudes do teachers and parents actually display that encourage boys and girls into sex-differentiated behavior? Few parents or teachers can be criticized for being unfairly sexist in their interactions with their children or students. Yet children absorb and incorporate into their self-assignment and value system information from parents and teachers about appropriate sex-role standards. One way to disentangle these influences is to closely observe the type and extent of interactions between parent and child, and teacher and child.

The most obvious parental socialization practice is direct positive and negative reinforcement. Some parents want their girls to play with dolls and household items and their boys to play with trucks and tools. They encourage the boys to be aggressive and competitive in games and set up times and opportunities for rough-and-tumble play. They may encourage girls to involve themselves in quiet, fine-detail activities by providing elaborate doll house and art materials. The sparse research done on this topic (Lansky, 1967; Fling & Manosevitz, 1972) shows that parents can tolerate girls playing with boys' toys. Both mothers and fathers, however, strongly discourage boys from playing with girls' toys or doing girlish things. They believe it is essential for a boy to preserve his masculinity at every age.

More often parents simply fall into uncritical patterns of supplying children with only sex-appropriate toys and encouraging only stereotypical activities. A parent who is concerned with the fullest development of the individual child may purposefully supply toys considered both "girls' toys" and "boys' toys" so that the child can learn all the skills and participate in all the fantasies that accompany the toys. A boy supplied with a doll, for example, may learn earlier how to be a vigilant and capable father, just as girls learn how to be competent mothers through playing with dolls. When they play, children learn about occupational roles and about possibilities for their future family. Concerned parents should be more closely involved in the games, toys, and television programs their children enjoy and learn from.

A review of the research literature suggests that parents generally treat boys and girls similarly (Maccoby & Jacklin, 1974). Boys, however, tend to receive more intensely directive interactions from parents than girls do. That is, they receive more criticism, but probably more direct praise and encouragement as well. Girls are given more generalized approval, while boys get specific critiques of their behavior, like strong discouragement for cross-sex play activities and toys. These parental behaviors are paralleled by the teachers' behaviors when the children are in school. The teachers' behaviors directly relate to current achievement issues and future plans of the children.

Teachers' Attitudes and Behaviors toward Boys and Girls

Since the avowed goal and personal commitment of teachers is to introduce the children to new skills and to stimulate their thirst for knowledge, teachers probably do not purposefully guide girls into limited future options and boys into more open and fulfilling aspirations. Currently, teachers are well aware of the concerns about sexism. In a survey of teachers from a variety of school systems, across grades and sex of teacher (Donovan, 1974), no teacher reported different feelings or treatment of boys and girls. Yet classroom observations of the same teachers revealed some clear differences in teacher–girl-boy interaction patterns. Unspoken beliefs about sex differences in boys and girls, their future occupational roles, and different parental expectations for the children seem to influence the dynamic interactions between teachers and students, although teachers may not be consciously aware of it.

Many teachers decide that boys and girls have different needs which must be met by differential treatment by the teacher. A recent study reexamined the issue of sex differences from an attitudinal perspective by focusing on how the teacher perceives the preferences of the class and other teachers. Ricks and Pyke (1973) carried out interviews with thirty male and thirty female teachers (age range twenty-five to fifty-seven years) from Ontario, Canada. As expected, a majority (73 percent) of the teachers in the sample reported that boys and girls perform or behave differently. The percentage was the same for male and female teachers. Another item asked whether students expected to be treated differently. Fifty-five percent of the females and fifty percent of the males thought that boys and girls expected differential treatment. A similar percentage indicated that teachers had neither the responsibility nor the right to influence children's attitudes toward sex roles. The rest of the teachers felt that by modeling in such a way as to keep nonsexist role images before the children they would change children's attitudes.

The picture these findings present is one in which teachers, aware that for educators sexism is taboo, nonetheless perceive boys and girls to be radically different, believe they want to be treated differently, and see the teacher's role as one of meeting rather than shaping these "needs." For the teacher to be a model of nonstereotypy is important, but it is not enough. On topics other than sex roles, children in the educational environment are accustomed to receiving directive guidance which provides information about new concepts and skills. Issues of competency, self-confidence, sensitivity toward people, and equality of opportunity are suitable for any classroom and are directly relevant to the discussion of sex roles.

Some studies of teachers' general attitudes toward boys and girls have set up hypothetical instances and asked the teachers to rate them and describe their feelings. For instance, one study (Levitan & Chananie, 1972) paired hypothetical boys and girls who showed characteristics of dependency, aggression, or achievement. Teachers were asked how much they approved of the student (denoting professional values), how much they liked the student (depicting personal values), and how typical the student was (reflecting realistic evaluations). Trends indicated that the dependent male received less approval than the dependent female, and the aggressive male and dependent female were acknowledged to be fairly typical. Teachers like the achieving girl and the dependent girl more than the dependent male. Perhaps in the school situation, where there is a demand for obedience and consistent performance, the dependent girl is the one who listens to the teacher, follows directions, and produces correct papers, becoming an achiever of a submissive kind. This study distinguished between attitudes appropri-

ate to the teacher's job and more personal evaluations of
boys and girls as likeable. The results of this study show
that both direct and indirect expectations and approval are
communicated to the dependent girl. She is liked. The
dependent boy is not. Yet it is independence, not dependence, which later correlates with creative intellectual
ability. Girls who are trained to be dependent grow up to
be dependent women who may demonstrate knowledge
on tests of achievement, but are seldom the innovators
and reformers of ideas or systems. Boys who are pres-
sured out of dependence may grow up to be the thinkers of
original thoughts and the problem solvers in our society.

    Although the direct effects of attitudes on behaviors
are difficult to evaluate, there have been many studies
about the concrete behaviors of teachers and students in
the classroom. These use systematic observational methods in which trained observers code and count specific
actions, e.g., "child asks questions," "teacher scolds,"
or "student ignores teacher." Diverse but significant sex
differences have appeared in many of these studies. One
of the earliest (Meyer & Thompson, 1956) tested the
hypothesis that boys receive more disapproval contacts
with teachers than girls do. In the sixth grade classes that
were examined, this hypothesis was upheld significantly.
A trend indicated that boys also received more praise than
girls did. Jackson and Lahaderne (1967) found sixth grade
boys had more prohibitory, managerial, and instructional
contacts with the teachers. There was a positive correla-
tion among the three kinds of contacts for boys, though
not for girls. Research on verbal interaction at the preschool level (Cherry, 1975) demonstrated that teachers
verbally interacted with boys more than with girls and
were more likely to initiate those verbal interactions.

The Teacher and Disciplinary Action

    Disruptive and dependent behaviors by students and
teachers' reactions to them were chosen as the focus of a
recent study of sex differences in preschool classrooms

(Serbin, O'Leary, Kent & Tonick, 1973). Classroom observations indicated that teachers reacted in a louder and stronger fashion to the aggressive behavior of boys than they did to the aggressive behavior of girls. Perhaps teachers believe that boys cause more disruption and need to be dealt with immediately and forcefully. Or perhaps teachers think they need to yell to make boys listen and behave. By measuring the distance between teacher and children, they learned that boys and girls receive equal amounts of attention *only* when they are very close to the teacher. Boys receive more attention than girls when they are out of the immediate vicinity of the teacher. This teacher behavior indirectly encourages girls to stay near the teacher and emphasizes all the supportive elements of physical contact, including nodding praise, slight helping, and eye contact. Boys who are appropriately at work in the classroom out of the teacher's reach still receive encouragement and attention from the teacher, supporting their adventurous and independent activities. This is a subtle yet powerful form of differential treatment by teachers. It supports a policy of training boys for independent behaviors and girls for socially approved behaviors.

Achieving boys receive substantially more praise and support than normal boys, while underachievers receive substantially more punitive reaction from the teacher (Martin, 1972). Girls fall in between the extreme ranges of praise and punishment given the boys. Female underachievers tend to be passive in the classroom rather than disruptive. Because of this they may be overlooked in a classroom, and receive little stimulation or guidance from teachers. Male underachievers are constantly directed toward achievement possibilities.

On the whole, it is clear that boys receive more behavioral criticism in elementary classrooms. They also seem to be generally more active and to have more interactions of all kinds with teachers. When differences are found on student-initiated contacts, it is in favor of boys. When a pupil is not called on, it is more likely to be a girl.

In teacher-initiated interactions, boys are called on more often and given more evaluative and elaborated feedback than girls.

If teachers tend to initiate more contact with boys and give them more evaluative feedback on their performance, this will help boys to realistically evaluate their own efforts and will help to lay the groundwork for independent intellectual activity. In contrast, if girls are given more global feedback, they will not be able to evaluate their own performance realistically or feel confidence about doing things on their own.

Teachers employ different strategies in dealing with the behavior of boys and girls in the classroom. The current patterns of teacher-pupil interaction may help the boys, but neglect the needs of the girls. Boys do receive the behavioral criticism and discipline contacts which will train them to be less impulsive. At the same time they get encouragement and attention in academic areas. Girls, who need to be encouraged in independent and assertive behavior, get less attention and feedback from teachers than do boys. The girls quite easily fall into obedience rather than aggressive thinking and socializing.

Teacher Evaluation of Boys and Girls

Teachers seem to know more about individual boys and what abilities they have and what qualities they lack. Jackson and Getzels (1959) and Jackson (1968) found teachers able to more accurately distinguish boys who were dissatisfied with school from those who were satisfied, though this was not the case for girls. Jackson et al. (1967) found that teachers made more negatively evaluative statements about boys, but their statements also indicated more overall personal involvement with boys.

Boys appear to be more salient in the eyes of their teachers: they are perceived more analytically and accurately, and are interacted with more differentially and frequently. To some extent, this may reflect actual differences in the children's behavior. Boys are more active and variable in behavior from birth. They show more learning and behavior disorders in the early grades, and some research suggests that this may have a constitutional basis. However, the differential perception and treatment of the sexes is undoubtedly largely a function of the teacher's different expectations and stereotypes.

The survey by Ricks and Pyke (1973) reports two interesting and consistent preferences. First, more teachers, especially female teachers, prefer male students to female students. Teachers reported that males were more outspoken, active, willing to exchange ideas, open, honest, and easier to talk with. The sole reason they gave for preferring female students was a lack of discipline problems. Second, 41 percent of the teachers believed that students prefer male teachers. Not one teacher felt that students preferred female teachers, although the female teacher was not evaluated as less effective. They reported that male teachers speak with more knowledge, authority, directness, and clarity than female teachers. There can be little doubt that prevalent beliefs such as these strongly influence the dynamic interaction between teacher and student.

Female versus Male Teachers

Periodically, suspicions and complaints arise about the feminine atmosphere in the elementary school and the female teacher's possible bias against boys. Do female teachers feminize boys, and in so doing hinder achievement for boys? What effects would male teachers have on boys and girls?

The much-cited work of Fagot and Patterson (1969) indicates that nursery school teachers reward both boys and girls for traditionally feminine activities. These investigators defined feminine behaviors as listening to stories, painting, doing artwork, playing in the doll corner, and playing in the kitchen. Masculine behaviors included playing in the block and truck corners, climbing and running, and riding tricycles. The researchers found that during the specified time period teachers rewarded the girls 353 times for "feminine" behavior and only 10 times for "masculine" behavior. The boys were rewarded only 232 times for any sex-typed behavior, but 199 of those were for feminine behaviors. Over the year, however, boys did not become more apt to prefer the feminine behaviors than when they started. Peer groups were noticeably powerful in reinforcing same-sex values by reminding each other that boys liked the "boy's toys," and boys did "boy things" together. Girls also kept to their stereotypically proper play groups and corners during free play.

Girls in the primary grades learn to read faster than boys. Boys repeat grades more often, and are referred for clinical help more often. Researching sex differences in reading, Felsenthal (1970) suggests that identity shifts of boys from femaleness (mother attachment) to maleness are complicated by the dominantly feminine environment of the elementary school. At early ages, boys neglect classroom achievement and performance because in their struggle to form masculine values, they receive strong cues against aggressive or independent behavior rather than encouragement toward achievement. Girls, on the other hand, flourish under the tutelage of a female teacher who expects docility and performance from them. They are not subject to the same conflict as the boys.

Theorists hold that boys benefit from teachers' external control as they learn to gauge limits and direct energies. But, the same process reemphasizes already existing conformity and dependency on the part of girls. Thus, girls are more solidly entrenched in behaviors which are stereotypically female. Even the role model close at hand of a strong, dependable, authoritative woman such as the teacher herself may do little to encourage independence in the girl at that age. It is the prescribed *role* of the teacher, rather than the female sex of the teacher, which predicts the teacher's type of interaction with boys and girls in the classroom. Although many people believe that male teachers revolutionize the classroom, it appears that male teachers, conscious of the delineated teacher role, also maintain sex-differentiated patterns of classroom interaction.

What happens in a classroom taught by a male? Can there be a "masculine atmosphere" in the classroom? Very few studies have been done which have controlled for sex of teacher because of the scarcity of male teachers in non-sex-segregated elementary classrooms. It is unclear what the exact influence of male teachers on boys and their achievements is. Nevertheless, the idea of male role models has been popularized as a reason for putting men into nursery and elementary school positions. There is some indication (Mueller & Cooper, unpublished, 1972) that in a preschool setting teacher teams of a man and a woman have the effect of increasing area use and social play for children of the opposite sex. Male teachers attract the girls to the blocks and trucks, while female teachers increase the boys' use of dressing up and art areas. The findings suggest that a male-female team teaching situation might maximize both boys' and girls' play with cross-sex-type toys, and may also increase cross sex cooperative and assertive play.

On the issue of teacher effectiveness, one study rather weakly asserts that a small number of young boys taught by a male teacher improved their reading achievement while a control group under a female teacher did not (Shinedling & Pederson, 1970). However, a variety of other projects (reported in Brophy & Good, 1973) indicate strongly that the sex of the teacher has little to do with increasing boys' reading ability. Variables like innovative techniques, programmed learning, teaching style, and enthusiasm more often predicted an increase in the verbal achievement of boys.

Good, Sikes, and Brophy (1973) set out to compare the behavior of male and female teachers with boys and girls in sixteen classes at the junior high school level. Interaction analyses showed the expected student sex difference: boys were much more active and interacted more frequently with the teachers. Proportionately, boys' interactions with teachers were more likely to be negative than were girls' interactions. Results showed that although males and females have different teaching styles, they do not treat boys and girls differently. Only one of the sixty-two measures of interaction between teacher sex and student sex reached significance, and even then it showed female teachers more likely to seek out boys on work-related topics. The same kind of sex differences recorded as repeatedly occurring in classes taught by females also appear in classes taught by males. The sex of the teacher per se apparently has nothing to do with changing sex typing. Evidently the profession of teaching in the current educational system maintains certain norms for the participating students. These requirements happen to coincide with stereotypically feminine values, and boys thus require more attention in order to fit them into the student role.

What Can a Teacher Change to Alleviate Sex-Role Stereotypy?

The question must be addressed: What innovations in the educational system will equalize treatment by sex while maximizing individual achievement? How can teachers socialize boys to control impulsive behavior and motivate girls to independent actions? How can boys be directed to verbal skills and school achievement and girls be encouraged toward independent creative thinking and problem solving?

Torrance, as part of his study on creativity, observed significant sex differences and attempted to manipulate these informally through the expectations of teachers (Torrance, 1963). First, he asked teachers to describe incidents in which they had rewarded creative behavior in the classroom, either by listening, helping, or allowing continuation. Teachers reported 224 incidents. In 172 incidents, the sex of the children was mentioned. The ratio of 26 percent girls to 74 percent boys suggests that teachers recognize the creative behavior of the boys more often and may possibly reward the boys for creativity, while they communicate conformity expectations to the girls. Other sections of Torrance's work show that children do much better at creativity tasks which are sex-typed. This suggests that girls may be choosing their level of creativity based on the sex-role appropriateness of the task. Torrance reports two studies which involve playing with science toys. The boys produced many more creative ideas with the science-toy stimulus. Torrance discussed the findings with teachers and parents and enlisted their aid in encouraging girls toward creative thinking with nonfeminine toys. The next year, when the children were retested, girls had significantly increased in creative behavior. However, during both years the student participants reported that the boys contributed better ideas than the girls.

Small-scale interventions such as this provide invaluable information about the capacity of children to change and the methodology through which the teacher can encourage change. This study identified sex-typed toys and playing as a source which limits children's creativity. This effect could be counteracted by attention which concentrated on the encouragement of play with cross-sexed toys. There are countless other factors, like classroom structure, science and math curriculum, classroom task assignment, seating arrangements, play groups, and sex-typed extracurriculars, that could benefit from observation and intervention. Our intervention study was an attempt, not to obscure the differences between males and females, but to release the developing child from those binds on abilities and aspirations that are the result of strict sex-role stereotyping.

CHAPTER
TWO

The Nonsexist Intervention Project

The scope of the nonsexist intervention project was wide. Educators and developmental psychologists worked in coordination to design the experiment and measures, and to develop the curriculum and teacher-training methods. The development of the nonsexist curriculum, school arrangements for the study, preintervention measures, the intervention itself, postmeasures, and the analyses of results extended over a busy two-year period. The sequence of activities included these steps:

1. The literature on sex-role stereotyping was reviewed. (See Chapter 1.)

2. Ways of measuring children's sex-role attitudes were developed (this chapter).

3. School systems, schools, and teachers were selected and contacted for participation in the nonsexist project.

4. Appropriate curriculum materials for early childhood, middle school, and high school were surveyed and selected. (See Chapters 3 to 6.)

5. Children's sex-role conceptions at the three age levels were measured before the intervention. (See Chapter 7.)

6. Teachers were trained in nonsexist interactions and discussed curriculum materials with staff.

7. The six-week intervention took place. Systematic classroom observations of teacher-pupil interactions were conducted throughout the intervention in all experimental and control classes.

8. Children's sex-role attitudes were reassessed. (See Chapter 7.)

9. Feedback about the nonsexist curriculum materials was monitored. (See Chapter 5.)

10. The data were analyzed (Chapter 4), and the results reported.

Details about each of these steps are provided in this chapter for educators who may wish not only to introduce nonsexist curricula and teacher-pupil interactions but also to assess the effects of such changes on children.

Three school systems in the Boston area participated in the intervention project. The research design (Solomon Four group) called for a minimum of four classrooms at every grade level (kindergarten, and fifth and ninth grades) in every school system. However, the number of classes was limited by availability at the kindergarten level. During the training period, a few teachers decided not to participate in the nonsexist project for personal reasons. A total of twenty-two experimental classrooms were fully involved in the project from beginning to completion. Because of the scarcity of men in elementary school positions, only four teachers were male: two in the fifth grade, two in the ninth grade. Fieldworkers on the project thoroughly interviewed 409 children.

Measuring Children's Sex-Role Attitudes

The measurement of children's sex-role concepts for boys and girls, men and women, has been difficult. Children's attitudes may change rapidly in relation to age and circumstance. A child who overhears a conversation between parents on the value of the women's movement may shift reported attitudes overnight. One is also not sure whether the child reports what he/she actually believes, or what he/she thinks is expected. Or the child's responses may be cryptic because he/she simply hasn't thought about it at all. Children at various cognitive levels understand sex-role concepts in very different ways. Comparison of attitudes across grades is important. Previous studies have not used comparable measures across grades, and this has made it difficult to understand how sex-role concepts change with age.

The sex-role measures which were developed for the study can easily be used in the classroom. They can be used both to reveal children's views and to start discussions about sex roles. The measures pick up the child's views of men and women in nontraditional occupations and in a variety of family and personality roles and his/her ideas of what typical and ideal boys and girls are like. In the following section, the various measures are described. A complete packet of measures is included in the Appendix.

THE PICTURE TEST: Children were shown pictures of men and women in stereotypical or nonstereotypical job roles. The child was asked to tell a story about each picture. A male mechanic and female teacher were the stereotypical occupations, while the female mechanic and male nursery school teacher were nonstereotypical. Children were asked to say what they were doing, why, and how they liked the job, and give any further ideas about the picture. If the child had difficulty talking, some questions were used to prompt the child, like: "What is happening in the picture?" "How did he or she get there?" "What will happen in the future?" "What is the person thinking and feeling?" In the data analysis, stories were coded for the unique details in the child's story, i.e., whether the job was full or part-time, what status it was, how successful the person in the job was, how much

trouble the person had getting the job, whether the job
was approved of, and whether the character was involved
in family or interpersonal relationships.

THE OPPOSITE-SEX STORY TEST: Children were asked to
name the jobs that women could have, and the jobs that
men could have. Children generated lists of occupations
or activities for each sex. As few as one or two, and as
many as twenty-five, jobs were named. Occasionally a
child, even with prompting, could not think of any occupations. Sometimes there was an empty list because the
child said that both men and women could do any job they
wanted. This was quite infrequent.

The children were also asked to describe men and
women: the way they are and the way they act. Children
often halted after three or four adjectives or phrases.
Later we asked the children to use the words which they
had generated for the men's list in a story about a woman,
and the women's list words in a story about a man. This
task tapped their flexibility in using both "masculine" and
"feminine" attributes in their description of a person. The
children reacted in a variety of ways to this request. Some
were delighted. They enjoyed devising creative and
unusual settings and plots for their stories about androgynous men and women. Some pushed their characters
beyond the unusual to the bizarre by placing them in
impossible, unrealistic situations. Some children were dis-
pleased with the task and refused to tell a story. Sometimes they misinterpreted the words or left them out.

' The data were analyzed by evaluating the jobs and the
personal adjectives which were listed along dimensions
like the traditionality of the sex-typed word, the interpersonal or instrumental nature of the job or adjective, the
status of the job, the desirability of the characteristic, and
the overlap between the male and female lists.

Stories varied widely among children and between
grades. The material ranged from bare character sketches
which simply reiterated an adjective in sentence form to

succinct character sketches like, "There was a woman who was *strong;* she worked *very hard* and enjoyed *sports*. She had a *good sense of humor* and told jokes a lot." (The *italicized* words were the adjectives the child originally generated for a man.) Often the stories were intricate and revealing as the child faced a task which required a shift in attitude away from the stereotyped male or female picture. This struggle is illustrated in the following story given by a fifth grade girl:

> Once there was a boy who all his life was very *gentle*. He never hit anyone or started a fight and when some of his friends were not feeling well, he was *loving* and *kind* to them. When he got older he never changed. People started not liking him because he was *weak, petite,* and he wasn't like any of the other men—not strong or tough. Most of his life he sat alone thinking about why no one liked him. Then one day he went out and tried to act like the other men. He joined a baseball team, but he was no good, he always got out. Then he decided to join the hockey team. He couldn't play good. He kept on breaking all the rules. So he quit the team and joined the soccer team. These men were understanding to him. He was really good at soccer, and was the best on the team. That year they won the championship and the rest of his life he was happy.

For this girl the implications of nonstereotyped behavior are clear. A man may choose to act out socioemotional abilities in relationships, but the consequence is social rejection. The man is well on his way to recovery if he can prove his masculinity in the all-male sports group. The strong impression of stereotyping revealed in this story was picked up by our coding system. Many children showed this pattern of presenting a nonstereotypical character, and then, in the course of the story, bringing the person back to "normal" or stereotyped roles. There was often an unwillingness to approve of a man with sex-reversed (but not necessarily negative) qualities.

The Opposite-Sex Story Test not only provided information about children's sex-role flexibility but also was later used as a teaching tool. Often it sparked students' enthusiasm and thought. Students had to expand their thinking and creatively present such changes within the disciplined format of the story. Frequently, children could handle the concept of androgyny for a woman by picturing a successful, authoritative woman who was not socially out of place. It was harder for them to imagine a male with the characteristics of gentleness and sensitivity without reverting to images of the weird transvestite or henpecked husband. This task can be used to help eliminate sex-typed words in the classroom. Using this task, children can explore the fact that many characteristics stereotypically assigned to one sex are actually shared by both.

THE TYPICAL DAY MEASURE: Children were asked to describe what a typical day in their lives would be like when they grew up. Boys' and girls' aspirations about future occupations and family life were thus revealed. Children were not asked to name their future activities in the abstract. Instead, they set them within the context of a normal day. This measure provided information on the daily routines they planned and the home and leisure activities in which they would participate, in addition to their chosen vocation. Other researchers (Iglitzin, 1972) have noted that stated occupational goals for the future sometimes conflict with what a child thinks he or she will actually spend time doing in the future. This inconsistency, we found, was common. For example, a girl said that she was going to be a nurse. Then she told a story about taking her own children to school, cleaning the house, working after lunch, and leaving work in time to pick the children up from school. Clearly, she wanted to be a nurse for two hours a day and homemaker for the rest of the time.

There were two further Typical Day measures. The child also was asked to tell a story about a typical day in the life of a hypothetical woman (named Barbara Smith) and a hypothetical man (named Robert Wilson) of about thirty years of age. Comparisons between the Typical Day stories for self and a hypothetical typical woman and man revealed useful information about the extent to which children believed they, as individuals, would have to fulfill stereotypical roles. Usually children told stories about housewives and professional men in these stories.

After the child told each of the stories, the interviewers carefully probed to discover the limits and qualifications of the child's statements. If the child had made the woman a homemaker, the interviewer checked to see what type of circumstances could induce the woman to take a job. Similarly, if the woman were working, the interviewer asked whether she were married, what her husband and children thought, whether her friends approved, what would happen if she no longer wanted to come home and cook dinner after a hard day at work, and other conflict-producing questions. The interviewer checked for what circumstances were necessary to relieve the man of his breadwinner role, and if the husband and wife could exchange work roles.

As an exercise in the classroom, the task focused the child's attention on expectations for the future, a task which revealed a considerable amount about the child's current estimation of him- or herself and his or her abilities.

SEMANTIC DIFFERENTIAL MEASURE: The Semantic Differential measure permitted an objective comparison between the child's perception of him- or herself, and his or her perception of the way most boys and girls are, and should be. A list of word pairs was selected, with words that had opposite meanings. One of the adjectives was sex-typed with either a stereotypical masculine or feminine quality. There were equal numbers of desirable and undesirable characteristics for each sex, and there were two neutral word pairs. These are labeled on the protocol example shown in the Appendix.

The children then marked the word pair lists five

times consecutively for: Self, Most Boys, Most Girls, Boys Should Be, and Girls Should Be. This provided information on what most fifth and ninth graders believe about how the sexes should be ideally, what they think the sexes are like now, and how they compare themselves with the typical and the ideal boy or girl. When categories are combined for Self description, the result is, in part, a measure of self-esteem.

SEX-ROLE PREFERENCE QUESTIONNAIRE: The final measure was a standardized test developed by Aletha Stein (1973). (See Appendix.) The child's attitudes toward items and activities which traditionally belong to the realm of men or women are picked up by this measure. Preferences for stereotypically girls' or boys' hobbies or activities are also recorded. The measure evaluates the extent to which the child enjoys performing traditional or nontraditional sex-typed activities, and his/her enjoyment in doing both masculine and feminine activities.

This variety of objective and projective measures provided ample opportunity to gather a rounded knowledge of the attitudes of children toward sex-role concepts. Many children enjoyed the open-ended tasks; others preferred the objective segments. Some measures were easy to code and evaluate; others were difficult. At some ages information gleaned from one measure was not strongly substantiated by other measures in a different mode. Usually, however, the results fitted together in a complex but coherent picture of the development of children's sex-role attitudes.

The Classroom Observations

The aphorism "actions speak louder than words" seems particularly appropriate when considering what goes on in a classroom. Do boys act differently than girls? Do teachers treat girls and boys differently? What happens to teacher-child interactions in the fast-paced schedule of a classroom session? Research (as delineated in Chapter 1) suggests that teachers and students get caught in a vicious cycle in which teachers, as they attempt to cope with sex-typed behaviors, subtly reinforce those behaviors. Can teachers who are consciously geared to acting in a nonsexist manner toward children produce any change over time in the type and quality of classroom interaction? With these questions in mind, teachers in the intervention project were introduced to past research on teacher-pupil classroom interactions and to new strategies for reducing sex-role stereotyping in such classroom interactions. Then, before, during, and after the intervention, the classroom interactions were observed and coded by pairs of observers. The techniques of classroom observation which were used included a quite specific counting procedure of numbers and types of behavior and interchanges during each class session. Since preschool classes are quite different from middle and late childhood classes, two different methods for classroom observation were used. A modified Serbin scale was used in the kindergarten classes, and a modified Flanders system was adopted for the fifth and ninth grades. Interaction categories were chosen to highlight any sex differences in classroom interaction patterns. The specific systems, which can be used by any teacher to evaluate teacher-child interaction in his/her own class, are summarized below.

OBSERVATIONAL SCALES, KINDERGARTEN: A kindergarten classroom is a busy place. An observational system is needed which can handle both verbal and nonverbal behaviors. The interaction analysis developed by Serbin and colleagues (1971) examined which behaviors on the part of boys and girls evoked what types of responses from the teacher. Trained observers scanned the class for 20 seconds and then recorded for 10 seconds how many of what types of behaviors were emitted by the boys and girls and how the teacher responded. Kindergarten children's behaviors recorded in the classroom observation sessions included:

1. Child offered information to the teacher, talked with the teacher, or attempted to get involved in a conversation with the teacher.

2. Child responded to a question; e.g., the teacher put forth a general question to the class and one child spoke up in reply.

3. Child requested assistance; the child asked for help on a project, or solicited help in a nonverbal way.

4. Child ignored the teacher. This was coded when a child's inattention was responded to by the teacher, either because the child wandered away or because the child directly refused to pay attention to the teacher.

5. A count of the number of boys and girls who participated in a current activity was used and compared with the number of boys and girls who shifted between the major focus of activity and any extra corner of interest.

6. A proximity measure was taken by the observer for any child who remained very close to the teacher for a full 20-second period.

There were nine teacher behaviors that were measured as responses to the chosen children behaviors. These behaviors were:

1. Soft reprimand—verbal scolding or negative evaluation audible only to child and child's neighbor

2. Loud reprimand—scolding audible to whole class; may be in loud, normal, or harsh tone

3. Praise—verbal praise, compliments, or positive evaluation

4. Touching—positive physical contact, patting, holding

5. Brief conversation—teacher asked or answered without giving directions or evaluation

6. Extended conversation—longer than one sentence

7. Brief direction—verbal direction to a specific child

8. Extended direction—descriptive directions, modeling a skill or activity for the child

9. Helping—doing something for the child; physical response to a child's request for help

The kindergarten observations did not show consistent boy/girl differences during the classes. The activity and approach of the teacher seemed to vary drastically at different classroom observation sessions. Few significant differences occurred in either the proportion of types of class contributions for boys and girls or in the way teachers responded to the children. Perhaps kindergarteners do not demand sex-typed behavior from the teacher. Rather it is their young age which predicts the teacher's response. The teacher's task is to settle the children down, focus them on individual projects, and keep them from harm. Observers commented that they sometimes had difficulty coding the activities, since they could not easily label the child's appearance as either male or female. Many kindergarten children wore bibbed coveralls, had shoulder-length hair, and threw dirt at each other. This lack of sharp sex differentiation in their appearance and in teachers' aims may prohibit much interaction between teacher and pupils which is sharply differentiated by sex.

OBSERVATIONAL SCALES, FIFTH AND NINTH GRADES: In the interaction analyses used in the upper grades, all talk that took place during a class period was coded. The Flanders observational system codes the type and amount of verbal behavior of teacher and students in a sequential fashion. Every 3 seconds a number was recorded which pinpointed who spoke at that moment. The twenty numbers coded within 1 minute specified who started and stopped talking and what type of talk occurred during each interval. The categories were broad and clear enough so that two observers maintained a high level of agreement throughout the coding of the interchanges.

The specific categories of the system are explained below:

1. Teacher accepts feelings from a student. This is a low-frequency behavior. When it occurs, it denotes an emotional interchange between teacher and student. It is coded when teachers handle affection from the student in a nonrejecting way, e.g., in a clarifying, feeling tone and in a nonthreatening manner.

2. Teacher praises or encourages a student. This category includes a teacher's extensive explanation of why a student's work is acceptable, or even a simple "good job," accompanied by a nod of the head.

3. Accepts or uses ideas of a student. This is coded when a teacher clarifies, builds, or develops the ideas or suggestions by a student.

4. Asks questions. The teacher asks a question about content or procedure with the intent that a student answer.

5. Lecturing. The teacher gives facts or opinions about content or procedure, expresses own ideas.

6. Giving directions. The teacher gives directions, commands, or orders with which the student is expected to comply.

The *student talk* category consisted of only two types of response:

7. Student talk—initiation

8. Student talk—response

These were coded for male or female. The "student talk—response" is defined as talk by students in response to the teacher. The teacher initiates the contact or solicits student statements. The "student talk—initiation" means spontaneously contributed talk by the students. The last two useful coding categories are (9) silence and (10) confusion.

For the analyses of classroom observations, the list of numbers were entered into a sequential matrix. This permitted the determination of the proportions of boys and girls who initiated talk or responded to the teacher. Those teacher behaviors which preceded (elicited) or followed (reinforced) particular student behaviors were also examined. These measures provided a complete general view of class interactions. The content and tone of the interactions were supplied by observers' descriptions of activities, their analysis of any peculiar interactions, and their maps of the seating arrangements in each classroom.

The Flanders-Dunbar system originated during an era of classroom procedures in which only one student spoke at a time, and a teacher responded and then called on another student who had raised his or her hand. Four of the classrooms in the study had seats arranged in rows and had structured, fairly formal in-class behavior. Four more of the classrooms were moderately organized. The others were totally unstructured. In these classes, students sat on carpeted floors and wandered in and out of the classroom. They worked on individualized or small group projects in irregular patterns. This meant that the teacher walked around the room speaking with individuals, at times inaudibly. There were also more class disruptions, yelling, or everyone talking at once. There was much physical interplay in these classrooms either in a spirit of reprimand or of affection. In the unstructured classroom, the teacher did not control the activities. Much more power fell to the strong peer groups. This factor critically influenced the effectiveness of the ninth grade nonsexist intervention

(Chapter 8), since the peer group could endorse or stifle the intervention attempts.

Developing the Curriculum

Preparation for the curricular program began with the purchase of several hundred trade books, ranging from picture books to adult material, as suggested chiefly by several bibliographies. Individual materials from other sources were also purchased. The project staff read through most of these books, sorting them into three age-level categories: early childhood, middle childhood, and adolescence. The books were informally rated on such characteristics·as interest, literary style, and degree of stereotyping in plot or character development. In effect, the trade books underwent two screenings: the first through the staff's use of bibliographies in which trade books had been screened or categorized on the basis of nonsexism; the second, by staff members themselves on this preselected group of books. A third screening was done by the curriculum director before the library books were assigned to specific classrooms.

Simultaneously, all known feminist resource organizations and/or research centers were contacted. All published curricular materials or information pertaining to such materials were ordered. These materials, recent journals, and unpublished materials were carefully examined for curricular possibilities. Activity cards listing all ideas culled from these materials were compiled for all three grade levels. Several general criteria were used in the final selection of these activity cards for inclusion in the curriculum notebooks prepared for each grade level:

1. Did the activities seem suitable for the cognitive level of each intended grade?

2. Were the activities as a whole adaptable for the range of abilities one could expect to find in a heterogeneously grouped class?

3. Did the suggestions as a whole reflect a balance between structured, carefully outlined activities and more open-ended, improvisatory ideas?

4. Did suggested reading materials for students (in grades 5 and 9) provide for a range of levels to match the usual range of reading levels in the average classroom?

5. Did teachers have sufficient variety to choose from, depending on their own interests and their class's schedule?

6. Were materials or ideas easily integrated into ongoing skill work in language arts classes?

7. Were opportunities for further traditional academic skill work through these suggested materials and ideas clearly apparent to the teachers?

8. Was there a balance between longer curricular units of one or two weeks' duration for teachers who so desired and short, more extemporaneous kinds of assignments?

9. Did the suggestions offer a balance between some whole-class activities to be led by the teacher and more individualized activities or projects?

All the above criteria are important considerations for curriculum planners when an attitudinally oriented intervention program is being integrated with a traditional academic program. The curriculum director prepared the curriculum notebooks for the teachers (see following sections) so as to select these general criteria.

The notebooks for each grade level were completed several weeks before the intervention program was formally initiated in the classroom. The notebooks were divided into four sections:

1. Background information for the teacher on sex-role stereotyping in order to supplement the outline

2. Suggested curricular materials or activities

   3. Bibliographies of nonsexist children's and/or adults' literature

   4. Curriculum evaluation forms for rapid evaluation of completed activities by the teachers

Each notebook included a cover letter from the curriculum director, an annotated table of contents, and a statement of the objectives for that grade level.

The following section delineates at each grade level the material provided to each teacher and the published sources for some of the suggested curricular activities. No sources are cited here for many of the short writing or discussion assignments included in the curriculum notebooks which were gleaned and adapted from a variety of materials or devised by the curriculum director.

The three kindergarten teachers received:

   1. A selection of nonsexist children's books

   2. The record *Free to Be . . .You and Me*

   3. Two sets of eight photographs of professional women and women in community jobs

   4. A variety of the following toys: plastic hard hats, hammers and saws, play cash registers, play telephones, template tracers, pots and pans, mixing and measuring spoons, and an apron

   5. The curriculum notebook, which included:
      a. Two journal articles
      b. "Recommendations for Eliminating Sex-Role Stereotyping in Elementary Texts"
      c. A bibliography

Grade 5 teachers received:

   1. A selection of nonsexist library books

   2. Multiple selections from the following list to be used with the Bement curricular unit (optional):

Brink, Carol Ryrie. *Caddie Woodlawn*. New York: Macmillan, 1974 (paperback).

Mirsky, Reba Paeff. *Thirty-one brothers and sisters*. New York: Dell, 1973 (paperback).

Uchida, Yoshiko. *Journey to Topaz*. New York: Scribner, 1971 (hardcover).

Wilder, Laura Ingalls. *On the banks of Plum Creek*. New York: Harper & Row (paperback).

3. The record *Free to Be . . . You and Me*

4. Two sets of eight photographs

5. The curriculum notebook, which included:
   a. Three journal articles
   b. Student Workbook: Discovering Sex-Role Stereotypes
   c. Sexism in the Fourth Grade
   d. Growing Up Male and Female in America
   e. Short biographies of Elizabeth Cady Stanton, Susan B. Anthony, Frederick Douglass, Ida Wells Barnett, Sojourner Truth, Mary McLeod Bethune, and Ah-Toy
   f. Preferred Qualities of Male/Female
   g. Recommendations for Eliminating Sex-Role Stereotyping in Elementary Texts
   h. Two bibliographies

Grade 9 teachers received:

1. A selection of fiction and nonfiction books (all nonsexist)

2. The curriculum notebook, which included:
   a. Two journal articles
   b. Student Workbook
   c. Conversational Clichés
   d. A literature-based writing assignment
   e. Susan B. Anthony Day Kit
   f. Article on women in politics

   g. Individual project choices
   h. Fact Bombardment
   i. Statistics on the status of women
   j. Preferred Qualities of Male/Female
   k. Career aspiration activity
   l. Description of class meeting
   m. Three bibliographies

The curriculum notebooks were delivered to all the teachers a week before the workshop meeting was held. Other materials and supplies were delivered during the initial weeks of the program.

Participation of Teachers

A teacher training workshop was held. Because teachers had been given an opportunity to read through their notebooks in advance, it was possible for them to discuss the curricular material in greater depth. The program consisted of: (1) a slide show and discussion of sexism in children's literature; (2) an overview of research on sex-role development and a summary of the curricular intervention program; (3) an overview of the curriculum by the curriculum director; and (4) a discussion of research on teacher-pupil interaction. The teachers were rotated according to grade level among discussion sessions on: (1) the use of the curricular materials; (2) teacher-pupil interactions; and (3) teacher goals.

During sessions on the use of the curriculum, the teachers were encouraged to raise questions about ways to integrate the suggested materials with their scheduled program. They were asked to voice any critical comments they may have formulated when reviewing the notebooks before the meeting. Several concerns of the teachers were discussed and clarified. Specifically, first, the teachers were assured they were not going to be observed or judged on the way in which they implemented the intervention program. There would be complete reliance on their own professional judgments. Second, the teachers were not expected to use all the suggested materials or ideas. They could freely pick and choose according to their own taste, and could adapt any of the materials to suit their class's needs or interests. Third, it was made clear that all materials would be delivered to their schools and that multiple copies for classroom use of any of the material in their notebooks would be supplied upon request. Little additional preparation or work was expected of the teachers; they were asked only to fill out curriculum evaluation forms so that a written record would be available at a later date for overall evaluation by the curriculum director.

At the workshop meeting it was agreed that weekly meetings outside of formal class time would be scheduled with the curriculum director so that the teachers in each school would have an opportunity to exchange ideas, information, and experiences with one another and with the director. These were very informal meetings. The teachers were encouraged to save for the curriculum director any interesting sets of classroom papers done by their students during the intervention program.

Within two weeks after the workshop, the teachers began to formally use the materials suggested in the notebooks. The curriculum director met with all the teachers at each participating school, either as a group, when possible, or individually, for three consecutive weeks after the initial week of the program. Books and materials ordered by the teachers were regularly delivered, either by the observers or the curriculum director.

THREE

Objectives and Curriculum for Early Childhood Classes

The Early Childhood Curriculum

The material presented in this section is suitable for use at preschool and early grades. In our intervention project, the following objectives were used with teachers at the kindergarten level:

1. To encourage children in nonsexist play activities

2. To encourage children to consider a variety of occupational roles

3. To encourage the children to see themselves and adults of both sexes in multiple family and personality roles

The rationale for these objectives was derived from theoretical, descriptive, and experimental research on the cognitive and social functioning of children at this grade level.

Socially, kindergarten or first grade represents the first real separation of the child from the home, and it is through this experience that children begin to develop ideas and concepts about extrafamilial roles and institutions. This age group has difficulty in thinking of people in multiple roles, e.g., that a woman can be a mother and a doctor at the same time. Five-year-olds are rigid and categorical in their thinking. They will insist that differences between the sexes exist because that is the way they *must* be.

The five-year-old fails to believe in the constancy of gender if physical appearances are altered. Thus, a five-year-old may insist that a boy cannot wear a dress and still remain a boy. Likewise the child does not separate functions of roles from physical appearance—a doctor is a doctor only if he or she wears a white coat.

Research on sex-role development has mainly focused on sex-role preferences. At age five, children prefer their own sex and reliably show sex-appropriate preferences. By age six, children reach the ceiling on gender identity and make 80 to 100 percent same-sex choices on sex-typed objects and activities. The equation of psychological differences with physical and activity differences by the child at this age are thought to lead to a belief in male superiority because strength and energy are equated with intelligence, aggression, and dominance. It is also true that the social world with which the child is interacting portrays men as more intelligent, aggressive, and dominant. The fact that males occupy more prestigious roles in this society must also affect the child's valuing of the male role.

Since the effectiveness of environmental influence largely depends on the match between the level of concepts being encountered and the developmental level of the individual, a curriculum for five-year-olds is concrete and closely tied to the everyday world of the child. Therefore, the kindergarten objectives were primarily positive in scope. They were intended to help make children aware of the real, not rigidly sex-typed, variations in the activities of children and adults they know.

For example, very young children are apt to indulge in many play activities which only later on become more sexually differentiated. Nevertheless, it is probably true that little girls engage in a wider variety of activities, ranging from the doll's corner to the carpentry bench, than do little boys, who may not venture as readily into the homemaking end of the activity spectrum.

Again, depending on experience and social class, young children probably *see* adults of both sexes in roles that are not as stereotyped as what they say. Children today are apt to see female doctors and male elementary school teachers, though they may believe doctors or teachers in general to be of only one sex.

Last, many children today see both adults in their homes performing tasks that fall outside media-influenced stereotypical categories. There are many mothers who work from choice or necessity and many fathers who help out with cooking, babysitting, and so forth. In many classrooms, teachers need only to point out what is already within their youngsters' actual experiences in order to broaden their intellectual awareness of the discrepancy between a social stereotype and reality.

Based on these perspectives of the young child, the following exercises and activities were developed for use in preschool or early grades to aid attitude change toward a nonstereotypical sex-role stance.

KINDERGARTEN: SEX-TYPED ACTIVITIES

Goal:
   To discover children's present sex-role concepts and expand, if limited.
Activity:
   1. Have children draw two pictures each: one of a man they like, the other of a woman they like, doing whatever activity they choose.
   2. When finished, in small groups, discuss what man or woman is doing. List on board suggested activities. When children have completed describing activity their pictures show, discuss whether activities are confined to one sex or other or could be both.

KINDERGARTEN: CHOOSING GIFTS

This unit provides a familiar framework for looking at stereotypical attitudes toward the sexes. Students will match gifts that they perceive as desirable to people of different ages and sexes. Discussing the reasons for these (perhaps) sex-typed choices provides an opportunity to illustrate cross-sex preferences. The lesson involves as a sidelight the dealing in monetary terms. This activity was developed by Educational Challenges, Inc., for the Resource Center on Sex Roles in Education of the National Foundation for the Improvement of Education.

Materials needed:
1. *Gift list,* paper labeled to represent a typical gift list for the family
2. *Money sheet,* copies of various denominations of monetary bills totaling $100

Procedure:
1. Use Ward's or Sears' or any other large catalog to cut out a variety of objects which might be gift items. (Avoid clothes.) Mount each item on construction paper and print a one-word label and the price in even dollars underneath each picture. Display the pictures on a table or bulletin board. If students prepare these pictures for the class, they may wish to display them in a store arrangement.
2. Cut apart the money sheets and distribute $100 to each student. Distribution can take place through student bankers.
3. Distribute gift lists and tell each student to choose gifts for each member of his or her family and to pay the storekeeping students the amount of each chosen gift. Note that gift lists allow personalization due to differences in families. For writing practice, have students write the names of the chosen gifts on their lists.

The economic lesson is optional, and therefore the money exchange may be eliminated. Beginning readers would benefit from copying gift words onto their list, but students could cut pictures from catalogs to paste on their sheets beside family names. If this plan is followed, more than one catalog will be needed.

4. When gift lists are completed, conduct a class discussion.

KINDERGARTEN: OCCUPATIONAL PICTURES

Goal:
To expand occupational interest and break down stereotypes.
Activity:
Have pictures of men and women in different occupational roles displayed around the room.

Ask children to describe what people in specific occupations are like, e.g., doctor, lawyer, plumber, electrician, janitor, truck driver, policeman, etc. Write descriptive words in relation to the occupations and sex they implied.

KINDERGARTEN: PRETENDING NONSTEREOTYPES

Goal:
Nonsexist role playing
Activity:
Have children make up little scenes that they think would be typical of occupational roles. Use props or symbols of occupations (hats, etc.) and choose girls to assume "typical" male occupations. Have children discuss how realistically the players make up their scene. At end of scene, discuss whether sex makes any difference in performance of job as children know it.

KINDERGARTEN: OCCUPATIONAL ROLE PLAYING

Activity:
Gather equipment for these roles: construction worker: hard hats, saws, hammers; salesclerk: cash register, money, merchandise, price tags; doctor: stethoscope,

charts, white coat; clothes maker: sewing machine, patterns, ruler, cloth, pincushion; fire fighter: fire hat, rain
coat, boots, ladder, shovel; cook: apron, pots, pans, spat-
ula, chef's hat; plumber: wrench, pipe, nuts and bolts

Goal:

The important aspect of this exercise is that the child
understand that within any vocation there is a wide range
of activities. Both men and women have some of the
qualities and abilities that will make them good workers at
parts of any job they choose. Maybe not all women would
make good construction workers, but some women could;
maybe not all men would be good cooks, but some men
would. Thus any profession needs to be exposed to the
children as an acceptable occupation for both males and
females, if so chosen.

The specific questions and settings listed below could
be utilized to lead the children to the aforementioned
conclusions.

1. What does the worker do?

Example: What does a fire fighter do?
Stops fires in houses.

But also: Rescues kittens from trees.
Saves people from drowning.
Checks on houses to see if they are safe.
Gives school fire drills.
Keeps all the equipment shined and ready.

2. How did she or he learn to do the job?

Example: How does one become a clothes maker?
Learns how to use a sewing machine.
Has good ideas about how clothes ought to
look on people.
Enjoyed handling material and putting it
together.
Practiced until really quick and efficient.

3. What type of person does this worker have to be to do the job well?

> Example: Salesclerk needs to act in what way?
> Needs to enjoy talking and smiling at people.
> Should be careful, neat, and precise.
> Should be strong to stand up for a long time and carry goods.
> Able to work with numbers and machines.

4. Why would this be a good job? Why a hard job?

> Example: What is a construction job like?
> Good because it is outside, up above other buildings, good pay, work with hands, watch a building grow, etc.
> Hard because must lift heavy things, sometimes it is cold or very hot, tiring work, maybe boring, etc.

KINDERGARTEN: OCCUPATIONAL ROLE-PLAY INTERACTIONS

Goal:

This exercise attempts to show how males and females within different occupations can work together without status conflict to make a community run efficiently. In the role-playing sessions, put two different occupations together and examine the interaction and exchange. In order to demonstrate the nonstereotypical roles, let a girl be in a traditionally masculine vocation, and a boy be in a traditionally feminine profession.

The teacher should continue adding new occupational roles and rearranging old ones and re-creating stories until the children see that (1) every person needs to work together since every role is necessary to the healthy community, (2) any role can be taken by either a male or a female, and (3) no status inequities arise in cooperation between males and females.

Activity:

Perhaps these types of questions and activities would be appropriate for helping the children in the role playing:

1. How can men and women in different jobs work together?

   Example: How could a fire fighter ever help a cook? Help children make up a story about a cook making a special dinner; his/her stove exploded; the kitchen caught on fire; the fire fighter put it out; the cook made a delicious dinner the next week for the fire fighters.

   Or In the emergency of a flood, the fire fighters pulled people out of the water, while the cooks made food for them.

   Example: One very cold weekend the pipes in the school building froze, and then burst. The plumber tried to fix them, but didn't have the right size pipe; so waited until Monday morning; went to the store early; the salesclerk was right on time; knew exactly where the pipe was that she/he needed; the salesclerk worked quickly and well so that the plumber could get back to fix the school pipes.

2. Expand the list of possibilities the child perceives as appropriate male or female activities. Focus on the main activity of an occupation and name as many related occupations or similar abilities as possible.

   Example: When talking about a clothes maker, mention other occupations like fashion designer, department store manager, sewing machine salesperson, shoe repair, bookbinding, etc.

3. Discuss jobs or roles in the classroom. What skills does it take to do specific tasks like passing out toys, opening windows, or watering plants? Point out that tasks can be

divided along non-sex-typed lines with girls moving furniture and boys cleaning dishes. Also that when boys and girls cooperate on hard jobs, they can be done very easily.

KINDERGARTEN: FAMILY ROLES

Goal:
To discover children's present sex-role concepts and expand if limited.
Activity:
Interview the children either in small groups or whole class. Write on blackboard activities mentioned under a heading for each question.

1. What do mothers do?

2. What do fathers do?

3. What are good things for a girl to do when she grows up?

4. What are good things for a boy to do when he grows up?

5. What is important to do?

Read off activities children have contributed under each list. Are there overlaps, complete separations, etc.? Discuss with children whether activities under any one sex could also be under the other. Can you provide some?

KINDERGARTEN: STEREOTYPY IN LITERATURE

Goal:
Develop awareness of sex roles presented in reading books.
Activity:
1. Have children collect a number of picture or reading books—sit together in a circle.

2. Have children tell who main characters are—boys or girls (or male or female young animals). Discuss meaning of "main character." Keep count on the blackboard.
3. Have children decide (if they can) what kind of activity the boy or girl does in the story.
4. Have children discuss what adult females in these books do. Also adult males (or animals).
5. Write some key words from discussion on board. Repeat them and see if any conclusion about the kind of representation of boys and girls they see can be drawn.
6. Ask them if the boys could do girls' activities and vice versa.

KINDERGARTEN TO FIFTH GRADE: RECORD—*FREE TO BE . . . YOU AND ME**

The starred selections are especially recommended for the grade levels indicated.

Side 1:
    "Free to Be . . . You and Me"—all grades
* "Boy Meets Girl"—grade 5
    "When We Grow Up"—grades K to 5
    "Don't Dress Your Cat"—grade 5
* "Parents Are People"—grades K to 5
    "Housework"—grade 5
    "Helping"—grade K
* "Ladies First"—grades K to 5
    "Dudley Pippin"
    "It's All Right to Cry"—grades K to 5

Side 2:
    "Sisters and Brothers"—all grades
    "My Dog Is a Plumber"—grades K to 5
* "William's Doll"—grade K

---

*This record, done by Marlo Thomas and her friends and recorded on Bell Records, Inc., is an exciting example of nonsexist audiovisuals. For more nonsexist multimedia materials, see listing in Chapter 6 of teachers' multimedia resources.

* "Atalanta"—grade 5
   "Grandma"—grade 5
   "Girlland"—grades 5 and up
   "Dudley Pippin"
* "Glad to Have a Friend Like You"—grades K to 5

CHAPTER
FOUR

Objectives and Curriculum for the Middle Grades

The Middle Grades Curriculum

For the interventions at middle grades, the objectives included those already formulated for the early childhood level, and an additional objective designed to develop the critical capacities of middle elementary students in relation to their reading materials and their cultural environment. Around the ages of ten and eleven, children are able to reflect in more abstract and objective ways about the kinds of experiences their culture provides and shapes for them.

The following objectives were given to grade 5 teachers in the intervention project:

1. To encourage students to consider a variety of occupational roles, regardless of sex

2. To encourage students to develop nonsexist attitudes about participation in sports activities

3. To encourage the students to see themselves and adults of both sexes in multiple family and personality roles

4. To help develop some awareness of the sex-role stereotyping that exists in literature, the media, and occupational roles

The rationale for these objectives derived from research literature suggesting that the ten- or eleven-year-old child is at the level of ego functioning called "conform-ist." In contrast to the five-year-old, the ten-year-old focuses on social roles as well as physical attributes. The child at this age is conforming and conventional, and firmly believes that social roles reflect social duties. The child justifies sex-role divisions as *necessary* to maintain the world as he or she knows it; e.g., a mother stays home to care for children because children need mothers to stay home and care for them. When the child does make psychological distinctions between the sexes the child sees these as based on wishes or interventions: girls are quieter because they want to be; boys are more active because they like to be, etc. While the child may assert the principle of "unlimited opportunity"—anyone can be anything he or she wants to be—the child is also likely to believe that people are in conventional social roles because they have chosen to do so.

By this age identification with same sex models has occurred and there is a clear bifurcation of sex roles for boys and girls. Both sexes differentiate male and female roles and interests for both adults and children and attach differential values to competencies associated with male and female roles. Sex differences in intellectual abilities appear. Girls show less self-confidence in their abilities and their judgment and exhibit greater dependency.

At this age children are beginning to be concerned with the gross inequities in society. While materials pre-senting men and women in nontraditional roles are still effective, one can also begin to introduce concepts of discrimination and prejudice. Reading materials can include biographies of pioneering women, as well as histo-ries that depict women's struggles for equal rights.

FIFTH GRADE: UNIT ABSTRACT

Goals:
    1. To make the children aware of unequal treatment given to females in society (and in classroom?)

2. To develop the feeling of freedom of association between sexes in the classroom

3. To examine how males and females are stereotyped into certain roles and the effects of such stereotyping

4. To help broaden the children's perspective of what they may do with their lives

Curricular activities:
1. To develop awareness of the issue in classroom
   a. Use mimeographed sheet provided for class.
   b. Adapt directions on Karkau, page 2, for your class.
   c. Teacher or small group of student assistants compiles list of adjectives on one chart.
   d. Discussion period: see examples of topics under item 4 (below) to bring up to keep discussion to the point.
   e. Discussion of adjective lists: from more general examples to immediate, concrete examples.

2. To develop small group discussion and interaction
   a. Use of advertisements to illustrate stereotypes. Teacher *or* students can bring in. Ask for specific number of male or female ads from each child from newspapers or magazines.
   b. Discussion of sex-stereotyping in ads.
   c. Possible written project at home for students: describe specific number of ads on TV for a two-hour period.
   d. Give more specific topic to children: e.g., "What kind of work will I be doing when I am twenty-five years old?" Important for girls to consider a specific vocation when they are adults for purposes of assignment.

3. To consider the effects of stereotyping today in the real world

     a. Movie to watch (or slide show on children's books)

     b. Discussion of apparent *and* real differences between men and women

4. Evaluation by students of unit materials

     a. Devise suitable kind of evaluation task for your students. For example, perhaps you might ask them for ways in which they think their attitudes have changed or not changed. (Content of paper not to be graded, but writing skills can be directed.) Perhaps provide them with list of topics (e.g., should men and women receive equal pay, could a woman be a good president, etc.?) and ask them for a one-paragraph response.

     b. Creation of some positive project showing nonsexist attitude, e.g., rewritten fairy tale, newspaper ad, TV ad, career job description, etc.

FIFTH GRADE: A CASE STUDY OF NONSEXIST TEACHING

This article was written by a student teacher concerned about sexism in his class. This describes his process for encouraging nonstereotypical behavior and interactions. He presents both the activities he used and the response from the students. His suggestions (at the end of the article) for expanding sex-role attitudes of children are particularly helpful for a teacher initiating a thorough nonsexist program in a class.

SEXISM IN THE FOURTH GRADE*

—Being an account of how I tried to make fourth-graders aware of sex roles, stereotypes, and POTOS; and how I in turn became

---

*Printed with permission. KNOW, Inc., P.O. Box 86031, Pittsburgh, Pa. 15221, August 1973.

aware of cooties, girl-touch, and the illegibility of fourth-graders' handwriting.

By Kevin Karkau

The fourth-grade open classroom where I student-teach is composed of 18 boys and 10 girls. A high percentage of the students at the school have a parent(s) who is a professional, and the income level is thus relatively high. In the classroom, two students are of oriental background, 26 are white, and the teacher is young, female, and white. The classroom is "open" in that there are no letter grades given, students may work at their own pace on designated workbooks and in areas of personal interest, and they are given 15 minutes of free time in the morning and the afternoon to do as they wish. There are some structured activities, such as art and music classes. Perhaps the greatest difference between the "open" and the "traditional" classrooms is that students are freer to move about in the "open" classroom.

The inspiration for the activities brought in was the behavior of the children. There was a definite problem, in that boys and girls rarely associated with each other. The children could place their desks wherever they wished, but the result was that boys and girls did not sit together. They formed two separate lines—one for boys and one for girls—whenever they went to art class or math lab although the teacher had never asked them to do so. Boys played soccer at recess while most girls played pom-pom or tag. In art class boys and girls sat at separate tables. In math lab, they played separate math games. They teased each other when someone touched a Person of the Opposite Sex (which I will call a POTOS), formed all-girl and all-boy groups for creative writing exercises, sat in two rows for music class, and worst of all, rarely talked with each other.

The children's segregated behavior could be attributed to a "natural stage" that children go through, but I believed that the behavior was a result of socialization processes. Surely this segregation was unhealthy and limiting for those people who wished to associate with a POTOS. I decided to implement some activities with the following goals in mind: (1) making the

children aware of unequal treatment given to females in society
and in their classroom, (2) getting the kids to feel more free
about associating with a POTOS, (3) examining how males and
females are stereotyped into certain roles and the effects of such
stereotyping, and (4) helping to broaden the children's perspectives of what they may do with their lives.

Change must first begin with the teacher. Teacher awareness will include substantially equal expectations for boys and
girls, equal attention, encouraging the children to interact more,
pointing out unfair or stereotyped treatment of females in textbooks, movies, readers, and people's attitudes, sharing of classroom responsibilities between boys and girls (running the pro-
jector, carrying books, reading aloud), playing equally with boys
and girls at recess, and, if oral reading is done by the teacher,
selection of non-sexually stereotyped books. Luckily, the
teacher in this class was excellent at not discriminating, but
there was also little encouragement to interact with a POTOS.

Learning by example can only lead so far, though. For this
classroom, some consciousness-raising activities were needed.
The first activity was discovered on page 33 of the tremendously
helpful booklet *Sexism in Education,* published by the Emma
Willard Task Force on Education of Minneapolis. The purpose
of the activity is to get a feel for the students' attitudes towards
men and women. The mimeographed sheet that was handed out
to the children is in the back of this report. Here are the
instructions I gave to the class:

1. Individually I would like each boy to think of some one-
    word characteristics of a man, and each girl to think of
    some characteristics of a woman. Then write the char-
    acteristics on the mimeographed sheet. If you have
    difficulty thinking of characteristics, think of a man or
    woman you know. If you don't think men or women
    have any special characteristics, list what an ideal per-
    son would be like. In any case, try to list at least five
    characteristics.

2. From your first list, choose the characteristics that you
    like and list them in the second column.

3. Now form groups of three to five people of your own sex. In your group, each one should read their lists out loud. If you don't know the meaning of a word, ask.

4. Decide, as a group, on ten characteristics that you believe are most important for a male (for the boys) or a female (for the girls) to have. Then rank these items from one to ten in order of importance. It is essential that you all participate in the decision.

The students were asked to work on characteristics of their own sex because it was felt that a freer choice of characteristics and more natural discussion of the importance of the items would result, but mixed groups and both sexes working the same sex are possible variations. This section of the activity required about one hour, and the first discussion took place four days later.

On looking over the groups' ideal persons, most of the characteristics that the groups decided on were unisexual—that is, they could be important to both sexes. But there were some differences, especially in the first column (the typical man or woman). There, the traditional views towards men and women showed up. Men were brave, strong, healthy, humorous, kind; women were gentle, pretty, good cooks, clean, and smart. In general, the children described men and women in terms of the traditional stereotypes. In the third column (the ideal man or woman), the differences were more subtle but still noticeable. Here are the seven groups' lists, with the number of people in each group in parenthesis:

FEMALES

GROUP I (5)		GROUP II (5)	
1. Understanding	6. Firm	1. Active	6. Fairness
2. Good-mannered	7. Smart	2. Work with men	7. Truthful
3. Gentle	8. Clean	3. Nice	8. Smart
4. Loving	9. Active	4. Generous	9. Humorous
5. Hard worker	10. Confident	5. Helpful	10. Faithful

MALES

		GROUP		
III (3)	**IV (3)**	**V (4)**	**VI (3)**	**VII (3)**
1. Nice	1. Healthy	1. Healthy	1. Perfect	1. Honest
2. Good personality	2. True	2. Educational	2. Smart	2. Fair
3. Good looking	3. Kind	3. Equal	3. Brave	3. Real
4. Good sport	4. Serious	4. Friendly	4. Lucky	4. Kind
5. Smart	5. Happy	5. Creative	5. Brainy	5. Helpful
6. Brave		6. Active	6. Cheerful	6. Humorous
		7. Patient	7. Nice	7. Imaginative
		8. Well-off	8. Quick	8. Peaceful
		9. Kind	9. Fast	9. Uncompetitive
		10. Intelligent	10. Funny	10. Smart

I make no great attempts at analyzing these lists, but notice that the girls tended to list qualities necessary for helping other people (perhaps defining themselves in terms of others), while the boys described qualities of a more individualistic nature.

The discussion required *two class periods of about 45 minutes each.* For the discussion, we all moved into a small corner of the room and sat on the floor. Almost everyone participated, except for three boys who played chess in the corner, but even they were partially listening. The plan was to *examine whether males and females should have completely equal opportunities in everything,* and to point out the discrepancy between the people the children had described and their behavior in the classroom. (For anyone attempting this activity, it is important to have some broad areas of study in mind, as one can easily get sidetracked during the discussion.)

Two lists were written on the blackboard (numerals I and V) and we discussed the question "to which sex does each list refer?" The children could determine easily that I referred to girls, V to boys. Next we went through the lists and put a check mark by the qualities that could apply to both males and females. Everyone agreed that all the qualities could apply, but there were disagreements over the order of importance. One boy objected strongly to placing "good mannered" (sic) second in importance. He conceived "good mannered" as meaning opening doors for women and seating women at tables. We then discussed why men perform such chivalric deeds, whether women should perform the same deeds, and whether such niceties are really necessary. The girls expressed no strong opinions about such actions, but most of the boys seemed to be repulsed by the idea of being polite to girls—probably due more to fear of being teased than a belief that girls could fend for themselves.

We next went to the third word on the boys' list—"equal"—and discussed its ramifications. How equal should men and women be? Should women have equal job opportunities? Should they have the freedom to be tough, strong, brave, active, as men are traditionally supposed to be? Should boys be able to cry freely and not be teased for it? Are there any qualities that are peculiarly masculine or feminine? *What does the word "stereotype" mean?* What can we do in the classroom to break down stereotypes? These were some of the questions asked in the discussion.

Everyone believed that men and women should have equal job opportunities. There was less vociferous consensus on the next question, which really asked "to what extent should people be able to behave as they wish?" General opinion among the boys was that "if girls *want* to act in a 'masculine' way, sure, that's fine"; but it could be seen that most boys didn't want girls to act like boys and couldn't understand why a girl would want to. When asked if boys should be able to cry freely, or play with dolls, the boys snickered a lot but said "sure, if they want to." It was clear that few of them wanted to. Females can certainly have the same job opportunities as males, but the boys were not quite ready to accept equality of personality opportunities. The girls were wholeheartedly in favor of such freedom.

We next discussed the word "stereotype." A boy read the dictionary definition—"a conventional and usually oversimplified conception or belief"—and we discussed how stereotypes work in everyday life. "How many of you have moms that work?" I asked them. "Does your dad ever cook? How many male elementary teachers and female principals have you seen?" Many children had moms that worked and dads that cooked. When the boys were asked if they ever cooked, most seemed a little offended and said "no, because we just don't want to."

I then asked the group if anyone could think of qualities that were peculiarly masculine or feminine. No one could think of any. Now was the time to bring out the discrepancy between their attitudes and behavior. "I don't understand something," I said. "Here you have listed characteristics that could apply to both men and women, you have agreed that males and females should have equal opportunities, that there are no distinctly masculine or feminine qualities; yet in the classroom and at recess, boys and girls hardly ever associate with each other. Why?" No one replied, so I moved the discussion to a more concrete area—that of sports. If equality in the sports area can be achieved, other areas quickly follow. I asked the class why girls didn't play soccer more at recess—was there any discrimination on the boys' part? Some boys were upset at that thought and quickly defended themselves. "They can play if they want to," said the boys, "but they just don't want to." I asked the girls if they felt free to play soccer. Most replied affirmatively, but said they simply didn't want to play soccer. But one girl who played soccer occasionally brought out some real reasons for the lack of female participation. "First of all," she said, "the boys never ask us to play. Then when we do play, only boys are chosen to be captains. And girls don't get the ball passed to them very often, and when a girl scores a goal, the boys don't cheer." I asked the boys if that was true, and they argued a great deal, but finally agreed that the girls had legitimate complaints.

Next I asked the class if they could think of other areas in their classroom where girls were treated unfairly. No one could think of any, so I pointed out the way they were currently sitting. It was as if a wall were separating the sexes—girls on one side, boys on the other. The children looked around as if they had never realized the separation before, then let out a collective sigh of amazement. I then asked them why they formed two lines whenever they went out of the classroom. Some of the boys said that the teacher had told them to do so.

But the teacher and the girls quickly corrected that statement. The teacher then asked if previous teachers had told them to form two lines. No teachers had, which showed that the segregation by sex was voluntary, and thus deeply socialized into the children by their experiences outside school.

The first discussion ended and the children went out for recess. There were some immediately noticeable results. Eight girls played soccer, more so than ever before. There were at least three occasions where boys and girls talked to each other. One girl kept touching a boy she liked, teasing him about his hair, but really seeking for some sign of interest. When the students returned and lined up for art class, one girl formed the girls' line on the side where the boys usually stood. "Hey, that's the boys' side," said some boys, whereupon the girls dared the boys to stand on their usual side. The boys weren't quite ready yet to stand close to girls, so that day two lines were still formed.

For the *second discussion,* the goals were to discover reasons why boys and girls interacted so rarely, to make them more aware of their behavior and its limiting effects on people, suggest activities where the kids could interact more with a POTOS (such as helping with classwork, integrating the art tables and lines), and, if they seemed ready, initiate a reward system (M&M's) for performance of integrating activities. All but the last goal was accomplished, as I decided that rewards would be punishing to those people who were not yet ready to interact freely.

One major reason why males and females don't interact so naturally in our society is that an overemphasis on physical attraction interferes. When a male and female are simply talking to each other, to many this connotes that a sexual attraction exists, even though there may be none. The problem manifests itself even in the fourth grade. I asked the class "why don't you talk with or even go near a POTOS more?" The answers— "People will think you're 'in love' with the person," said many girls; while for the boys, "if you touch a girl you get 'cooties' or 'girl-touch'" (a mysterious quality which can only be removed by saying "no gives"). Obviously, those who act on their

feelings are subject to ridicule or embarrassment, in the fourth
grade and in society. So I asked the kids why people say such
things, and why they themselves take the sayings seriously.
There were no explanations, except that people have always
done it, and everyone agreed that the sayings were not necessarily true, but that it was difficult to ignore the laughter and
ridicule. Getting this point into the open helped to ease the
tension in interactions with a POTOS. Everyone believed pri-
vately that talking with or touching a POTOS signified next to
nothing in itself, but as long as the group enforced its opinion on
interactions, it was difficult to disregard the group.

I next attempted to show some negative effects of sexual
stereotyping through personal experience. When I was in grade
school, I would become very frustrated at failure and break out
in tears. Crying only made me feel worse, though, because I was
a boy, and boys weren't supposed to cry. This previously untold
revelation was difficult for me to relate, but the kids seemed to
understand completely. Hopefully it made them realize that
expression of emotion should not be limited to one sex.

In the *third section of the discussion* I asked the children if
they could think of specific activities they could perform in the
classroom to help reduce the separation between the sexes.
"Invite the girls to play soccer," said one boy. "Stand in the
boys' line," said a girl. After that, though, there were no other
suggestions, and although many people were interacting more
with a POTOS, some were clearly uninterested in the whole
issue. I decided to simply list some activities they could do with
a POTOS, but not reward people with candy (simply praise) for
doing the activities. The list included sitting near, helping, standing in line, talking, playing sports, saying something nice about a
POTOS, and not laughing when people associated with a
POTOS.

There was a group of about four boys who seemed to take
no interest in the subjects of sex stereotyping and interaction
with a POTOS. The reason was fairly simple. In changing their
behavior to a situation where unlimited opportunities for living
one's life are available, many people lose their security of an
already-defined role. The boys didn't understand the long-term

benefits of such a change, and felt threatened by loss of their male status. Perhaps even worse, they were afraid of being coerced into changing their behavior. They didn't want to talk with girls or play sports with them, and when someone talked to them about changing roles and interacting with a POTOS, they turned their minds off in fear. Individual attention and explanation is necessary for such people, but they must also be given the option of not changing.

The next logical step, since the class as a group was not completely prepared for natural interaction, was small group discussions. I brought in *some advertisements* that showed women and men in stereotyped manner, and prepared some questions on the effects of advertising. *Two discussions of about a half-hour each* were held over the same material, with volunteer groups of six people each. I had previously asked the four boys who seemed uninterested in the subject to volunteer, and two of them did so.

The ads showed women in passive roles, concerned with beauty and pleasing men; while men were shown in tough, outdoorsy roles, such as racing, canoeing, and herding horses. Such ads can be found in almost any magazine; my sources were *Glamour, Cosmopolitan, Esquire,* and *Newsweek.* The general goals were to show the overemphasis on beauty in advertising, how sex and glamour are used to sell products, and how ads reinforce stereotyped attitudes about men and women. The points came across well, as everyone understood and could think of other television and magazine ads that furthered sex typing.

But more important than the discussion that day was a change in the children's behavior. Four days had elapsed between the second discussion and the small group discussions, and in that time the girls and boys occasionally played together at recess, and another good discussion over an article in the weekly news-magazine had taken place. The article concerned sex roles, and the kids were strongly critical of some unfair views in the article. I state these facts to illustrate how long it took for some fundamental behavior changes to occur.

Anyway, after the small group discussions, two girls

decided to integrate the boys' line. The lines were just forming and the two girls stepped behind two boys, while I was the only male in the girls' line. Immediately the two boys left the line and tried to stand behind me, but some girls arrived first. The boys looked around, realized they would have to stand next to a girl, and as the rest of the class arrived, the lines dissolved into one big integrated line. There was much excited teasing and talking between boys and girls as we walked to the art room, and once there, boys and girls sat together at tables, although not too closely. It was gratifying, to say the least, to see such behavior changes.

Two days later, another major change occurred in the classroom. The same two girls who integrated the lines moved their desks into a boys' group (after asking the boys first). Other girls quickly followed suit and asked to join boys' groups. I suggested to two girls that they ask two of the shyest boys in the classroom to sit with them. The girls were also too shy to ask however, so I served as intermediary and persuaded the boys to sit with the girls. After sitting all year in a corner of the room, the boys moved to the center of the room and sat in a group with girls. There was a tremendous amount of noise and confusion with the desks scraping on the floor and boys and girls talking, teasing, and flirting with each other. At recess, everyone played pom-pom (a traditionally girls' game at the school). By the end of the day, there were three integrated groups of ten, five, and five people, plus various other all-male groups.

An activity on jobs was partially implemented. The students were asked to write on the following subject: "Imagine you are grown up. Describe a typical day." The purpose was to discover if boys conceived of their adulthood in terms of career goals, while girls conceived of it in terms of domestic life, as in the Iglitzin-Fiedler study ("A Child's Eye View of Sex Roles," *Today's Education*, December 1972, pp. 23–25). If so, a study of job opportunities would be helpful in expanding the children's awareness of options. But the essays did not turn out well— some children did not understand whether to write about a job they might be doing or just a typical day's activities; others expressed no ideas about their future; while others had spring fever and couldn't write much. So nothing further was done with the subject.

Another discussion was held to examine the children's feelings towards the changes in the classroom and to suggest or entertain ideas for further change. The consensus was that people enjoyed the opportunities for increased association with a POTOS, felt more free to interact, and teased others less when they interacted with a POTOS. But there were no further suggestions for change, except to try individually to be less sensitive to unjust ridicule.

For the final week, two movies were shown to the class. The first one, *Psychological Differences between the Sexes*, portrayed men and women in a stereotyped manner and attributed personality differences between the sexes to natural occurrences, not socialization processes. For example, men were typified as being blunt, tending toward direct action, and naturally stronger. Women were shown as more concerned with physical appearance, took general comments personally (more sensitive to criticism), and were more romantic.

I asked the children to write some reactions immediately after the film was over. Here is a sample of their comments:

- It was not true about a man is stronger than a woman. Because there was a woman who could rip a coat of chain mail with her bare hands.

- It isn't always true that just women think about what is said about another person. I do sometimes.

- It was stupid because the man was doing all the work and the lady was picking up little sticks.

- I don't think girls are like they said. I am not like that at all.

We then discussed the film and the classroom in greater detail. The most interesting information from the discussion was that while teasing people for associating with a POTOS had decreased within the classroom, the change had not transferred to outside the classroom. There, the children still experienced

teasing that was difficult to ignore. I asked them why other
people teased them. There was a long silence, then one girl gave
exactly the right answer—"because they've probably been
teased too." We decided that the best way to handle such a
situation was either to ignore it or to explain to the other person
why it was wrong to tease someone for associating with a
POTOS.

Two days later the kids saw another film entitled *Anything
You Want to Be*. It concerned a girl's career goals (doctor,
chemist, class president) and what she actually ended up doing
(nurse, mixing baby formulas, class secretary). People kept
telling her that she could be anything she wanted to be, but
because she was female, the dreams never came true. Even
after two showings, the children had a difficult time understanding the idea, as the movie was full of fantasy, subtlety, and
symbolism. Also, being young and in a liberal community, the
children had not yet experienced society's full oppression
against women. Perhaps the ideas contained in this movie will
make more sense to the kids as they grow older.

The last activity was a student evaluation of the changes in
the classroom. Twenty-four evaluations were turned in, and as
can be seen, a high percentage indicated that they felt more at
ease in various activities with a POTOS:

1. Since the activities and discussions began on sex stereotyping and male and female behavior, how much at
   ease do you feel with people of the opposite sex in each
   of the following situations?
   a. Talking with them
        much less 1 less 0 same 7 more 11 much more 5
   b. Standing in line
        much less 0 less 0 same 9 more 6 much more 9
   c. Sitting next to them
        much less 0 less 0 same 8 more 9 much more 7
   d. Helping (in any way)
        much less 1 less 0 same 11 more 8 much more 4
   e. Playing at recess
        much less 1 less 0 same 13 more 5 much more 5

f. Touching

much less 1 less 0 same 11 more 8 much more 4

2. In the classroom, do you think there is less or more teasing when a boy and a girl associate (talk, touch, etc.)?

much less 9 less 10 same 1 more 1 much more 0

3. Outside the classroom, do you think there is less or more teasing when a boy and a girl associate?

much less 3 less 5 same 11 more 5 much more 0

4. Have any of your ideas about men and women changed?

yes 12 no 10

5. If your ideas have changed, please describe at least one change (more if you can).

6. Please use the space below to list any other comments you may have about the activities—use the back of this paper if necessary. Please think hard. Thank you for filling out this evaluation.

For the last two questions, only nine people wrote about a change in their ideas or commented on the activities. But the attitude changes towards men and women seemed to be healthy, and the comments were all favorable. Here are some examples:

5. Most boys in the class don't mind sitting with, talking to, and touching girls.

At least in our classroom I think everyone likes people more.

They seem to like each other more now because of standing in line together, etc.

6. I think these activities have helped a lot.

I think you have changed the class a little but it helped.

I think outside the classroom is the same—girl-touch, being teased, and so on.

I liked it except the discussions.

I think boys and girls should get jobs just as easy and they should be equal.

Student evaluations must always be taken with a grain of salt, however, as young children tend to answer as the teacher wants them to. There is also the possibility that they will misunderstand the questions; and where are the comments of the people who were uninterested in the activities? But taking into consideration the behavior and attitude changes in the classroom, there is no other interpretation then that these evaluations represent fairly accurately the increased association of boys and girls on a more natural basis.

There have been some definite and seemingly permanent behavior and attitude changes. There is more communication between the sexes, boys and girls feel freer to sit, talk, and play together, and they are more sensitive to sexual stereotyping. The five goals stated at the beginning of this report were accomplished with most of the class. For those who didn't become more free to associate with a POTOS, there was nothing completely wrong with that, either. They must certainly be allowed the option of not associating with a POTOS, as the goal was not to *force* people to interact, but to *expand* their opportunities for interaction.

For anyone attempting similar activities, here are some suggestions:

1. *Keep an overall view of your goals* and ways of implementing them, but also be flexible enough to match the children's moods.

2. Don't go too fast, and be ready to backtrack. Children learn at different rates. (The activities described required only about eight class hours, but it took fifteen days for behavior to change significantly.)

3. Be very sensitive to the interactions between the boys and girls. Try to understand what a change in role means for a boy and girl, and provide some viable role alternatives.

4. Devise some relevant questions for consciousness-raising periods. *Tailor the discussion to the problems of the classroom, not just society.*

5. If something has affected you deeply, share it with the students. They'll sympathize and perhaps reveal some of their own experiences.

6. *Never coerce the students to act in a manner which is clearly not to their desires.*

In a way, these activities have required the children to act in a more mature way than adults do—to ignore a person's gender as a measure of ability, to allow people to define their own role, to tolerate various behaviors—but that is exactly the point of education. The value of such education can be seen in the increased associations between boys and girls in the class-

CHARACTERISTICS OF A WOMAN (OR MAN)	WHICH OF THE CHARACTERISTICS DO YOU LIKE?	IN YOUR GROUP, SELECT 10 ITEMS FROM THE COMBINED LISTS THAT ARE MOST IMPORTANT AND RANK THEM IN ORDER OF IMPORTANCE
		1.
		2.
		3.
		4.
		5.
		6.
		7.
		8.
		9.
		10.

room, in their more sociable personalities, and in their positive comments about the activities. The difficulties of the project, such as lack of interest inside the classroom and non-understanding outside the classroom, are only symptomatic of what the children may face in the future. In that sense, the final value of the project depends on the degree to which the ideas I have attempted to communicate can help the children in their future.

FIFTH GRADE: WOMEN WORKERS

A set of statistics compiled by the Women's Bureau of the U.S. Department of Labor provides an illustrative example of the new woman worker. (See the profile on the opposite page.) Besides being an exercise in mathematical concepts, it allows interesting speculation about the future woman worker. What conclusions can be drawn from the data?

FIFTH GRADE: ACTIVITIES CONCERNING JOB OPPORTUNITIES

Writing assignments—occupational:
   1. a. Teacher lists (or has class help) about twenty to thirty occupations on board.
      b. Have each student select ten and make up five descriptive words to go with each role. State whether job is for male, female, or both.
      c. Why?
   2. a. Have students review want ads in a Sunday paper. Have them make a list of jobs that want women and those which want men. What jobs have no qualifications? (Each student should collect a list of twenty to thirty jobs.)
      b. Collate lists in class and discuss rationale (or lack of) for sex-specific jobs.
      c. Possibly have student come to own conclusion before class discussion.
   3. a. Have class compose questionnaire about male or

PROFILE OF THE TYPICAL WOMAN WORKER: 1920 AND 1970*

	1920	1970
Age	28 years old.	39 years old.
Marital status	Single.	Married and living with her husband.
Occupation	Most likely to be a factory worker or other operative. Other large numbers of women in clerical, private household, and farm work. Occupational choice extremely limited.	Most likely to be a clerical worker. Many other women in service work outside the home, factory or other operative work. About 500 individual occupations open to her.
Education	Only 1 out of 5 seventeen-year-olds in the population a high school graduate.	High school graduate with some college or post-secondary-school education.
Labor force participation	Less than one-fourth (23 per cent) of all women 20 to 64 years of age in the labor force. Most apt to be working at age 20 to 24 (38 per cent). Participation rate dropping at age 25, decreasing steadily, and only 18 per cent at age 45 to 54.	Almost half (49 per cent) of all women 18 to 64 years of age in the labor force. Most apt to be working at age 20 to 24 (57 percent). Labor force participation rate dropping at age 25 and rising again at age 35 to a second peak of 54 percent at age 45 to 54.
	Less than 1 out of every 5 (18 per cent) women 35 to 64 years of age in the labor force.	Can expect to work 24 to 31 more years at age 35.

What conclusions can be drawn from the data?

---

*Reprinted with permission from U.S. Department of Labor, Women's Bureau.

female job opportunities, requirements, or descriptions.

b. Have them interview six adults in own neighborhood. Have them learn how to compile data and display in a matrix.

c. Have class write up results.

4. **a.** Have all students write in 10 minutes what work they want to do when they finish their education.

b. Teacher collects papers by sex and gives back each pile to *opposite* sex.

c. Have male students defend a student's career expectation as if it were his own, if he can, and vice versa.

FOURTH, FIFTH, AND SIXTH GRADES: GROWING UP FEMALE AND MALE IN AMERICA*

The following unit, entitled "Growing Up Female and Male in America," was developed by Susan Bement, Director of the Women's Studies Program of the Berkeley Unified School District. It was developed during the 1972–1973 academic year for use in grades 4, 5, and 6.

Study questions can be used with many reading books, sexist or nonsexist, to pinpoint the attitudes of the author and characters toward sex roles, or to open discussion about the class's feelings about sex-role stereotypes. Many books focus on children's difficulties in adjusting to their roles (e.g., *Queenie Peavy*) or on children's expectations for adult behavior. For example, Natalie Savage Carlsen's *Ann Aurelia and Dorothy* is a favorite with upper elementary students. Chapter 8, "The Surprise Party," shows Ann Aurelia and Dorothy's mistaken assumption about why their much-loved teacher, Miss Bennett, is going to leave school. Assuming she is going to get married (why else would she leave?), they plan a surprise party replete with poems and a wedding cake, only to discover too late that Miss Bennett is going back to graduate school. Through guided class discussion and questioning, the students in your class

---

*The Women's Studies Program, Berkeley Unified School District.

should be able to see the kind of stereotype Ann Aurelia had for single adult women. This can lead to an examination of the class's feelings about unmarried women, about the kinds of things adult women do. See the student bibliography for further suggestions.

I. INTRODUCTORY IDEAS
A. *Goals*
1. Begin to learn how to research around an idea
2. Gain understanding of what it means to be female and male
3. Gain understanding of what sex-role behavior is learned and serves a social function, and what behavior is innate
4. Gain understanding of sex-role behavior from a multicultural perspective
5. Gain understanding of sex-role behavior from an historical perspective
6. Create a product that embodies and communicates this understanding

B. *How to begin*
1. *Lesson plan 1:* What does it mean to be female and male? Use of magazine pictures for role definition.
2. *Lesson plan 2:* Behavior observance.
3. *Lesson plan 3* (optional): How did females and males learn the sex roles they play? Are boys and girls taught differently in other cultures? Use films about cultures that show behavior patterns different from those we would consider traditional.
4. *Purpose of unit:* To look into these questions—
   a. Whether females and males act out the same sex roles in all cultures in the United States
   b. How our learned definitions of female sex role and male sex role have developed historically

II. GETTING DOWN TO WORK
A. *Lesson 4:*
Historical fiction books with information on the above

questions are brought into the class. Each student
selects a book to read and works in a group with the
other students who have selected the same book. As
they read they are to keep in mind: In this book, what
kinds of things do females do, males do, and why? The
books selected could be drawn from the following areas:

1. Indian tribes 17th–19th centuries
2. White farm/pioneer life, 19th century (sample:
   Caddie Woodlawn)
3. Immigrant urban life, 19th century
4. Asian immigrant life, 19th–20th centuries (sample: *Journey to Topaz)*
5. African family life (sample: *31 Brothers and
   Sisters)*
6. Black family life (sample: *Sounder)*
7. Chicano family life
8. Poor white family life
9. White suburbia, 20th century
10. Teenage culture today

B. *Study questions:*

Study questions should be developed for each book (see
samples). Time must be allotted for the groups to meet,
discuss their books and the study questions, and to put
together a report to be presented in class. The purpose
of the reporting is to share with the class the information
each book gives about:

1. The culture and historical period involved
2. The male and female sex-role behavior described
3. How the sex-role behavior is influenced by the
   historical situation
4. Information on what is considered "typical" or
   "atypical" sex-role behavior

This information can be presented in traditional report
form, or via skits, cartoons, etc. The reports must be brief
and to the point. Observers should have a simple chart
which they fill in with the information each reporter gives
them re the above questions. (See sample enclosed.)

C. *Lesson 5—class discussion:*
Everyone should have her/his charts completed before discussion begins.
   1. Tack a long sheet of paper on a bulletin board. List on it the name of each book read and under it put Male and Female. Have students fill in the sex roles played by the males and females in each book, based on the information on their charts.

SOUNDER		PLUM CREEK		JOURNEY TO TOPAZ	
MALE	FEMALE	MALE	FEMALE	MALE	FEMALE

   2. Read the information on the woman's role across the chart. What role behaviors are most common? What are the exceptions?
   3. Read the information on the man's role across the chart. What role behaviors are most common? What are the exceptions?
   4. Can we draw any conclusions about what is typical among all these cultural groups for female sex-role behavior? for male sex-role behavior? and what is atypical behavior for both females and males?

III. CONCLUSION: GROUP ACTIVITY
Lesson 6—creative writing assignment:
Students are to write a story about a person, living or imaginary, who:
   1. Is a representation of typical female sex role behavior or typical male sex role behavior but is an

> *exaggeration* of that stereotype. (Examples: Mike
> Fink, Mississippi boatman; Priest in Superfly;
> movie actresses; Archie Bunker.)
>
> *or*
>
> 2. Lives a life where she or he crosses over the
> barriers of typical sex role behavior and is shown
> living on the other side. (Examples: *Story of X* in
> *Ms.,* December 1972 issue; "Male Dancers," *S.F.
> Chronicle,* Tuesday, March 6, 1973, p. 17; *Pene-
> lope and the Mussels;* reverse roles in Sendak's
> *Where the Wild Things Are.*)

LESSON 1: GROWING UP FEMALE AND MALE*

I. INTRODUCTORY DISCUSSION (*5 minutes*)
Take a brief poll of the class: How many girls in this class
want to grow up to be a boxer, a pilot, a plumber, an engineer? How many boys want to grow up to be a nurse, a
housekeeper, a secretary, a plane steward? Take each profession, one at a time, seeing if you get any hands, then go on to
the next profession. Why is it so few boys are interested in
any of the occupations in the second grouping, and so few
girls interested in the occupations in the first grouping?

The professions asked of the girls are the kinds of things
men usually do; those asked of the boys are the things women
usually do. Today we are going to look into this question of
what men do and what women do.

II. MATERIALS NEEDED
Scissors, paste
Magazines (Students can bring from home. Make sure of
variety—Life, Ebony, etc. Also, make sure pictures of a
nontraditional nature are represented.)
Cardboard boxes

----

*Bement, Susan Groves. "Growing up Male and Female in America."
The Women's Studies Program, Berkeley Unified School District.

III. INSTRUCTIONS *(30 minutes)*

    A. Divide class into small groups, each group having basic equipment.

    B. In the middle of the room is a box. Labeling one side of the box for each of the following purposes, the students go through the magazines cutting out pictures of:

        1. Things only women do

        2. Things only men do

        3. Things both do

    The pictures are then pasted onto the designated sides of the box.

    C. If students can think of something for which there is no picture, they can draw a picture, cut it out, paste it on the box.

IV. CLASS DISCUSSION *(20 minutes)*

    A. Compile a list on the board based on the students' research of the things only women do, etc., discussing the suggestions as they are made to see if there is agreement.

    B. Controversies:

        1. Reproduction. Although women give birth, men supply sperm.

        2. Child care. Men show maternal instincts when put in the position of having sole responsibility for their children.

        3. Tough jobs demanding strength. Discuss different kinds of strength, i.e., lumberjacks and pioneer women.

    C. *Conclusions:*

    What can we conclude are things only women do? only men do? *Aim: To show how interchangeable sex roles are today.* That's the reality. It may be important to acknowledge that many people desire to keep the traditional sex role patterns.

    Is this what it means to be female and male? Let's look at ourselves to see if we can observe ourselves

doing the same kinds of things we saw in the magazines.
(See lesson 2.)

Make poster of the final list so it can be seen for
later use.

STUDY QUESTIONS FOR YOSHIKO UCHIDA,
Journey to Topaz

A. Let's work on the historical setting in which this story takes
place:

QUESTION	ANSWER
1. At what time (approximately) does it take place?	1.
2. In what part of the United States?	2.
3. Were the Sakanes American citizens? Explain.	3.
4. Where did they come from & why did they come to the United States?	4.
5. Were there quite a few people who came to the United States as they did?	5.
6. Why, according to the author, were the people of Japanese ancestry forced to leave their homes and jobs and move into "relocation" camps until the war was over?	6.
7. Is there any reason why people of Italian ancestry were not treated in the same way since the United States was at war with Italy as well?	7.

B. *Research theme:*

What kinds of things did females do, what kinds of things did
males do and why?

1. See if you can make a list under the following columns.

You may have to go back and look at the book in order to get as much information as you can.

THINGS ONLY FEMALES DID (MOTHER SAKANE)	THINGS ONLY MALES DID (FATHER, KEN)	THINGS THEY DID TOGETHER

2. Can you make a general statement based on the above list, that sums up what their "roles" were?
3. It is pretty clear that the women in this book did certain kinds of work, and the men did other kinds of work most of the time. Why do you think they worked things out this way rather than, let's say, decide that Mother Sakane would be the breadwinner while Father Sakane would stay home and do the cooking, cleaning and sewing?
4. Even under extreme conditions (such as camp life) where the routines of normal life were upset, Mother Sakane basically kept the feminine role. Can you give several illustrations that show this?
5. When Father Sakane was arrested he gave Ken his role of leadership in the family. Why do you think he didn't give that role to the Mother?

C. *Conclusion:*
1. Many Americans of Japanese ancestry came from families similiar to the Sakanes. How different are the roles played here by the Mother and Father from the roles played today by your Mother and Father? Let's look at your family for comparison. Make a chart like the one in B-1, only describe what goes on in your family under the following headings:

MY FAMILY

THINGS ONLY FEMALES DO (MY MOTHER, SISTERS, ME)	THINGS ONLY MALES DO (MY FATHER, BROTHER, ME)	THINGS DONE TOGETHER

2. Would you say the things your Mother does as a woman are quite similar to Mother Sakane? or different? and what about your Father as compared to Father Sakane?

STUDY QUESTIONS FOR CAROL BRINK'S *Caddie Woodlawn*

A. Let's work on the historical setting in which this story takes place:

QUESTION	ANSWER
1. At what time does it take place?	1.
2. At this time the North and South were at war. What events are described in this book that let us know how the war affected frontier families like the Woodlawns?	2.
3. In what part of the United States does the story take place?	3.
4. The author describes Western Wisconsin as being on the "outskirts of civilization." Can you give several examples to illustrate this was so?	4.

5. Why did this family choose   5.
to live on the edge of
civilization rather than in a
city?

6. The author gives us a special   6.
insight into the wars between
the white settlers and the
Indians. Can you describe
what she says about this?

B. *Research theme:*
What kinds of things did females do, what kinds of things did
males do and why?
1. See if you can make a list under the following columns.
You may have to go back and look at the book in order
to get as much information as you can.

THINGS ONLY FEMALES DID: MOTHER, CLARA, ANNABELLE	MISS PARKER	CADDIE

THINGS ONLY MALES DID	THINGS THEY DID TOGETHER

2. Can you make a general statement based on the above list, that sums up what were the "roles" of the men and of the women?
3. Why was Caddie an exception to the rule on how little girls should be reared?
4. The author makes it clear that if one had to choose between the childhood of Caddie and her brothers, and the childhood of Clara and Annabelle, it wouldn't be a difficult choice at all—Caddie's life was much more fun and exciting. Why do her Mother and Father agree that after she gains her strength Caddie must begin to learn "to be a lady"? Do you agree with their decision?
5. Can you describe what Caddie's life might be like were she not trained to "be a lady," and left to grow up like her brothers?
6. Caddie's father was the one who insisted she be allowed to run in the woods with her brothers. He was also very important in convincing her that she should, after gaining back her good health, begin to think about being a lady. How does he explain this to her in a way that convinces her and changes her life? What does he describe as being a woman's responsibilities? What does he feel are a man's responsibilities?
7. Caddie is an unusual girl. She is quite a contrast to Clara. But she does do some things that are usually described as typically female even though she is a tomboy. Can you name a few?

C. *Conclusion:*
1. Many of today's Americans came from pioneer farm roots such as the family in this book. In many families today, Mothers and Fathers play basically the same roles we have read about here. Let's look at your family for comparison. Make a chart like the one in B-1, only describe what goes on in your family under the headings at the top of page 93.
2. Would you say the things your Mother does as a woman are quite similar to Mother Woodlawn? or dif-

MY FAMILY

THINGS ONLY FEMALES DO (MY MOTHER, SISTERS, ME)	THINGS ONLY MALES DO (MY FATHER, BROTHERS, ME)	THINGS DONE TOGETHER

ferent? and what about your Father as compared to Father Woodlawn?

STUDY QUESTIONS FOR 31 BROTHERS AND SISTERS
By Reba Mirsky

A. First, let's work on the setting in which this story takes place.

QUESTIONS	ANSWERS
1. In what part of Africa does the story take place?	1.
2. Around what tribe does the story focus?	2.
3. The way this family is defined is quite different from the way a family is defined in the U.S. Can you describe some of the differences?	3.
4. The way the tribe operates, for example on the elephant hunt, is quite different from the way we are used to. Can you describe some of the practices that are different?	4.
5. What was the main difference between the Zulus and the Pygmies?	5.

B. *Research theme:*

What kinds of things did females do, what kinds of things did males do, and why?

    1. See if you can make lists under the following columns. Refer back to your book for specific answers.

THINGS ONLY FEMALES DID:
MOTHER   NOMUSA AND HER SISTER

THINGS ONLY MALES DID:
FATHER   BROTHERS

THINGS FEMALES AND MALES DID TOGETHER:

---

    2. Can you make a general statement, based on the above list, that summarizes the "roles" of the men and of the women?

    3. Nomusa is considered a very unusual girl because she knows how to do all the things that boys are supposed to know how to do. Can you describe what kinds of things a girl is supposed to do? (Use Sisewe, her sister, as an example.) Now, describe the kinds of things that Nomusa does that are considered "boy's territory."

4. Nomusa's brother, Mdingi, is criticized by his father for not caring enough about doing the things boys are supposed to do. Where does Mdingi fail, in his father's estimation? What kinds of things would he rather do?

5. In this story, Nomusa is rewarded for what she does, even though she is acting like a boy. Mdingi is not rewarded. See if you can guess what will happen to Nomusa and Mdingi as they grow older. Do you think they will continue to rebel against what they are supposed to do, or do you think they will conform? Explain.

6. A very important part of being a woman in this story is serving food to your husband and waiting on him while he eats. If he belches, you know he has enjoyed the food. What do you think is the purpose of this custom of the woman serving the man?

C. *Conclusion:*

1. Many of today's Americans came from Africa. Many Americans have roots in the African culture. Let's compare the way your family divides responsibilities and roles with the way it was done in this book. Make a chart like the one in B-1, only describe, under the following headings, what goes on in your family:

MY FAMILY

THINGS ONLY FEMALES DO (MY MOTHER, GRANDMOTHER, SISTER, I)	THINGS ONLY MALES DO (FATHER, BROTHER, GRANDFATHER, UNCLE, I)	THINGS DONE TOGETHER

2. Would you say the things your mother does as a woman are quite similar to Nomusa's mother, or different? And what about your father, as compared to Nomusa's father?

FIFTH GRADE: WOMEN IN DIFFERENT SOCIETIES AND ERAS IN HISTORY*

This is an assignment for a research project to be given orally in class. Before you give your presentation, you should ditto up an outline to pass out in class the day of your report. The outline should cover the *main* points of your presentation, and also include the sources you have used for your research. (You should use a *minimum* of three different sources). In your report, answer as many of the following questions in A, B, C, and D as you can, in depth. If you are doing a period of American history, be very sure to cover D in depth.

I. QUESTIONS TO BE COVERED IN YOUR ORAL REPORT
    A. In this society, how did most people feel about:
        1. The nature of women
        2. What traits were feminine and masculine
        3. What were possible and proper roles for women
    B. What was the *status of women* in this society or era:
        1. Their legal rights (to property; rights in marriage; of divorce)
        2. Their educational possibilities
        3. Their work possibilities
    C. What *goals,* if any were women striving for in this era:
        1. What methods did they use?
        2. How successful (if at all) were they in achieving their goals?
    D. Discuss the lives of the most important or significant women in this era. (What obstacles did they face in

---

*Reprinted with permission from Patricia Silvers.

achieving their goals, and in living the kind of lives they wanted to live?)

You are free to do your presentation in whatever way you think will be most effective. Remember that two factors are very important to a good presentation:

1. Getting across the necessary information
2. Holding the attention and interest of the class for the duration of the report

Use whatever materials or strategies you like. You might choose to use photographs, pictures, paintings, role playing, skits, costumes, etc.

II. THE CHOICES

A. *American history:*
1. 17th and 18th century: The colonial women; women in Puritan New England; the frontier women.
2. 19th century women
   a. General—the Victorian era
   b. Pre-Civil War southern belles
   c. Pre-Civil War feminists (the early women's rights movement)
3. The World War One era: the Suffragettes
4. The 1920's: the Flapper
5. The Depression
6. The 1950's: Dr. Spock and the era of Domesticity
7. The Black Woman in America (17th century to the present)

B. *Traditional societies:*
8. The Japanese women (the geisha; the wife)
9. Eskimo women
10. Indian women (of India)
11. African women
12. Arab women

C. *Women in liberated (?) societies today:*
13. The Scandinavian women

    14. The Israeli women
  D. *Communist countries (compare women before and after the revolution):*
    15. Russian women (1917—Russian Revolution)
    16. Chinese women (1949—Chinese Revolution)
    17. Cuban women (1957—Cuban Revolution)

FIFTH GRADE: RECOMMENDATIONS FOR ELIMINATING SEX-ROLE STEREOTYPING IN ELEMENTARY TEXTS*

In every society, social roles are assigned to individuals on the basis of sex. Individuals are generally expected to engage in certain kinds of behavior and to refrain from others, to possess certain skills and aptitudes, and to exhibit emotional characteristics according to whether they are male or female. Specific sex-role behavior differs greatly from culture to culture, and what may be "male" behavior in one culture may be considered "female" behavior in another. Research indicates that children in all cultures learn at a very early age what behavior is expected of them in terms of sex, and can identify toys, occupations, colors, and clothes as "male" and "female."

Our world is one of rapid change. Today, the stereotypes and the code of expected sex-role behavior commonly presented in school textbooks is no longer consistent with reality. The perpetuation of traditional stereotypes through school materials can have a damaging and inhibiting effect on the development of both boys and girls.

Education includes not only the acquisition of skills and knowledge, but also the development of a sense of self. It is important that each student come to an understanding of his or her full worth as an individual in an atmosphere free from bias; one that does not classify without regard to individual preference and aptitude, and does not assume restrictions without providing opportunities. Those involved in the development of

---

*Copyrighted © 1974 by Laurie Olsen Johnson. Reprinted with permission of The Feminist Press.

educational materials are undoubtedly key figures in the shaping of the aspirations of the young. The textbooks used throughout the country define much of what will and what will not be taught in the classroom. In addition, children look to them as a major source of information about the world.

For these reasons, we feel it is important that curriculum eliminate what sex-role stereotyping does exist. To this end, we offer the following guidelines.

In general, if you are directing a project, watch to see that there is a balance in the number of "boy" stories and "girl" stories, and try to construct your anthologies or projects to reflect as nearly as possible a 50/50 ratio of boys to girls.

PORTRAYAL OF GIRLS

In curriculum materials, girls are generally portrayed as passive individuals who are dependent on the male figures in their lives. They are seen as neat, domestic, and well-behaved individuals who are fairly incompetent when it comes to any type of activity outside of domestic household chores and child care. They are also unable to undertake tasks which require physical strength or endurance. Most school materials indicate that a girl's main goal in life is to become a wife and mother. Any career aspirations which happen to be part of a girl character's make-up tend to be for careers which will not conflict with the role of wife and mother. To correct this problem, try the following:

- Show girls achieving academically and being rewarded for such achievements.

- Portray girls as mischief-makers every once in a while.

- Portray girls as decision-makers.

- Show that girls do have determination, guts, and a willingness to stand up for what they believe is right.

- Show girls participating in outdoor activities which require physical coordination and some strength, such as camping and athletics.

- Have girls doing adventurous and exciting activities.

- Portray girls cooperating with other girls in various adventures or creative situations. Avoid the stereotyped situations in which girls are seen doing silly things, or competing with each other for male attention.

- Show that girls who are not particularly attractive according to present-day standards may still lead active and exciting lives.

- Show that girls who are smart, academically inclined, or leaders can still be popular among their peers, both male and female.

- Show girls working toward a wide variety of career goals. Portray girls who are interested in science, electronics, computers, law, politics, economics, or business, as well as girls who want to become homemakers, models, teachers, beauticians, nurses, or entertainers.

PORTRAYAL OF BOYS

According to most schoolbooks, boys are brave adventurers, problem-solvers, mischief-makers, and seldom show emotion. There is nothing wrong with portraying boys as daring and adventurous, but a realistic balance should be attempted. In real life boys are often frightened, display emotion, and generally function in nonadventurous situations. To achieve a realistic balance, try the following:

- Show boys having fun indoors doing quiet activities (or outdoors doing nonathletic or not particularly adventurous activities). For example boys learn to play musical instruments, cook, paint, read, and study.

- Show that boys can experience a whole range of emotions. They can be frightened or upset, can feel like crying, and sometimes even cry. Show that the ability to honestly display emotion, or to face deep feelings, is a good trait.

- Show that boys can be helpful to other beings besides girls and mothers. Portray boys helping other boys, their fathers, pets, and other adults in their lives.

- Show boys who are quiet, gentle, sensitive, and sometimes passive.

- Show that boys can be self-sufficient. Boys can make their own lunches, repair clothing they have torn, or clean up after they have made a mess.

- Show that boys can be perplexed about the solutions to problems, and can seek answers from girls.

- Show some boys as well-behaved and have them rewarded for their good behavior. In doing this, use realistic boy models. Some boys really are concerned with cleanliness, grooming, being polite, living up to their responsibilities, trying not to hurt people's feelings, and allowing others to be leaders.

PORTRAYAL OF BOYS AND GIRLS IN MIXED SITUATIONS

When boys and girls are shown working or playing together in textbooks, the boys are generally portrayed as the leaders of the group, or as the oldest, most knowledgeable, most dependable, or most innovative members of the group. To achieve a more realistic balance, try the following:

- As you show girls and boys actively involved in an activity, have the girls participating in decision-making on an equal par with boys.

- Have girls as well as boys coming up with problem solutions, and have the female problem solvers recognized for their good ideas by the other boys and girls in the group.

- Show that it's all right for a boy to be helped by a girl, and that this does not necessarily make the boy any less of a person, or any less of a "man."

- When presenting boys and girls interacting, avoid having the children doing activities generally connected to one or the other of the sexes. For example, avoid having the girls cleaning up a mess created by boys.

- Eliminate scenes in which boys and girls toss sarcastic, flip, or derogatory comments at each other because of their sex, unless such scenes are central to a conflict situation which is resolved. Comments like "You're just a girl," "You're pretty smart for a girl," and "Ick! Dolls!" or "Boys are always a lot of trouble," "Boys will be boys," "You're just a boy. You wouldn't understand," or "Ick! Baseball!" lead to unfortunate and unrealistic stereotyping.

PORTRAYAL OF MOTHERS AND ADULT WOMEN

Mothers are generally portrayed doing household chores or caring for children. For the most part they are seen in textbooks cleaning, cooking, or serving meals. Yet mothers usually have many interests outside the home. They enjoy reading, working at hobbies, gardening, being active in civic affairs, playing instruments. They balance checkbooks, drive cars, fix things around the house. They are involved in hundreds of things schoolbooks never hint at. Further, mothers make important decisions in the home, yet fathers are generally shown making all important decisions independently.

Many adult women—including four out of ten mothers—hold jobs. They work in a wide range of occupations. Yet when women are shown working they are seen in a limited number of occupations. They are generally portrayed as teachers, nurses, or secretaries. Rarely, if ever, are they portrayed as bus drivers, lawyers, doctors, chemists, or in the large variety of occupations at which they actually work. To achieve a more realistic portrayal, try the following:

- When women are shown in the home, have them doing things other than housework.

- Avoid having women fall apart in crisis situations and needing a man to rescue them.

- Show women as decision-makers, both in the home and in occupational situations.

- Show mothers playing with, enjoying, helping, and showing things to their children—not just feeding and cleaning up after them.

- Portray women in the full variety of occupations in which they work. Show women doctors, engineers, police officers, and biologists, as well as women secretaries, teachers, and nurses.

PORTRAYAL OF FATHERS AND ADULT MEN

In textbooks, fathers are for the most part portrayed as highly competent, dependable, tall, and strong. In the family they are usually seen as the breadwinners and decision-makers. They seem to be the parent who does the fun things with the children, taking them on trips, helping them solve problems, and buying them treats. Fathers are rarely seen helping around the home, except as "fix-it" men or gardeners. Adult men in general are rarely seen showing any emotion. More balance should be brought into this portrayal. To achieve a more realistic portrayal, try the following:

- Show men involved in domestic chores. Men do dishes, put children to bed, clean, cook, discipline children, and help set tables.

- Show that men can be self-sufficient when it comes to running a household, cooking, cleaning, and mending clothes.

- Show men supporting the female members of the family in their efforts to accomplish things for themselves such as seeking careers, creating things, or studying to improve their work or themselves.

- Show that men do show emotion and do have feelings. Fathers get angry with their children, get mushy, and hug their children with joy. Adult men sometimes show disappointment.

- Show fathers sharing in decision-making with their families.

PORTRAYALS IN ARTWORK AND ILLUSTRATIONS

The illustrations in our textbooks and school materials provide visual statements on what the world is like. Taken as a whole, these statements are largely inaccurate. Girls are shown in dresses and neat attire even when involved in activities where this might be highly impractical. Mothers are usually portrayed in dresses, high heels, and aprons. Boys are consistently drawn taller than girls, and a single standard for "normal" physical appearance for both boys and girls is maintained. Boys are portrayed as active, moving, and are placed in the foreground, while girls are quiet and on the sidelines. Adult men are portrayed as tall, strong, and good-looking. Finally, 40 percent of our work force is female; this is not reflected pictorially in schoolbooks even when the opportunity is present. To correct this problem, try the following:

- As a general rule, have people wearing clothing appropriate to the activity in which they are involved. Show girls in casual play clothes when they are playing on a slide or in a sandbox. When mothers are cleaning house, have them dressed in casual work dresses or slacks; avoid having a mother cleaning the house while she is wearing high heels.

- When portraying a group of children of the same age, make sure that they are different heights. Have some girls who are taller than the boys.

- Allow boys to be portrayed in quiet, passive postures.

- Avoid having only girls watching the action from the sidelines.

- Have a smattering of both girls and boys in glasses, with freckles, with lost teeth, or with braces. Do not use a single standard of physical appearance; use reality as your guide.

- Avoid linking colors with sex. Both boys and girls should be portrayed in bold colors, as well as in pastels.

- Portray women in a variety of vocations. Women can be bank tellers, managers, secretaries, nurses, doctors, police officers, lab technicians, bus drivers, etc.

- Give men a variety of physical appearances. Some men are tall, strong, and handsome, but others are short, fat, and have bald spots.

FIFTH GRADE: STUDENT WORKBOOK: DISCOVERING SEX-ROLE STEREOTYPES*

This workbook guides students into observing television, school books, and real life for stereotypes of characteristics of the sexes. It was developed by Laurie Olsen Johnson for use in upper elementary classrooms.

SEX ROLES

To understand how human beings learn *sex roles,* you have to observe yourself and others. This workbook will help you discover and record sex roles and sex-role *stereotypes.*†

What do you feel it means to be *male* or *female?* Check off everything on the list that you feel applies to you.

BOYS ONLY:	GIRLS ONLY:

Because I am a boy,
I would not
____ cook
____ knit
____ wash dishes
____ help my mother around
       the house
____ wear a dress in a play
____ cry
____ hit a girl
____ kiss my father
____ wear beads or jewelry
____ babysit
____ back out of a fight

Because I am a girl,
I would not
____ wear curlers in front of a
       boy
____ dress like a man in a play
____ climb a tree
____ wear a necktie
____ play baseball
____ beat a boy at a sport or
       game
____ try to join a boys' club or
       team
____ hit a boy
____ kiss my mother
____ get in a fist fight
____ get a crew cut

What would be different about your life if you were born of the other sex? Finish the sentence below:

(girls) If I were a boy _____

_____

(boys) If I were a girl _____

_____

Would you rather have a brother or a sister? Why?

_____

_____

What would you like to be some day? Would it be different if you were of the other sex?

_____

_____

Make a list of words that describe what you think it means to be male:

_____

_____

Make a list of words that describe what you think it means to be female:

_____

_____

The picture we carry around in our minds of what it means to be male or female is what is called a *sex-role stereotype*. People act differently depending on whether they are male or female because they *learn* to act differently. We learn what kind of behavior we should show if we are a boy or a girl from our parents, from TV, from books and magazines, and from school.

OBSERVING SEX-ROLE STEREOTYPES ON TV

Spend two hours watching TV programs. Answer the following questions about each program you see.

Who are the main characters in the program?

_____

_____

What clothes do the women/girls wear? What do they look like?

_____

_____

What clothes do the men/boys wear? What do they look like?

_____

_____

What kinds of things do the adult women do? What do they worry about?

_____

_____

What about the girls?

_____

_____

The boys?

_____

_____

The adult men?

_____

_____

Describe the personality of the main adult woman (silly, stupid, intelligent, mean, grouchy, sweet, etc.).

_____

_____

Do the same for the main adult male.

_____

_____

The leading girl.

_____

_____

The leading boy.

_____

_____

What kinds of things happen to the people in the program?

_____

_____

What kinds of things do they do together?

_____

_____

Now think about what TV shows us it means to be a male or a female and fill in the blanks.

TV tells us that to be male means:

1. _____

2. _____

3. _____

4. _____

TV tells us that to be female means:

1. _____

2. _____

3. _____

4. _____

Is this the same or different from what *you* think it means to be male or female?

Answer the following questions about yourself and your family:

Does your mother, sister(s), or yourself (if you are a girl) dress like the females on TV? How are they the same or different?

_____

_____

Does your father, brother(s), or yourself (if you are a boy) dress like the males on TV? How are they the same or different?

_____

_____

What kinds of things does your mother do? Your aunts?

_____

_____

What kinds of things does your father do? Your uncles?

_____

_____

What kinds of things do your brothers do?

_____

_____

What kinds of things do your sisters do?

_____

_____

What kinds of things do you do?

_____

_____

What kinds of things happen to the people in your family?

_____

_____

What kinds of things do your family do together?

_____

_____

Compare the TV world to your own. Think about how it is different from your life, what kinds of things you do that are not shown on TV. Do you think your life would make a good TV program? Why or why not?

OBSERVING SEX ROLES IN SCHOOL BOOKS

Look through your school reading book. Don't read the words, just look at the pictures and record this information:

Name of the book

_____

Number of women in the pictures   _____

Number of men in the pictures   _____

Number of boys in the pictures   _____

Number of girls in the pictures   _____

Things the women are doing in the pictures

_____

_____

Things the men are doing in the pictures

_____

_____

Things the boys are doing in the pictures

_____

_____

Things the girls are doing in the pictures

_____

_____

Look at what you have observed. Were there more boys than girls? Were they doing different things? Are men doing more things than women in the book? Different things?

_____

_____

What kinds of things do girls do that weren't in the book?

_____

_____

What kinds of things do boys do that weren't in the book?

_____

_____

What kinds of things do women do?

_____

_____

What kinds of things do men do?

_____

_____

What do the illustrations tell you it means to be a female or a male?

_____

_____

For a whole day carry a pencil and paper around with you and listen very carefully. Every time you hear a comment about how a boy should act, or how a girl should act, write it down.

COMMENT	WHO SAID IT TO WHOM	SITUATION IN WHICH IT WAS SAID
"Big boys don't cry."	Teacher to first-grade boy	Boy fell down on playground, hurt himself, and began to cry

SUMMARY

List three ways that we learn sex-role stereotypes

1. _____

2. _____

3. _____

Describe the stereotype of how a girl should act:

_____

_____

_____

Describe the stereotype of how a boy should act:

_____

_____

_____

Do you act and feel like the stereotype of how you should act as a boy or a girl? How are you different? How does that make you feel?

FIFTH GRADE: ACTIVITIES CONCERNING SOCIAL STEREOTYPES

Goal: Awareness of social stereotypes and real world conditions

I. DISCUSSION ASSIGNMENT—WOMEN IN LEADER-SHIP ROLES
   A. What can women do that men cannot?
   B. What can men do that women cannot?
   C. Should a woman get paid as much as a man?
   D. Could a woman be president?
      Consider other world leaders: Golda Meir, Indira Gandhi.
   E. What female political leaders do they know of? Nationally, locally?

   F. Do they think there are restrictions on women in
   politics?
   What kinds? Are they realistic or not?*

II. WRITING ASSIGNMENTS
   A. For two students, along with discussion of women in
   leadership roles.
      1. Have them take notes.
      2. Read back to class what they have abstracted
      from class discussion.
      3. Ask class to formulate conclusions to topic.
   B. Have students draw and/or write up the "ideal"
   woman and "ideal" man. Have students describe:
      1. Physical characteristics
      2. Emotional characteristics (personality)
   C. Group activity
      1. Girls write: "I would (not) like to be a man
      because. . . ."
      (At least 2 paragraphs).
      Boys write: "I would (not) like to be a woman
      because. . . ."
      2. Divide class up into two groups, choose a
      recorder, have them collate reasons.
      3. Discuss reasons.

---

*Talk in class by some female politician, if possible.

FIVE

Objectives and Curriculum for Junior High School

The Junior High Curriculum

At the early high school level, the objectives encompassed those formulated for earlier grade levels, but also sought to extend the critical capacities of adolescents by creating an awareness of the socialization process which they themselves were undergoing and the way this process was abetted or distorted by specific environmental influences. The objectives presented to the grade 9 teachers in our intervention project were as follows:

1. To encourage students to consider a variety of occupational roles, regardless of sex

2. To encourage students to develop nonsexist attitudes about participation in sports activities

3. To encourage students to consider multiple family and personality roles

4. To help students develop critical awareness of existing sex-role stereotyping in schools, occupational roles, the media, and literature

5. To help students think critically about the limiting aspects of historical sex-role socialization processes

Early adolescence begins with the "growth spurt" of puberty that produces marked development of the primary and secondary sex characteristics and a rapid change in the nature of hormonal secretions. Extremely rapid growth in height and weight occur. Socially, the child shifts from the neighborhood elementary school to the more remote junior or senior high school. Generally there are more male teachers, particularly in areas like science and mathematics. Boys and girls are assigned different subjects (e.g., home economics or shop) or different treatments (e.g., in physical education). By age thirteen there is interest in opposite-sex peers accompanied by the beginning of dating. A new component of responsibility is added to one's role as son or daughter. Own-sex peers become very important as well as opposite-sex peers. Boys show an increasing devotion of energy to the instrumental area (achievement and independence) and receive in return the approval which supports their sense of competence and self-determination. Girls are increasingly directed toward the expressive area, especially in the development of those interpersonal skills which yield approval.

Cognitively, children have begun to achieve the level of formal operational thought. They can begin to deal with hypothetical situations, and think about possibility as well as actuality. Children of this age group have well-developed role-taking abilities and there is the beginning of a shift in thought about social rules and morality and politics, away from an authoritarian, social-order-maintaining stance toward relativistic ideas of individual rights and social roles.

Sex differences tend to increase and become more internalized at this age. Projective measures indicate that at puberty boys show an increase in assertive and sexual themes while girls show an increase in the self-abasement themes of self-damage and self-disparagement. Early adolescent girls express satisfaction with traditional concepts of the female sex role. Sex typing increases with respect to attainment values in school. This is true in spite of the fact that psychological sex differences, the basis at this age for differentiating male and female sex roles, are freed from fixed and prescribed social sex roles. This can allow more individual choice in expressing sex-differentiating traits since sex-role stereotypes are not seen as binding in either the rational-logical or moral sense. Since girls increase their value of traditional feminine roles, it may be that during puberty social pressure from peers and adults increases. The fifteen-year-old's sex-role stereotypes closely parallel adult stereotypes.

Curriculum at this age could include films, slide shows, records, and books aimed at broadening notions of sex-role-appropriate behavior. Less structured activities may include discussions of what it feels like and means to be a man or woman, and why and how it might be different. Cross-cultural norms may be studied. Children in the ninth grade also can comprehend materials on sexism in the system. Role playing and examination of sexist curriculum materials can be used at this age.

JUNIOR HIGH SCHOOL: SEXISM IN LANGUAGE

Activity—vocabulary game:
  List female words:

spinster	the little woman
old maid	the weaker sex
the office girl	tomboy
gal	authoress, heiress, etc.
career woman	dame
housewife	slang—chick, babe, bird, etc.
little old ladies	

  List male words:
    the better half
    sissy

Questions:
  1. What is the parallel word for males?
  2. Is it a negative word?
  3. Does it connote status?
  4. What are other kinds of words referring to, male or female? What assumptions are reflected?
  5. Try adjectives too. (Negative ones!)

FEMALE	MALE
shrill	cocky
hysterical	henpecked
nag	

NINTH GRADE: QUOTABLE QUOTES

These quotations and statements can be used for motivation, discussion, further inquiry, and research. A similar possibility involves surveying poetry which portrays all types of images of women and men, separately and together. One might introduce for comparison samples of poetry from modern feminist poets such as: Denise Levertov, Adrienne Rich, Elizabeth Bishop, Sylvia Plath, and Anne Sexton.

It's a man's world—woman's place is in the home.

I don't think brains have any sex.
> (Margaret Mangam, New York State Supreme Court Justice)

Indeed it is difficult to imagine any creature more attractive than an American beauty between the ages of fifteen and eighteen. There is something in the bloom, delicacy and innocence of one of these young things that reminds you of the conceptions which poets and painters have taken of angels.
> (James Fenimore Cooper, "Conspectus," I, *Annals of America,* 1828, p. 346)

I ask no favor for my sex. All I ask of our brethren is that they take their feet off our necks.
> (Sarah Grimke, 1837)

We hold these truths to be self-evident: that men and women are created equal. . . .

> (Seneca Falls "Declaration of Sentiments and Resolutions," July 18, 1848)

We will have every arbitrary barrier thrown down.
We would have every path laid open to women as freely as to men.

> (Margaret Fuller)

JUNIOR HIGH SCHOOL: FOR CLASSES READING *ROMEO AND JULIET*

I. SHAKESPEARE'S PORTRAYAL OF WOMEN IN THE PLAY
    A. Role
    B. Activity

II. WHAT DO YOU THINK WAS THE STATUS OF WOMEN IN JULIET'S TIME?
    A. Proper role
    B. Legal rights (property, marriage, divorce)
    C. Educational possibilities
    D. Work possibilities

III. CONTRAST WITH LIFE OF SOME SIGNIFICANT WOMAN IN THIS ERA (problems in achieving goals, etc.)

IV. CONTRAST WITH LIFE OF WOMEN IN:
    A. Colonial times
    B. Frontier life
    C. Pre-Civil War southern belles
    D. Early nineteenth-century feminists
    E. The black woman in America
    F. Other societies
        1. Traditional (Japanese, Arab)
        2. Modern (Israeli, Scandinavian)
        3. Communist (Cuban, Russian, Chinese)

CONVERSATIONAL CLICHES*

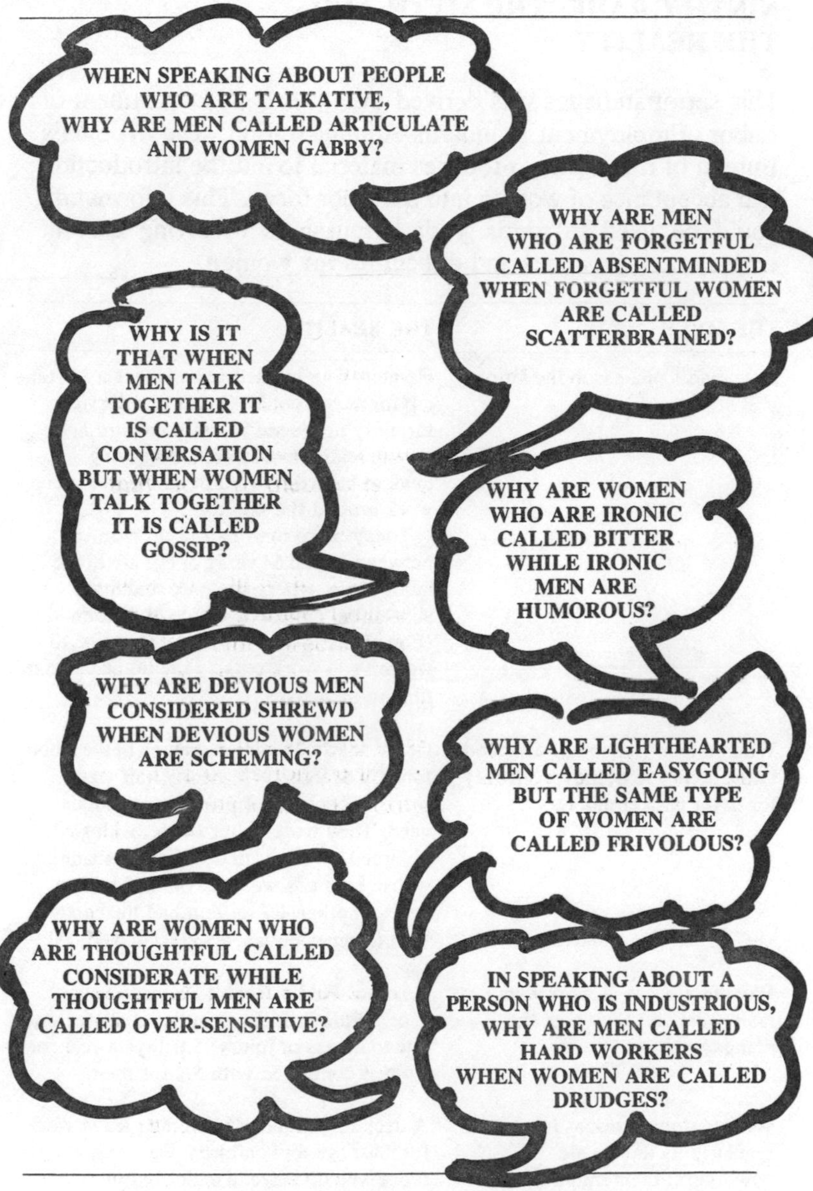

Because of Sexism in Language

NINTH GRADE: THE MYTH AND
THE REALITY

This set of statistics was derived from the U.S. Department of
Labor, Employment Standards Administration. The Women's
Bureau of this agency produces material to aid the introduction
and acceptance of women into the labor force. This information
could be used in ninth grade discussions involving current
employment practices and difficulties for women.

THE MYTH	THE REALITY
A woman's place is in the home.	Homemaking in itself is no longer a full-time job for most people. Goods and services formerly produced in the home are now commercially available; laborsaving devices have lightened or eliminated much work around the home. Today more than half of all women between 18 and 64 years of age are in the labor force, where they are making a substantial contribution to the Nation's economy. Studies show that 9 out of 10 women will work outside the home at some time in their lives.
Women aren't seriously attached to the labor force; they work only for extra pocket money.	Of the nearly 34 million women in the labor force in March 1973, nearly half were working because of pressing economic need. They were either single, widowed, divorced, or separated or had husbands whose incomes were less than $3,000 a year. Another 4.7 million had husbands with incomes between $3,000 and $7,000.
Women are out ill more than male workers; they cost the company more.	A recent Public Health Service study shows little difference in the absentee rate due to illness or injury: 5.6 days a year for women compared with 5.2 for men.
Women don't work as long or as regularly as their male coworkers; their training is costly—and largely wasted.	A declining number of women leave work for marriage and children. But even among those who do leave, a majority return when their children are in school. Even with a break in employment, the average woman

THE MYTH	THE REALITY
	worker has a worklife expectancy of 25 years as compared with 43 years for the average male worker. The single woman averages 45 years in the labor force.
	Studies on labor turnover indicate that net differences for men and women are generally small. In manufacturing industries the 1968 rates of accessions per 100 employees were 4.4 for men and 5.3 for women; the respective separation rates were 4.4 and 5.2.
Married women take jobs away from men; in fact, they ought to quit those jobs they now hold.	There were 19.8 million married women (husbands present) in the labor force in March 1973; the number of unemployed men was 2.5 million. If all the married women stayed home and unemployed men were placed in their jobs, there would be 17.3 million unfilled jobs.
	Moreover, most unemployed men do not have the education or the skill to qualify for many of the jobs held by women, such as secretaries, teachers, and nurses.
Women should stick to "women's jobs" and shouldn't compete for "men's jobs."	Job requirements, with extremely rare exceptions, are unrelated to sex. Tradition rather than job content has led to labeling certain jobs as women's and others as men's. In measuring 22 inherent aptitudes and knowledge areas, a research laboratory found that there is no sex difference in 14, women excel in 6, and men excel in 2.
Women don't want responsibility on the job; they don't want promotions or job changes which add to their load.	Relatively few women have been offered positions of responsibility. But when given these opportunities, women, like men, do cope with job responsibilities in addition to personal or family responsibilities. In 1973, 4.7 million women held professional and technical jobs, another 1.6 million worked as nonfarm managers and administrators. Many others held supervisory jobs at all levels in offices and factories.

THE MYTH	THE REALITY
The employment of mothers leads to juvenile delinquency.	Studies show that many factors must be considered when seeking the causes of juvenile delinquency. Whether or not a mother is employed does not appear to be a determining factor. These studies indicate that it is the quality of a mother's care rather than the time consumed in such care which is of major significance.
Men don't like to work for women supervisors.	Most men who complain about women supervisors have never worked for a woman. In one study where at least three-fourths of both the male and female respondents (all executives) had worked with women managers, their evaluation of women in management was favorable. On the other hand, the study showed a traditional cultural bias among those who reacted unfavorably to women as managers. In another survey in which 41 percent of the reporting firms indicated that they hired women executives, none rated their performance as unsatisfactory; 50 percent rated them adequate; 42 percent rated them the same as their predecessors; and 8 percent rated them better than their predecessors.

NINTH GRADE: ENGLISH CLASSES

Writing assignments:

Ideas for these suggested topics come from an informative questionnaire devised by Mary Beaven. Her work is reported in *Research in the Teaching of English,* Spring 1972, pp. 48–68.

1. List the five fictitious characters you most admire: consider all the reading you have done—both in and out

of school. *To the teacher:* have several students collate lists of characters according to sex when assignment is completed. Have class discussion about percentage of males and females and why imbalances may be revealed.

2. Name and discuss a character in a book you have read for an English class with whom you have experienced a strong identification. *To the teacher:* collate list and discuss with class.

3. Consider the literature you have read in English classes. What women have you admired in these readings?

> *Girls:*
> a. What female character that you have read about in English class would you like to resemble? Why?
> b. What female character that you have read about in English class would you like to have as a mother? Why?
>
> *Boys:*
> a. What female character that you have read about in English class would you like to have as a mother? Why?
> b. What female character that you have read about in English class would you like as a future wife? Why?

NINTH GRADE: A FAMOUS WOMAN

Activity:
Read one book on a famous woman in our history. See the following list for suggestions of historical characters.

1. Age in which woman born:
   a. Social and political background of the times
   b. Family background
2. Childhood:

   a. Specific interests
   b. Family influence on activities: encouragement or
      discouragement
   c. When choice of vocation made
3. Adult career:
   a. Specific work done
   b. Obstacles before or during chosen career (by
      society, men, women)
   c. Contribution to society then
4. Influence on other men or women then and now.
5. Was her contribution to society uniquely a woman's
   achievement or could a man have achieved the same
   goals? To the same extent?

Important American Women:

1. Jane Addams (Nobel Peace Prize winner)
2. Louisa May Alcott (writer)
3. Marian Anderson (singer)
4. Susan B. Anthony (suffragette)
5. Jacqueline Auriol (test pilot)
6. Mary McLeod Bethune (educator)
7. Elizabeth Blackwell (doctor)
8. Nelly Bly (reporter)
9. Evangeline Booth (Salvation Army)
10. Rachel Carson (ecologist)
11. Carrie Catt (suffragette)
12. Shirley Chisolm (politician)
13. Prudence Crandall (educator)
14. Marie Curie (atomic energy)
15. Dorothea Dix (mental health)
16. Amelia Earhart (aviator)
17. Mary Baker Eddy (religious leader)
18. Elizabeth Gurley Flynn (labor leader)
19. Althea Gibson (athlete)
20. Emma Goldman (anarchist)
21. Fanny Lou Hamer (leader in emancipation and education)
22. Anne Hutchinson (religious rebel)
23. Helen Keller
24. Fanny Kemble (actress, abolitionist)
25. Mary Elizabeth Lease
26. Juliette Lowe (Girl Scouts)

27. Lisa Meitner (atomic energy)
28. Maria Mitchell (astronomer)
29. Lucretia Mott (suffragette)
30. Ellen Richards (chemist)
31. Eleanor Roosevelt
32. Ernestine Rose (suffragette)
33. Deborah Sampson (Revolutionary War soldier)
34. Margaret Sanger (birth control)
35. Elizabeth Cady Stanton (suffragette)
36. Lucy Stone (suffragette)
37. Harriet Beecher Stowe (abolitionist and writer)
38. Maria Tallchief (ballerina)
39. Sojourner Truth (leader in freedom movement)
40. Harriett Tubman (leader in underground railroad)
41. Emma Willard (educator)
42. Clara Barton (founder of Red Cross and nurse)

NINTH GRADE: ORGANIZED DEBATES

Activity—plan a debate:
Class can be divided into three groups: pro, anti, and an audience or jury. Each prepares its own set of questions or arguments. Topics are to be researched, sources listed, and outline or paper prepared by each individual.
Possible topics:
1. Should women be given the right to vote? (historical)
2. Should women be given equal pay and equal job opportunities? (occupational)
3. Should women and men share equally the responsibilities of housework and child care? (family and personality roles)
4. Should all sports activities be entirely integrated? Should school athletic budget be equally divided between boys' and girls' sports? Should some segregated sports activities be permitted? (Students can research own school budget and athletic department facilities.)

NINTH GRADE: SHORT WRITING ASSIGNMENTS

Activity:
   I.   A. Have boys list all famous women they can
            (sports, science, politics, no movie stars or first
            ladies).
         B. Have girls do the same; compare lists.
   II.   A. Have boys and girls write one paragraph each on
            following four topics:
               1. What I like most in women
               2. What I hate most in women
               3. What I like most in men
               4. What I hate most in men
         B. Divide class into four groups, each group chooses
            recorder, collates reasons, and reports back to the
            whole class.
   III. Rewrite, "Love is. . . ."

NINTH GRADE: INTERVIEWING CELEBRITIES

Activities:
   I. ROLE-REVERSAL GAME
         A. Students read an interview in a newspaper or
            magazine with a prominent male or female.
         B. Compare and discuss questions asked male or
            female, e.g.:
               1. How to combine marriage and career?
               2. Favorite home repair techniques?
               3. What size suit do they wear?
               4. How to keep young and handsome?
   II. WRITING ASSIGNMENT: Satire on interview with
       male being asked "female" type questions

NINTH GRADE: EQUAL RIGHTS

The following set of materials provides information with which
to discuss the meaning of rights both personally and legally. This

discussion is particularly meaningful as one considers both the past and current legislation aimed at eliminating sex discrimination. The worksheet on women's rights was developed by Martha Gershun for the National Education Association's Conference on Sex Role Stereotypes, November 1972.

WHAT DO WOMEN WANT? RIGHTS IN AMERICAN HISTORY/HERSTORY*

1. 1974: Write a list of at least 10 different rights you believe women should have, now.

_____

_____

_____

_____

_____

2. If the American women's rights movement had a motto, it was:
   Men, their rights and nothing more;
   Women, their rights and nothing less.
Read the attached Declaration of Sentiments adopted at the first Women's Rights Convention, Seneca Falls, New York, July 19–20, 1848.
   a. What are the rights these women wanted?
   b. How would you have gone about attaining any of these rights in 19th century America?
   c. Have women achieved all the rights set out in 1848, more than 100 years ago?
   d. Do our 1974 rights lists include any rights that the women of 1848 omitted?

_____

*Reprinted with permission from Martha Gershun.

e. What is the picture of women's actual place in American society that you get from the 1848 and 1974 lists?

THE IDEA OF "RIGHTS"

In the Western tradition the idea came into prominence in the 18th century based on the concept of "natural rights."

The ideologies of the American and French Revolutions expressed this belief: all men are created equal. Following the publication of the French Declaration of the Rights of Man (1789), Mary Wollstonecraft published *A Vindication of the Rights of Woman* (1792).*

* What are the rights of woman?

* Are women's natural rights different from men's? Are women different from men?

* The Equal Rights Amendment now awaiting ratification reads in part: "Equality of rights under the law shall not be denied or abridged by the United States or by any State on account of sex."

* Can you think of any instances in which laws should be different for females and males?

* If men and women are different, does equality imply sameness?

THE EQUAL RIGHTS FOR WOMEN CONVENTION AT SENECA FALLS, NEW YORK, JULY 19, 1848

A little over a century ago, July 19, 1848, the Equal Rights for Women Movement came into being in the United States at a small gathering at Seneca Falls, New York. This was the first Equal Rights for Women meeting ever held in the United States and, as far as is known, the first Equal Rights for Women meeting ever held in the entire world.

---

*Published in paperback by W. W. Norton and Co., New York, at $1.75.

At this meeting, women demanded the vote. They demanded the right to enter schools and colleges, to enter the professions, to hold political office, to control their own property, to earn a living for themselves and their dependents, to control their own earnings. They demanded equal guardianship of their children, the right to make contracts, the right to make a will, the right to sit on a jury, the right to conduct a business. In short, as set forth in one of their "Declarations":

> We insist that they [women] have immediate admission to all the rights and privileges which belong to them as citizens of the United States.

The Declaration and Resolutions adopted at this historic meeting are given below:

DECLARATION OF SENTIMENTS

When, in the course of human events, it becomes necessary for one portion of the family of man to assume among the people of the earth a position different from that which they have hitherto occupied, but one to which the laws of nature and of nature's God entitle them, a decent respect to the opinions of mankind requires that they should declare the causes that impel them to such a course

We hold these truths to be self-evident: that all men and women are created equal; that they are endowed by their Creator with certain inalienable rights; that among these are life, liberty, and the pursuit of happiness; that to secure these rights governments are instituted, deriving their just powers from the consent of the governed. Whenever any form of government becomes destructive of these ends, it is the right of those who suffer from it to refuse allegiance to it, and to insist upon the institution of a new government, laying its foundation on such principles, and organizing its powers in such form, as to them shall seem most likely to effect their safety and happiness. Prudence, indeed, will dictate that governments long established should not be changed for light and transient causes; and accordingly all experience hath shown that mankind are more disposed to suffer, while evils are sufferable, than to right themselves by abolishing the forms to which they were accustomed. But when a long train of abuses and usurpations, pursuing invariably the same object, evinces a design to reduce them under absolute despotism, it is their duty to throw off such government, and to provide new guards for their future security. Such has been the patient sufferance of the women under this government, and such is now the necessity which constrains them to demand the equal station to which they are entitled.

The history of mankind is a history of repeated injuries and usurpations on the part of man toward woman, having in direct object the establishment of an absolute tyranny over her. To prove this, let facts be submitted to a candid world.

He has never permitted her to exercise her inalienable right to the elective franchise.

He has compelled her to submit to laws, in the formation of which she had no voice.

He has withheld from her rights which are given to most ignorant and degraded men—both natives and foreigners.

Having deprived her of this first right of a citizen, the elective franchise, thereby leaving her without representation in the halls of legislation, he has oppressed her on all sides.

He has made her, if married, in the eye of the law, civilly dead.

He has taken from her all right in property, even to the wages she earns.

He has made her, morally, an irresponsible being, as she can commit many crimes with impunity, provided they be done in the presence of her husband. In the covenant of marriage, she is compelled to promise obedience to her husband, he becoming, to all intents and purposes, her master—the law giving him power to deprive her of her liberty, and to administer chastisement.

He has so framed the laws of divorce, as to what shall be the proper causes, and in case of separation, to whom the guardianship of the children shall be given, as to be wholly regardless of the happiness of women—the law, in all cases, going upon a false supposition of the supremacy of rank and giving all power into his hands.

After depriving her of all rights as a married woman, if single, and the owner of property, he has taxed her to support a government which recognizes her only when her property can be made profitable to it.

He has monopolized nearly all the profitable employments, and from those she is permitted to follow, she receives but a scant remuneration. He closes against her all the avenues to wealth and distinction which he considers most honorable to himself. As a teacher of theology, medicine, or law, she is not known.

He has denied her the facilities for obtaining a thorough education, all colleges being closed against her.

He allows her in Church, as well as in State, but a subordinate position, claiming Apostolic authority for her exclusion from the ministry, and, with some exceptions, from any public participation in the affairs of the Church.

He has created a false public sentiment by giving to the world a different code for men and women, by which moral delinquencies which exclude women from society, are not only tolerated, but deemed of little account in man.

He has usurped the prerogative of Jehovah himself, claiming it as his right to assign for her a sphere of action, when that belongs to her conscience and to her God.

He has endeavored, in every way that he could, to destroy her confidence in her own powers, to lessen her self-respect, and to make her willing to lead a dependent and abject life.

Now, in view of this entire disfranchisement of one-half the people of this country, their social and religious degradation—in view of the unjust laws above mentioned, and because women do feel themselves aggrieved, oppressed, and fraudulently deprived of their most sacred rights, we insist that they have immediate admission to all the rights and privileges which belong to them as citizens of the United States.

In entering upon the great work before us, we anticipate no small amount of misconception, misrepresentation, and ridicule; but we shall use every instrumentality within our power to effect our object. We shall employ agents, circulate tracts, petition the State and National legislatures, and endeavor to enlist the pulpit and the press in our behalf. We hope this Convention will be followed by a series of Conventions embracing every part of the country.

RESOLUTIONS ADOPTED AT SENECA FALLS
CONVENTION OF 1848

Resolved, That such laws as conflict, in any way, with the true and substantial happiness of woman, are contrary to the great precept of nature and of no validity, for this is "superior in obligation to any other."

Resolved, That all laws which prevent woman from occupying such a station in society as her conscience shall dictate, or which place her in a position inferior to that of man, are contrary to the great precept of nature, and therefore of no force or authority.

Resolved, That woman is man's equal—was intended to be so by the Creator, and the highest good of the race demands that she should be recognized as such.

Resolved, That the women of this country ought to be enlightened in regard to the laws under which they live, that they may no longer publish their degradation by declaring themselves satisfied with their present position, nor their ignorance, by asserting that they have all the rights that they want.

Resolved, That inasmuch as man while claiming for himself intellectual superiority, does accord to woman moral superiority, it is preeminently his duty to encourage her to speak and teach, as she has an opportunity, in all religious assemblies.

Resolved, That the same amount of virtue, delicacy, and refinement of behavior that is required of woman in the social state, should also be required of man, and the same transgressions should be visited with equal severity on both man and woman.

Resolved, That the objection of indelicacy and impropriety, which is so often brought against woman when she addresses a public audience, comes with a very ill grace from those who encourage, by their attendance, her presence on the stage, in the concert, or in feats of the circus.

Resolved, That woman has too long rested satisfied in the circumscribed limits which corrupt customs and a perverted application of the Scriptures have marked out for her, and that it is time she should move in the enlarged sphere which her great Creator has assigned her.

Resolved, That the equality of human rights results necessarily from the fact of the identity of the race in capabilities and responsibilities.

Resolved, therefore, That, being invested by the Creator with the same capabilities, and the same consciousness of responsibility for their exercise, it is demonstrably the right and duty of woman, equally with man, to promote every righteous cause by every righteous means; and especially in regard to the great subjects of morals and religion, it is self-evidently her right to participate with her brother in teaching them, both in private and in public, by writing and by speaking, by any instrumentalities proper to be used, and in any assemblies proper to be held; and this being a self-evident truth growing out of the divinely implanted principles of human nature, any custom or authority adverse to it, whether modern or wearing the hoary sanction of antiquity, is to be regarded as a self-evident falsehood, and at war with mankind.

Resolved, That the speedy success of our cause depends upon the zealous and untiring efforts of both men and women, for the overthrow of the monopoly of the pulpit, and for the securing to woman an equal participation with men in the various trades, professions, and commerce.

NINTH GRADE: WOMEN'S ROLE IN AMERICA

This section provides an outline of important issues concerning the history of women in America. It delineates possible projects, debate topics, and independent research for high school students. This is only one part of an experimental curriculum designed by the staff of the Bureau of Social Studies, New York Board of Education. This section is reprinted with permission.

I. HOW WOMEN PLAYED AN IMPORTANT ROLE IN EARLY AMERICA

    A. Indian Women and their role
    B. With explorers and early settlers
        1. At Jamestown
           Pocahontas
           "Tobacco Brides"
        2. On the Mayflower and at Plymouth

II. WHAT WAS WOMEN'S STATUS IN COLONIAL DAYS
    A. As Colonial farmer's wife
        1. Life and activities
        2. Some female proprietors
    B. Dissenters
      Anne Hutchinson
    C. Lack of opportunities
        1. Legal, social, and political restrictions
        2. Educational discrimination
    D. Indians and blacks

III. HOW AMERICAN REVOLUTION STARTED WOMEN
ON THE ROAD TO FREEDOM
    A. Women's first great cause
    B. As colonial politicians without the vote
        1. Use of courage, wiles and ingenuity
        2. Boycott of Tories and British goods
    C. Case studies: Abigail Adams and Mercy Otis Warren
    D. Women in the war

IV. HOW WOMEN WENT WEST
    A. Some who went West
    B. Pioneer farms
      A partnership of man and wife
      Women's responsibilities
    C. Case study: Sacajawea

V. HOW WOMEN FOUGHT AGAINST SLAVERY
    A. Women in slavery
    B. Abolitionists
        1. Black—Sojourner Truth, Harriet Tubman
        2. White—Grimke Sisters, Harriet Beecher Stowe
    C. Women's struggle for rights of others

VI. WHAT WERE THE EFFECTS OF CIVIL WAR ON WOMEN
   A. Impact of the war on women and family structure
   B. New tasks, responsibilities, and occupations
      1. Paid employment as female clerks, bookkeepers, secretaries
      2. Government service—nurses, hospital attendants, and cooks
      3. Few women served as soldiers, spics, scouts, guides, and saboteurs
   C. After the war—black and white women
      Teachers in freedman's schools, pension claims agents, rehabilitation workers with soldiers and refugees
   D. Case studies:
      Clara Barton
      Dorothea Dix
      Charlotte Forten

UNDERSTANDINGS AND RELATED CONCEPTS

UNDERSTANDINGS	CONCEPTS
1. Women contributed to development of America	Societies draw upon ideas from other cultures.
2. Women were in the forefront in the fight for human rights and freedom	Change is an inevitable condition of life.
3. Women were discriminated against in early America.	Democratic governments provide protection for the rights of individuals and minority groups.
4. Women made their mark in war and peace.	The environment in which a person lives greatly affects opportunities for personal growth and development.
5. Black and white women fought slavery.	All persons are born free and equal in dignity and rights.
6. Women showed strength in managing and caring for their families during wars.	Change at variance with goals has also taken place.
7. Women demonstrated courage.	Human beings are much more alike than different.

Persons and terms to define:

Addams, Jane

American Woman Suffrage
  Association

Anthony, Susan B.

Atkinson, Ti-Grace

Barton, Clara

Mary McLeod Bethune

Bloomer, Amelia

Coeducation

Dix, Dorothea

Fifteenth Amendment

Fourteenth Amendment

Garrison, William Lloyd

Grimke Sisters

Howe, Julia Ward

Lyon, Mary

Miner, Virginia

Mott, Lucretia

Mott, Lydia

National Woman Suffrage
  Association

Nightingale, Florence

Oberlin College

Pankhurst, Emmeline

"The Revolution"

Roosevelt, Eleanor

Sanger, Margaret

Second-class citizen

Stanton, Elizabeth Cady

Stowe, Harriet Beecher

Steinem, Gloria

Thirteenth Amendment

Sojourner Truth

Tubman, Harriet

Vassar College

Willard, Emma

Wollstonecraft, Mary

W.C.T.U.

Wright, Frances

Topics for debates or panel discussions:

- *Resolved,* That the objection of indelicacy and impropriety, which is often brought against woman when she addressed a public audience, comes with a very ill-grace from those who encourage, by their attendance, her appearance on the stage, in the concert, or in feats of the circus.

- *Resolved,* That woman has too long rested satisfied in the circumscribed limits which corrupt customs and a perverted application of the Scriptures have marked out for her, and that it is time she should move in the enlarged sphere which her great Creator has assigned her.

- *Resolved,* That it is the duty of the women of this

country to secure to themselves their sacred right to the elective franchise.

- *Resolved,* Marriages and motherhood for girls, education and careers for boys.

NINTH GRADE: CIVICS CLASSES

Activity—mock trial of Susan B. Anthony (see kit):
1. Resource materials will be provided.
2. Multiple copies of short biographical summaries will be provided.
3. One book report of a biography of a famous American woman should be done by each student. Outline of report is included.
4. Discussion topics on page 144 of Susan B. Anthony Kit can be used.
5. See attached list of additional research topics for individuals or small groups. Research reports should be written up before mock trial enacted.
6. Arguments pro and con women's right to vote should be gleaned from textbooks provided or research papers.
7. Visit to the classroom by a local female politician.
8. Class may develop questionnaire to probe attitudes of constituents (adult neighbors) about women in politics.
9. Follow-up activity: Role playing of a woman running for office. Class prepares questions about her competence to run for and hold political office.

SUSAN B. ANTHONY DAY KIT*
February 15
To the Teacher:
　　We hope you will join us on February 15 in making that day a celebration that brings together the struggle of all women.
　　Included in this kit are materials designed to help you deal with the concerns of women in the 19th century (and today).

---

*Bement, Susan Groves, The Women's Studies Program, Berkeley Unified School District.

Please read the materials before using in order for you to be able to adapt them to their best advantage. We would appreciate your evaluative comments after having worked with the materials in the kit. If you are interested in the other curriculum materials we have developed please contact me. Good luck.

SUGGESTIONS FOR DRAMATIC ENACTMENTS

Mock Trial of Susan B. Anthony:

By 1870, the 14th and 15th Amendments to the Constitution had been ratified. These amendments stated that all U.S. citizens were to be given the equal protection of the law, the full privileges of U.S. citizenship, and that the right to vote was not to be denied on account of "race, color, or previous condition of servitude." In 1872, Susan B. Anthony registered and voted in the presidential election of that year. She was arrested and brought to trial on the charge of illegal voting. (Women were not granted the right to vote until 1920 when the 19th Amendment to the Constitution was passed.)

Stage a mock trial in the classroom. The boys take the parts of judge, jury, prosecuting attorney, and have the task of developing arguments why women should not vote. The girls are the audience. They meet in a group beforehand and determine the arguments Susan should use in her defense.

Excerpts of the trial: see separate sheet.

Sojourner Truth:

Sojourner Truth often made an appearance before gatherings of white men and women who had come together to discuss women's rights or man's superiority. This situation could be acted out in the classroom. Sojourner Truth was a tall black women whose back had been stooped under the lash in Mississippi cotton fields. She had an eloquence about her as she walked. When she rose to speak before these groups the derisive catcalls were plentiful—referring to her race and her sex. With her head erect and her eyes shining she spoke in a rich, powerful voice. And before long a hush would fall over the audience.

- Part 1: Boys and girls present arguments for and against the superiority of the male sex, Eve's sin, the "proper sphere" theory that a man's sphere is public and gives him the right to govern and a woman's sphere is private and is restricted to the family and the home.

- Part 2: Sojourner Truth listens on the sidelines and then rises and asks to speak. Catcalls. Sojourner speaks of her experiences as a black woman, an ex-slave, and these experiences go far beyond the bounds of a "woman's sphere." They point out the shallowness of that argument and speak to the difficulty of using the proper sphere theory to deny any group of people their rights.

The man over there says that women need to be helped into carriages and lifted over ditches, and to have the best place everywhere. Nobody ever helps me into carriages or over puddles or gives me the best place . . . and ain't I a woman?

Look at my arm! I have ploughed and planted and gathered into barns, and no man could head me. . . . and ain't I a woman? I could work as much and eat as much as a man—when I could get it—and bear the lash as well. . . . and ain't I a woman? I have borne thirteen children, and seen most of 'em sold into slavery, and when I cried out with my mother's grief, none but Jesus heard me . . . and ain't I a woman?   Sojourner Truth, 1851

BIOGRAPHICAL SUMMARIES
1. Susan B. Anthony and Elizabeth Cady Stanton
2. Sojourner Truth
3. Frederick Douglass
4. Ida Wells Barnett
5. Mary McLeod Bethune
6. Ah Toy

These biographies are meant to give students information on important 19th century women, on people whose contributions to the Women's Rights Movement were invaluable, and on women whose struggles spotlight the problems of their people.

These biographies were written by Barbara Christian, Mimi Yang, and Susan Bement.

SUGGESTIONS FOR ART WORK AND CREATIVE WRITING

1. Students work in groups on posters depicting scenes from the lives of people about whom they have read.
2. Students write an essay on: The connections between the things these people fought for and the issues being raised by people in the women's movement today; the relevance of the problems as defined by these 19th century people to their own personal lives today.
3. Each of these leaders fought for the right of all people to become what they were capable of being. Students write or draw their conception of themselves twenty years from now. (For teacher's use: does a student see herself/himself actually doing what she/he aspires to be? Can you help?)
4. The Office of Human Relations has sent out to all school libraries photos of Bay Area women at work in a variety of occupations. You may want to put these photos to use in the classroom today. The set is labeled, "Women In Their Varied Occupations."

SUGGESTIONS FOR DISCUSSION TOPICS

1. Select from the biographies those study questions you want to discuss with the class as a whole.
2. What methods would you have used, what arguments, were you in the position of the 19th century feminists? You want the laws changed, but what political power do you have to accomplish that? Who are the lawmakers, governors, judges, political representatives of any kind? Your only tool is persuasion. What would you have done?
3. Women today (Black, White, Asian, Chicano) are not as concerned with the right to vote as with other problems. Discuss what these problems are for each of these groups.
4. The women's movement is very broad and includes a wide variety of viewpoints. Do you know what some of the differences of opinion are within the movement?

What groups in Berkeley represent these different perspectives?

5. Do you see ways in which the women's movement improves the lives of men?
6. Have there been any changes in your home, or in how you look at things, as a result of the movement?
7. What does it mean to be masculine, to be feminine? How can you observe these sex-role definitions in the behavior of the students in this room? Among the teachers and administrators in this school?
8. What do these sex-role definitions inhibit boys from doing? Is that good or bad? What do these sex-role definitions inhibit girls from doing? Examples:

Why don't girls play football?
Why don't boys play jacks? Field hockey?
Why isn't the principal of your school a woman?
Why are most of the teachers in your school women, and the principals of all the 4–6 schools men?
Why do girls do better in reading and writing and boys do better in P.E.?
Are girls and boys given different jobs to do at home? Is there any reason why?
Are girls and boys given different jobs to do at school (traffic, cafeteria and service girls)? Is there any reason why?

SUGGESTIONS FOR OTHER CLASSROOM ACTIVITIES

1. The concerns of the feminists were often strikingly different from those of working women. Contrast the concerns of Susan B. Anthony with those of:
   a. Black women
   [See, e.g., *Harriet Tubman,* Ann Petry; *Jubilee,* Margaret Walker (post-Civil War); *Lay My Burden Down,* Botkin (accounts of slave women).]
   b. The women who worked in the factories of the East Coast (See, e.g., Mother Jones, Elizabeth Gurley Flynn, Emma Goldman.)

   c. Pioneer women of the West
      (See, e.g., *Heroines of the Early West,* Ross;
      Some Went West, Johnson.)

2. Investigate the role played by women in the Anti-
   Slavery Movement. (Fanny Kemble, Sojourner Truth,
   Lucretia Mott, Harriet Tubman, Sarah and Angelina
   Grimke.)

3. Investigate the role played by men in the Women's
   Rights Movement. (Frederick Douglass, William Lloyd
   Garrison, Theodore Weld, James Mott.)

4. Susan B. Anthony worked very hard to get women
   admitted to colleges and universities. Because of her
   work, women were admitted to Stanford. Why was it
   felt that girls needed less education than boys? Who was
   Emma Willard (besides the person for whom Willard Jr.
   High School is named?)

5. Ah Toy was an unusual Chinese woman in that she was
   economically independent and did not play the role
   usual to Chinese women. What role did Chinese women
   play when they came to the U.S.? Have you read *Fifth
   Chinese Daughter* by Jade Snow Wong? What can you
   find out about the experiences of Chinese and Japanese
   women in America in the late 19th and early 20th centuries? (See *Asian Women.*)

6. How did women finally get the right to vote in 1920?
   (See *Petticoat Politics* by Faber, *Century of Struggle* by
   Flexner.)

7. Many women who wanted to be active were unhappy
   with the clothing that convention dictated they wear.
   They experimented with "bloomers" but found them to
   be a detraction: Critics focused on their dress rather
   than their words. Who designed the bloomer? What
   roles did Amelia Bloomer and Fanny Kemble play in
   advancing dress reform?

8. When Susan B. Anthony became a teacher she was
   paid half the salary of the teacher she replaced, a man
   whom she had known and helped in school. (As a
   student he had been unable to do long division!) Explore

this topic of working conditions for women in the 19th century.

9. Women with a public life in the 19th century were always told to stay in their "proper sphere," the home. Where did this idea develop that a woman's place was in the home, a man's place was in the world?

10. Lucy Stone was an important feminist. When she married she refused to change her name. What was her contribution to the movement?

ACCOUNT OF THE PROCEEDINGS OF THE TRIAL OF SUSAN B. ANTHONY ON THE CHARGE OF ILLEGAL VOTING AT THE PRESIDENTIAL ELECTION IN NOVEMBER, 1872:

Miss Anthony: Yes, your honor, I have many things to say; for in your ordered verdict of guilty, you have trampled under foot every vital principle of our government. My natural rights, my civil rights, my political rights, my judicial rights, are all alike ignored. Robbed of the fundamental privilege of citizenship, I am degraded from the status of a citizen to that of a subject; and not only myself individually, but all of my sex, are, by your honor's verdict, doomed to political subjection under this, so-called, republican form of government.

Judge Hunt: The Court cannot listen to a rehearsal of arguments the prisoner's counsel has already consumed three hours in presenting.

Miss Anthony: Your denial of my citizen's right to vote, is the denial of my right of consent as one of the governed, the denial of my right of representation as one of the taxed, the denial of my right to a trial by a jury of my peers as an offender against law, therefore, the denial of my sacred rights to life, liberty, property and . . .

Judge Hunt: The Court cannot allow the prisoner to go on.

Miss Anthony: All of my prosecutors . . . not one is my peer; . . . had your honor submitted my case to the jury, as was clearly your duty*. . . . Not one of those men was my peer; but, native or foreign born, white or black, rich or poor, educated or ignorant, awake or asleep, sober or drunk, each and every man of them was my political superior; hence, in no sense, my peer. . . . Precisely as no disfranchised person is entitled to sit upon a jury, and no woman is entitled to the franchise, so, none but a regularly admitted lawyer is allowed to practice in the courts, and no woman can gain admission to the bar—hence, jury, judge, counsel, must all be of the superior class.

Judge Hunt: The Court must insist—the prisoner has been tried according to the established forms of law.

Miss Anthony: Yes, your honor, but by forms of law all made by men, interpreted by men, administered by men, in favor of men, and against women; and hence, your honor's ordered verdict of guilty, against a United States citizen for the exercise of "that citizen's right to vote," simply because that citizen was a woman and not a man. But, yesterday, the same man-made forms of law, declared it a crime punishable with $1,000 fine and six months' imprisonment, for you, or me, or any of us, to give a cup of cold water, a crust of bread, or a night's shelter to a panting fugitive as he was tracking his way to Canada. And every man or woman in whose veins coursed a drop of human sympathy violated that wicked law, reckless of consequences, and was justified in so doing. As then, the slaves who got their freedom must take it over, or under, or through the unjust forms of law, precisely so, now, must women, to get their right to a voice in this government, take it; and I have taken mine, and mean to take it at every possible opportunity.

SUSAN B. ANTHONY AND ELIZABETH CADY STANTON

In the days before the Civil War, when Susan B. Anthony and Elizabeth Cady Stanton were children, little girls of their class

---

*The judge instructed the jury to return a verdict of guilty.

were raised like hothouse geraniums. They should be shy and retiring, spend large amounts of time practicing stitchery, and vigorous physical exercise was not only unladylike, it was impossible. Their everyday dress included a stiff corset, drawers, petticoats, a high-necked dress with long sleeves, a tight bodice and a full, long skirt!

Although there are no pictures of Susan B. Anthony riding a bicycle with her skirts flying, she was not one to let fifteen pounds of petticoats interfere. Susan grew up in a Quaker abolitionist family where social issues were much discussed. She must have developed a sense of injustice at a very early age. Her family recalled little Susan insisting that her mother keep the rent money rather than hand it over to her father. Had she not done all the work for which the rent was paid? She was also unhappy to learn from her mother's experience that when a woman married, her inherited property was put under the control of her husband. Did women have no rights? Susan loved her father, but she thought the laws that denied a married woman the right to the money she earned and the property she inherited were unjust.

At the age of 17 Susan went to work as a teacher. She was offered $2.50, which was exactly half of the salary paid the previous teacher. He had been a man. True then, and true today, women were not getting equal pay for equal work. Although most of Susan's early reform energies went into anti-slavery and temperance work, it did not take Elizabeth Stanton long to convert Susan to the cause of women's rights. She had been active in female temperance and anti-slavery societies because women were not allowed by the men to participate in their own organizations. Susan remembered a Teachers Convention she attended where, although two-thirds of the members were women, teaching being a profession open to women, only men were allowed to address the convention. This was a common experience for women with a public life.

Elizabeth's father was a judge, and she grew up amidst sisters in a wealthy home in upstate New York. Her only brother died at a young age, and nothing any of the girls did could ever make up to their father for the fact that he had no son. "I tried to comfort him by telling him I had joined a class of boys at the Academy to study Latin, mathematics and Greek. I jumped across all the ditches and fences, and longed to hear my father say, 'Well, a girl is as good as a boy, after all.' But he never did.'' Elizabeth developed a keen resentment of the inferiority attached to being a girl.

Elizabeth married Henry Stanton, an ardent abolitionist, and honeymooning in Europe they attended the World Anti-Slavery Convention being held in London. Elizabeth and Lucretia Mott, founder of the Philadelphia Female Anti-Slavery Society and delegate to the Convention, were forced to sit in the galleries and prohibited from participating in any of the proceedings. That society at large frowned upon women participating in political activities was one thing; that the leading male radicals, those most concerned with social inequalities, should discriminate against women was quite another.

Refusing to keep to their "proper sphere," the home, Lucretia and Elizabeth determined it was time to hold a convention of their own.

On July 19, 1848, the first Women's Rights Convention was held in Seneca Falls, New York. It was attended by over 300 men and women who came from miles around. Lucretia's husband opened the meeting, but no man was allowed the platform after he had finished. Elizabeth read the Declaration of Rights she had written. "We hold these truths to be self-evident: that all men and women are created equal. . . ." The most controversial of all the resolutions, the right to vote, almost failed to be adopted. With the vigorous supporting speech of the great black leader, Frederick Douglass, Elizabeth was able to secure enough votes to pass it. For most of the women at Seneca Falls, the vote seemed a remote concept, and not nearly as pressing as most of their demands: equal rights to a free education, equal pay for equal work, freedom to enter all fields of endeavor, the right to own property and be guardians of their own children, the right to speak whenever and wherever they chose.

It was shortly after this that Susan B. Anthony and Elizabeth Cady Stanton met. They took an instant liking to each other. Of very different talents, these two women worked together for over 50 years. To Elizabeth writing came naturally. Susan, on the other hand, was a worker and organizer. Unmarried and free from domestic responsibility, Susan could provide the drive and energy both women needed if they were to accomplish their goal. Susan was included in the Stanton family life, which freed her from loneliness and her friend for work. And so it was Elizabeth who wrote the speeches, developing the rhetoric and philosophical arguments for the movement, and it was Susan who provided the facts and the statistics and traveled around the country delivering the speeches and doing the organizing. She traveled everywhere in all kinds of weather. On the most severe days of winter, with the temperature well below zero, the snowdrifts high, she would be out speaking, collecting signatures on a petition, urging change of one state law or another. She became so well known that girls who were tomboys were called "Susan Bs." And when, after her death, the Constitution was amended to give women the vote, the 19th Amendment was called the "Anthony Amendment."

Study questions:

1. With which of the women's rights were the women attending the Seneca Falls Convention most concerned?

2. Susan B. Anthony and many of the women who had been abolitionists saw a similarity between the slavery they had been fighting against and the situation of women. Can you name some of the similarities? What were the differences?

3. When Elizabeth Cady Stanton and Frederick Douglass pushed the suffrage resolution (suffrage means the right to vote), many women opposed the idea. See if you can give some of the arguments Stanton and Douglass might have used to convince them that the vote was important.

SOJOURNER TRUTH

Sojourner Truth was a black woman who spent 40 years as a slave and 40 years as a free woman fighting for others to be free. She was born in New York around 1790 and was named Bell by her master. And for Bell, as for so many others, slavery was harsh and bitter. She was sold many times, saw all her brothers and sisters sold, and was finally married off to an older slave by whom she had five children. But even when slavery was abandoned in New York, she remained a slave. Finally when her master sold her five-year-old son, Peter, she could not stand it any longer and ran away with her baby. Bell was finally freed in 1827.

But that was not the end of Bell's struggle. She tried to get back her son Peter and finally won his freedom through a court case. After that victory she did what so many black women have had to do. She worked as a domestic.

While she was working in New York, she had religious visions, as did other black freedom seekers, such as Nat Turner. Her vision commanded her to go out and preach to the people. So in 1843, she left New York City and all her possessions behind her. She called herself Sojourner because she was to travel and preach, and Truth because she was to tell the truth to everyone.

With her powerful figure and voice, her feeling for the richness of freedom and her conviction in what she was saying, she became a famous speaker. She spoke to audiences in the North about the inhumanity of slavery. Her strength and forcefulness of speech revealed to people truth about the injustices done to black men and women. She talked about the hardship of being a black woman and declared that black men could not be free unless black women were free too. She advocated the vote for both black men and black women.

Even in her last years she worked to free others. She put together a plan for blacks freed after the Civil War to resettle in the West. When she died in 1883, she had spent 40 years as a free woman doing everything within her power to free others so that the day might come when everyone might own their own soul and body.

Study questions:

    1. Sojourner Truth's vision commanded her to leave her possessions behind and preach to the people. What was the message she was to preach?

2. She talked of the hardship of being a black woman. Can you describe several examples she could have used?

3. Sojourner declared that black men could not be free unless black women were free too. This was a radical belief for that time. Why do you think she felt this way?

FREDERICK DOUGLASS

Born and raised a slave, Frederick Douglass is easily one of the intellectual giants of American history. His oratory ringing with fervor throughout the land helped more than any man's voice to arouse the North against slavery and to make the abolition of slavery a primary issue in the years preceding the Civil War. America would most likely be a different place if this slave had not run away to the North and made his life-time work the abolition of slavery in all its forms.

In addition to his voice, Douglass lent a mighty pen to the cause of anti-slavery. He wrote editorials in his paper, *The North Star;* his speeches are as effective in written form as they are spoken, and his autobiography, "The Life and Times of Frederick Douglass," is a recognized classic in American literature.

Frederick Douglass was also a statesman, active as well as reflective in approaching the major issues of his day. After the Civil War he spoke to Presidents Lincoln and Johnson in behalf of black men and women. He argued brilliantly for the case of the Negro franchise. And he insisted that blacks had worked to make America rich and that they belonged here, and should not be recolonized in Africa. He held such high positions as Minister to Haiti and President of the Freedman's Bank.

Douglass was one of the few black men to speak out in favor of the vote for women. Just as the vote must be extended to include black men, so must it include women as well, he argued.

He was a man who embodied the finest qualities of his age and who saw the problems of the future. We can still learn much from the writings of Frederick Douglass, for he knew that the legal abolition of slavery was only a beginning in the black American's journey to freedom.

Study questions:
1. What does "franchise" mean? Why would it do little good to end slavery and not extend the vote to the ex-slaves?

2. Why did Douglass feel blacks should not be recolonized in Africa?

3. Although Douglass was exceptional, as a man, in supporting women's right to vote, how does his position on this question follow from his stand as an abolitionist?

IDA WELLS

A little known but important black woman, Ida Wells Barnett was a fighting black journalist who almost single-handedly campaigned against lynching and also helped to mobilize black women in the struggle for black liberation.

As one of the two owners of the *Memphis Free Speech,* she wrote dynamic columns about racial discrimination in the South. The year 1892 was a turning point in her journalistic career, for in that year, Ida Wells attacked the white community of Memphis for the lynching of three black men who had committed no other crime than that they were economically successful. Because of her exposé, her newspaper offices were destroyed and her life threatened. But rather than discouraging her, this assault spurred Ida Wells on to becoming a one-woman crusader against lynching in the U.S. Her attack on lynching was basic. She exposed the myth that black men raped white women and instead exposed the facts: it was the other way around, white men raped black women.

One of the high points of her lectures against lynching occurred in Great Britain. Ida Wells accused Frances Willard, a leading abolitionist and suffragist who influenced many white women in America, of defending the white Southern attitude on race. A public debate took place between the two and Miss

Willard unwittingly revealed herself as a supporter of the Southern point of view. Possibly as a result of the debate, Miss Willard publicly spoke out against lynching.

Between 1865 and 1919, it was estimated that 3,360 black men were lynched. Ida Wells' campaign against lynching resulted in the NAACP's work on lynching, which helped to substantially reduce lynching and to make America aware of this hideous crime.

In addition to her anti-lynching work, Ida Wells helped to found the first black women's club in Chicago, as well as the first black women's political club, the Alpha Suffrage Club of Chicago. These black women's clubs, and subsequent women's clubs, have been significant factors in the education and political consciousness of black communities across the country.

If you would like to learn more about Ida Wells, black journalist and political organizer, she has written an autobiography called *Crusade for Justice*. Perhaps you would like to read it.

Study questions:
1. What is lynching?

2. Explain why it took real courage to speak out against lynching as Ida Wells did.

3. How did black women stand to benefit from Ida Wells' work?

4. Can you explain how, during that time, Frances Willard could be an abolitionist (someone who works to end slavery) and accept the white Southern attitude on race?

MARY MCLEOD BETHUNE

Mary McLeod Bethune (1875–1955) is one of the great educators in American history and one of the great women of this country. Born the first free person in her family, she yearned after knowledge from her early youth. As a teenager, working in the cotton fields, she had a vision to teach and educate those of her race

Buttressed by that vision she created from almost nothing the Bethune-Cookman College, an institution which has educated hundreds of thousands of blacks. She started the college on a dumping ground called "Hell's Hole," raising the downpayment for the land by selling ice cream and sweet potato pies. For the rest of her life she would raise funds for the school, develop materials students would use in the classroom, acquire land, nourish and sustain this institution, often with audacity and eloquence.

In addition to being president of Bethune-Cookman College from 1904–42, Mary Bethune founded the National Council of Negro Women. This organization, representing over one million Negro women, sought to improve the lot of black women and give them the political and social tools that would benefit them and their people. This great woman believed that the true worth of a race must be measured by the character of its womanhood and that the black woman had emerged from being the most pathetic figure in America to becoming an impressive contributor to the progress of blacks and of Americans in general.

Because of her outstanding work in education, Mary Bethune was appointed Director of the Division of Negro Affairs of the National Youth Administration by President Franklin Roosevelt, thus becoming the first black in this country to hold federal office. During the postwar years she was appointed to other positions by various presidents, even as she continued to develop the Bethune-Cookman College. For in spite of the honors piled on her, she felt her true home to be the South and the college she had founded. These words reflect her energy and commitment:

> For I am my mother's daughter and the drums of Africa still beat in my heart. They will not let me rest while there is a single Negro boy or girl without a chance to prove his worth.

Mary McLeod Bethune did not rest in her efforts to create opportunities for blacks until her death in 1955. Her energy, commitment, and astuteness were phenomenal.

Study questions:

1. Vocabulary. From the dictionary find the meaning of each of these words. Use one in a sentence describing Mary Bethune.

   audacity
   eloquence
   commitment
   phenomenal

2. Explain why Mary Bethune was so committed to education for black boys and girls.

3. Mrs. Bethune founded the National Council of Negro Women. Why did she feel it important for black women to have an organization like this to belong to?

AH TOY: THE GIRL IN THE GREEN SILK PANTALOONS

California's first Chinese settlers, two men and one woman, reached San Francisco in February 1848, from Canton. Sometime later that year a second Chinese woman arrived. This was Ah Toy, who was only twenty years old. For several years, these two women were the only Chinese women in California, while their male countrymen numbered in the hundreds and soon the thousands. This trend persisted. And it was in this way that Chinese immigration to this country differed from the immigration patterns of most other peoples. By 1890, there were 34 Chinese men to every Chinese woman.

There were several reasons for this imbalance. Because the Chinese had very strong family ties, the young men came to America to earn enough money to be able to return to China and buy land there. Their stay would be temporary; they would return to the land of their ancestors. This characteristic gave the Chinese immigrants the name of "sojourners."

It was the male's duty in Chinese tradition to provide not only for his wife but for his parents and family as well. When men left China, the wife remained to fulfill this obligation and take care of his parents while he was away. It was another aspect of Chinese tradition that a respectable woman simply did not leave the part of the country considered her home.

Even if the husband had been free of these traditions and was free to come with his wife, the expense of the trip was very great. In many cases, money had been borrowed to purchase one ticket. Bringing another person was, in most instances, simply out of the question.

In the 1880's, the United States passed immigration laws aimed at excluding the Chinese laborer. These Chinese immigrants were seen as competing for jobs with white males and were also seen as a threat because they were willing to work for very low wages. The racial and cultural differences of the Chinese were used to arouse white support for these discriminatory laws. While the immigration laws did not exclude the Chinese males already here, they excluded new Chinese laborers from entering, and the wives were excluded from joining their husbands already in America. The laws also made it difficult for Chinese men to make visits to their families in China because of the uncertainties of being readmitted to the United States.

Many of the men were separated from their wives for years. Single men were forced to marry back in China because of the shortage of Chinese women in America. In order to produce heirs, Chinese men had to save the money needed to return to China, either temporarily or permanently. Many immigrants were able to do neither and had to remain in the United States where they died without a family and an heir, a traditionally important responsibility in the Chinese family.

Besides disrupting the Chinese family, these immigration patterns also gave rise to a lucrative trade of prostitutes. In 1852, several hundred Chinese prostitutes arrived by ship from Hong Kong. A large majority of these women were not originally prostitutes but had been sold by their poverty-stricken families to others as servants. They were later sold against their will by men who could profit by the prostitution trade. There was much money to be made in the business which was controlled and run by men. Many Chinese women, therefore, came to California as slaves and prostitutes and remained so for life. Perhaps it was not unfortunate that the average life expectancy of a prostitute in Chinatown was short.

It is against this background that Ah Toy's story must be told. In some ways Ah Toy was unusual. Although she was a prostitute, she was not a slave. She was not owned by a man, nor did she work from a house owned by a man. She owned her own house and was in business for herself.

Whereas we know very little about the lives of individual Chinese women who came to America toward the end of the 19th century, we do have information about Ah Toy. Perhaps this is because she was a colorful character; perhaps it is because she appeared in court, and when she did, she made such a vivid impression. We know that in 1849 a letter came from a man in Hong Kong claiming that he was Ah Toy's husband. He insisted that the courts return her to him. Ah Toy denied that she was married; she was *Miss* Ah Toy, born in Canton, twenty-one years old, and she had come to San Francisco in order to enjoy a better life. The judge let her stay in California.

At other times Ah Toy appeared in court to seek payment from the customers whom she claimed cheated her. There is one description of her entering the courtroom wearing an apricot satin jacket, willow green pantaloons, a pretty pair of slippers on her tiny feet. She charmed the judge, embarrassed the men in the audience whom she knew and, in general, provided entertainment for all. On this occasion she had come claiming she was being paid with brass filings instead of gold. Her dramatic presentation won her admirers but not her case.

No matter how colorful Ah Toy was, like all prostitutes and slaves, she was still a victim of oppression. Not only did she bear the brunt of white prejudice because she was Chinese, she also had to bear the humiliation accompanying her profession.

For Chinese women connected with the American experience during the 19th century, whether they themselves came, or stayed in China as the wives of the men who did come, the

forces promoting disintegration of their family life were omni-
present. It was this experience which was shared in common by
the Chinese women on both sides of the Pacific Ocean.

Study questions:
    1. List several reasons why so few Chinese women came to
    this country before 1900.

    2. What were the consequences of this imbalance for
    Chinese men and women?

    3. Why is there so little information about Chinese women
    immigrants? Why do we have information about Ah
    Toy?

    4. In what ways was Ah Toy unusual as a Chinese
    prostitute?

    5. Chinese women who came to America in the 19th
    century had no rights. If you were a Chinese woman
    living at that time, what rights do you think would have
    been most important to you?

    6. In what respects was the plight of these women similar
    and different from that of the other women in this
    series?

NINTH GRADE: CAREER EXPLORATION
FOR HIGH SCHOOL WOMEN

These few exercises provide an opportunity to evaluate current
stereotypes about occupations and to speculate on the future of
stereotypes about occupations. These exercises involve fantas-
izing and role playing, which are fairly difficult teaching techniques in large groups. These activities were developed to be
used primarily in a counselor-directed, volunteer program for
high school girls. Originators of this prevention of occupational
stereotypy model were Janice Birk (Ph.D.) and Mary Faith
Tanney (Ph.D). Sections of their workshop presented at the

National Education Association's Conference on Sex Role Stereotypes are presented below.

WHAT NOW IS: ROLE PLAYING THE STEREOTYPES

1. *Goal:* The purpose of the role playing exercise is to sensitize the students to the stereotypes we share about men, women, parents, children, counselors, etc. It is posited that we frequently act according to the stereotypes we maintain rather than to the actual demands of people and situations. Becoming aware of the pervasiveness of this role or sex stereotyping is perhaps the first step toward freeing people from the limitations it imposes. This exercise can be conducted with only the women students participating or it can be expanded to include 5 male students or a male faculty or staff member invited by the counselor.

2. *Time requirement:* Situation 1, 15 minutes; Situation 2, 25 minutes

3. *Preparation:* The counselor asks for volunteers from the class and describes what "role playing" means and how it fits in to the program (see: Goal section). One way of explaining it is as follows: The volunteers are offering to take the parts of characters in scenes they will be given. They will make up the action and the dialogue as they go along according to how they imagine the character they are playing would react in the situation.

4. *Process:* The counselor, after soliciting the proper number of volunteers for the situation, reads the description of the scene to the entire group of students. The students are assigned roles within the situation (or they can select the one they wish to explore) and the scene begins. The counselor may want to reverse the roles the students are playing in the middle of the role playing. Following each situation the entire group is asked to

react to the presentation in terms of accuracy of presentation, evidence of stereotyping in mannerisms, dialogue, resolution of the situation, etc.

Situation 1:

a. Solicit two volunteers.

b. Read: Situation 1—In a law office, the female lawyer and her male secretary are discussing his performance. The secretary is attempting to get a raise.

c. Role play the above situation. Allow 8 minutes.

d. Total group reaction to the role playing. Allow 7 minutes.

Situation 2:

a. Solicit five volunteers.

b. Read: Situation 2—A female student is discussing her goal of becoming an Industrial Arts (shop) major with: (1) her parents (allow 5 minutes); (2) with her boyfriend (allow 5 minutes); (3) with her guidance counselor (allow 5 minutes).

c. Role play the above situations, allowing five minutes for each of the three scenes.

d. Total group reaction to the role playing. Allow 10 minutes.

WHAT CAN BE: FANTASIZING THE NONSTEREOTYPES

1. *Goal:* The goal of this exercise is to sensitize the students to the changes which might occur within the next five years in society, human relationships, and their own perspectives of appropriate behavior. The range of considered alternatives to dilemmas will hopefully be expanded and thoughtful planning of life styles will be encouraged by the presentation of the following situations.

2. *Time required: 25 minutes*

3. *Preparation:* The group of students is asked to form groups of 6. The counselor distributes a copy of the

fantasy situations to each student. The students are instructed to follow the instructions provided at the conclusion of each fantasy situation and are told that they will have approximately 15 minutes to complete the two assignments. During the time the students are considering the fantasies the counselor may drift from sextet to sextet observing the types of solutions, alternatives, etc., which are suggested.

THE FANTASIES (THE YEAR—1999!)

Patricia J. is just completing the first semester of her senior year in high school. Her boyfriend Scott and she have been dating for 7 months and, although their relationship is quite satisfying and important to her, it is currently causing her much distress. Scott has been accepted to a college in a distant state and has decided to attend. He would like Patricia to also go to school there (on a whim she applied and was accepted). Pat is unclear about what she would like to major in (if she goes to college at all—she really is not convinced she wants to do that), but several of the majors in which she is somewhat interested are not offered at Scott's school. Her parents want Pat to attend their alma mater and also want her to major in a subject which would guarantee employment upon graduation.

Instructions—Finish the story. (Insert any steps you think Pat might take to assist her in making this decision.) Remember—it's 1999! Imagine what *could* be.

Anne and Allan Johnson have been married for four years and they have one child, Jamie, age 2½. Anne and Allan met while both of them were in high school. Allan was 2 years older than Anne and when he graduated went immediately into the service. When he was discharged two years later they were married and then immediately moved across the country so Allan could attend college. While Allan was in the service Anne had worked as a sales clerk

in her father's store. Currently Allan is attending college
and also working to supplement the support the GI Bill
provides. He is majoring in business and hating it.
Recently he decided that he really wanted to be an engineer and, with only one year of school remaining to complete his Business degree, wants to switch majors although
that would necessitate another 3 years of college. Anne,
who has not been working at all since Jamie was born is
quite disappointed. She and her husband had agreed that
after he had completed college, she would be able to begin
whatever training she desired. An intense feud rages.

Instructions—Finish the story. (Insert any suggestions
you can think of which would help Anne and Allan to
resolve their problem.) Remember—it's 1999! What kind
of suggestions can you make as to what steps Anne and
Allan could have taken to prevent this conflict?

4. *Process:* After reading the situation, the students complete the account according to the instructions. As the
   students discuss the fantasies, the counselor may occasionally comment (as a reminder) that these events are
   taking place in the future and encourage the students to
   project into their solutions the changes they predict (or
   wish) will take place in 5 years. *After the fifteen minutes
   of group time* have elapsed the counselor may ask each
   group to briefly report to the entire class on the fantasies
   they constructed for the situations. The counselor may
   at this time make process observations or remark on any
   aspects of the fantasy construction ("This group felt
   that the situation was unlikely to occur in a few years
   time, and therefore, found it very difficult to flow with
   the sequence of events." Or "Apparently this family
   reminded you very much of your own in the way they
   developed priorities of who would be educated first.")
   This aspect of the exercise should take *no more than ten
   minutes.*

WHAT WE CAN BE: EVALUATING PERSONAL STEREOTYPES

1. *Goal:* The purpose of the triad exercise is to provide an opportunity for students to share their perceptions of each other in terms of an unconventional (for a woman) occupation. The exclusion from consideration of all traditional (e.g., teacher, nurse, secretary) occupations would provide impetus to expand alternatives in the realm of possible careers. The feedback provided by having others suggest occupations and provide rationales for their selection should help sensitize the students to their "images" or how they are construed by their peers.

2. *Time required:* 15–20 minutes

3. *Preparation:* Following the fantasy each group of 6 is asked to split into 2 groups of 3 by the counselor.

4. *Process:* Each member of the resulting triads is to take turns completing the following roles which are described by the counselor.

   a. Speaker—The task of the speaker is to share her perception of the receiver in terms of an UNCONVENTIONAL occupation (i.e., different from the traditional nurse, teacher, secretary roles typically filled by women) (e.g., "I see you as an airline pilot or perhaps a chemist"). Following this the speaker is to give the rationale for her choice(s) (e.g., "I see you as quite precise, calm . . .").

   b. Receiver—The task of the receiver is to listen to the remarks of the speaker and then share her reaction (e.g., "I was amazed you chose those fields because I see myself as less exact than that occupation would require").

   c. Observer—The task of the observer is to enforce the completion of the roles for the speaker and the observer, and then report to them what seemed to have taken place between them, e.g., "You seemed unable to explain clearly why you saw her (the receiver) as an agronomist." Or, "You didn't seem very happy with her choice of occupation for you. Were you? Why?"

Approximately five minutes should be devoted to each role (speaker, receiver, observer). After five minutes, the counselor announces, "Please switch roles. If you were assuming the role of Speaker, e.g., now assume the role of Receiver or Observer."

5. The final five minutes of the activity could be devoted to any reactions the students may have to the triadic interaction. These reactions could be shared with the total group. The counselor may ask specific questions to promote this brief discussion.

THE SOCIALIZATION OF WOMEN AND THE IMAGE OF WOMEN IN THE MEDIA*

Project choices:
    Collage with written or oral analysis
    Slide tape presentation
    Written or oral report
    Act out an original skit
    1. Pick at least one (you may do more than one if you like) of the categories listed below, and analyze a good number of examples of it. Describe the female characters, and analyze (make conclusions about) your descriptions. Some questions you might include and answer in your analysis are:

    a. What do these say about the average, normal, or "ideal" girl or boy?
    b. What should be the roles and goals of such a boy and girl?

---

*Thanks go to Patricia Silvers for some of the ideas in this section. Reprinted with permission from *Colloquy* magazine, November 1973, *6*, 9. Copyright © 1973 by the United Church Press.

  c. What type of people (consider their characteristics) are the girls presented here?
  d. Do you consider this *sexist* (degrading to women)? Does the image portray them as inferior, superior, equal, or something else?
  e. How do you think the images you're analyzing might influence other people who view them?

TV shows (the position of women in situation comedies, variety shows, shows starring men or women, etc.)
Adult commercials
Children's commercials
TV cartoons
Children's reading books (elementary school)
Magazines (for men, women, or general interest)
Comic books
Comic strips in newspapers
Etiquette books and columns
Advice to the lovelorn columns
Soap operas
TV news programs
True-Life confession magazines

2. Write an "unbiased" children's story, perhaps reversing the roles for the sexes, or including women in a number of different roles. Compare it with Dick and Jane readers, or other elementary books used in schools today.
3. Write and act out your original soap opera. Analyze what type of life is being presented. (Watch some soaps on TV. Try to figure out what makes them so popular, and analyze their effect on viewers).

FACT BOMBARDMENT

WOMEN IN THE U.S. POPULATION

In 1970, women made up 51.3 percent of the United States population. Characteristics of women in the population are:

CATEGORY	PERCENTAGE OF FEMALES
White	51.2
Black	52.4
Other races	49.9
Spanish heritage	50.5
Under 18	49.0
Voting age	52.5
In college	40.6
In labor force	37.2
Family heads	10.8
Married	50.0
Widowed	82.1
Divorced	61.1
Living alone	67.7
Below low-income level	58.1

WOMEN IN THE EDUCATIONAL PROFESSION

Three-fifths of women professional workers are teachers. Despite their participation in the teaching profession, they do not represent large numbers of school personnel in administrative and supervisory positions.

CATEGORY OF PERSONNEL	PERCENTAGE OF WOMEN
All full-time professional staff of public schools	64
Administrative and Supervisory staff	20
Teachers	67
Elementary School Principals	21
Senior High Principals	3
Superintendents	6
Assistant Superintendents	
Chief State School Officers	5

EARNINGS OF WOMEN

Despite their participation in the work force, women earn less than men. The average annual income for women who work full-time is $5,700, or 59 percent of the $9,630 average for men who work full-time. Mean income for families with female heads was $5,100, or 47 percent of the $10,930 median for families with male heads.

Women's entry into the work force has been a natural outcome of their rising years of education. Their educational advantage, however, has not been the same as that of males.

MEDIAN INCOMES OF PERSONS 25 YEARS AND OLDER BY SEX AND EDUCATION: 1971

EDUCATIONAL ATTAINMENT	ALL-INCOME RECIPIENTS		YEAR-ROUND FULL-TIME WORKERS	
	MALE	FEMALE	MALE	FEMALE
Elementary school				
Less than 8 years	$ 3,883	$ 1,503	$ 6,310	$ 3,946
8 years	5,469	1,883	7,838	4,440
High school				
1 to 3 years	7,570	2,581	8,945	4,889
4 years	9,088	3,594	9,996	5,808
College				
1 to 3 years	10,303	3,732	11,701	6,815
4 years or more	13,126	6,620	14,351	9,162

EMPLOYMENT OF WOMEN

Women have entered the work force in steadily increasing numbers. In 1900, they made up 20 percent of the nation's work force. By 1970, they had risen to nearly 40 percent. The types of work women do has also changed dramatically. In 1900, only 8 percent of women workers were professional, technical, or similar workers; 4 percent clerical workers; and 4 percent sales workers. In 1970, about one-third of all employed women were working as bookkeepers, secretaries, typists, file clerks, and the like. About 17 percent were service workers, beauticians, waitresses, attendants, etc. Another 16 percent were professional, technical, and kindred workers such as teachers, nurses, technicians, physicians, and lawyers. Two-fifths of the women in this last category were elementary or secondary school teachers.

JOBS WOMEN HOLD

OCCUPATION	TOTAL	WHITE	BLACK	SPANISH HERITAGE
Professional and technical workers	15.7%	16.3%	11.3%	9.6%
Sales workers	7.4%	8.1%	2.5%	6.0%
Clerical and kindred workers	34.9%	36.7%	20.7%	30.0%
Operatives, except transport equipment	13.9%	13.5%	16.1%	23.7%
Service workers, except household	16.6%	15.3%	25.5%	18.5%
Private household workers	3.8%	2.0%	17.9%	4.0%

The comment is often made that women work for "pin money" rather than out of economic necessity. The fact is that many women work out of need. Listed below are the percentage of working women and their marital status.

MARITAL STATUS	WHITE WOMEN	MINORITY GROUP WOMEN
Single	54.0	45.4
Married (husband present)	39.7	52.5
Widowed, divorced, or separated	37.6	43.1

EDUCATION OF WOMEN

Thirty million girls and women, three to thirty-four, are in school: 14 percent of girls three to six are in nursery school or kindergarten. Virtually all girls seven to fifteen are in grammar or high schools. Ninety-five percent of the girls sixteen to seventeen years old are in high school and 4 percent in this age group are in college.

Young men are more likely than young women to continue their education. Among young people eighteen to twenty-four, one out of three men but only one out of five women are in college.

Both women and men are completing more years of formal schooling. Listed below is the median school years completed by race and sex during the past thirty years.

MEDIAN SCHOOL YEARS COMPLETED BY RACE AND SEX:
1940–1970

							SPANISH	
	PERSONS 25 AND OLDER							
	TOTAL		WHITE		BLACK		HERITAGE	
CENSUS YEAR	M	F	M	F	M	F	M	F
1970	12.1	12.1	12.1	12.2	9.4	10.0	9.9	9.4
1960	10.3	10.9	10.7	11.2	7.7	8.4	*	*
1950	9.0	9.6	9.3	10.0	6.4	7.1	*	*
1940	8.6	8.7	8.7	8.8	5.4	6.1	*	*

Data for Spanish heritage not available before 1969.

THE STATUS OF WOMEN: SOME STATISTICS*

Women make up 51 percent of the American population:

1. How many women work?
   44% of American women over 16 work. They make up 40% of the American work force.

2. What type work do they do?
   More than 64% of the women who work are employed as clerical, service, and sales workers, or domestic workers (all relatively low-paying jobs). Of all working women:
   31% are secretaries

U.S. News and World Report. April 13, 1970, 35–37.
Time. March 20, 1972, 80–81.
The future of the sexes. *The Boston Globe*, Dec. 21, 1971, 33.
Report of the President's task force on women's rights and responsibilities. April 1970, 18. In Elsie Gould. *The American woman today.* Englewood Cliffs, N.J.: Prentice-Hall, 1972, 14.

15% are waitresses or servants
14% are factory workers
13% hold professional jobs

3. How does this type of women's work compare to men's work?
   About 70% of the men who work are employed as professional and technical workers, managers, proprietors, craftsmen, foremen, or factory workers (jobs that pay better than most of the jobs held by women).

4. How much do women earn, compared to men?

● There is a large gap between women's and men's earnings, and it is *increasing* as time goes by. In 1955 the average female employee earned 64% of the wages paid to similarly employed men; in 1970 she earned only 59% as much!

● The average woman today who works full time earns only $3 for every $5 paid to a man with a similar job.

● In 1970 the average median earnings for full-time workers was about:
   White men $7300
   Black men   4700
   White women   4200
   Black women   3100

● In 1968 a woman with a college degree was typically earning about $6600 a year, while a typical male college graduate was earning $11,700 a year. A woman college graduate can expect to earn $446 less per year than a white male who has only graduated from elementary school.

5. What percentage are women in different American professions?
   Women make up:

   7% of American doctors

3% of American lawyers
1% of American engineers
9% of American scientists
19% of college level faculties (in 1940 it was 30%)

By way of comparison, in western Europe 18 to 25% of the doctors are women. In West Germany 33% of the lawyers are women. In the Soviet Union women are 75% of the doctors, 36% of the lawyers, 28% of the engineers, and 38% of the scientists.

A summary of these trends:

- Most women workers are in lower-paying jobs than most male workers.

- Women earn less than men in all kinds of jobs.

- The gap between men's and women's earnings is getting wider, not narrower.

- The unemployment rate is higher for women than for men, and the gap is widening.

- The more education a woman has, the greater the gap is between the income she earns and that earned by a male worker with an equal amount of education.

CLASSROOM ACTIVITIES FROM FEMINISTS FOR NONSEXIST EDUCATION*

Four concerned women in the San Francisco Bay Area—Adele Meyer, Royetta Rule-Boyd, Shirley Olsen, and Elizabeth Roe—formed the Feminists for Nonsexist Education to study textbooks used in the public schools and to develop strategies for change. One of their activities was to devise and lead activities in the classrooms which attempted to make students aware of how their sex affects their expectations for themselves.

---

*Copyrighted © 1974 by Laurie Olsen Johnson. Reprinted with permission of The Feminist Press.

Career aspiration activity:
We had very interesting results with this game which we presented to four classes in a suburban junior high school.

- Ask each student to write down in a short phrase what
  she/he plans to do or be when she/he finishes her/his
  education.

- Collect the papers and divide the room in half according
  to sex, with each half of the room facing each other, i.e.,
  rearrange the desks.

- Exchange the papers at random, giving the girls the
  boys' expectations and the boys the girls'.

- Going down the row, ask the students facing each other
  to enter into a debate, first one then the other challeng-
  ing the expectation. Each student should defend the
  expectation against the challenge to the best of her/his
  ability. Where the words housewife/mother appear, the
  boys should change it to word househusband/father.

- After the debates ask the students what they noticed
  most in each other's reactions and why and what conclusions they have drawn.

- It is important that the monitors of this game remain as
  neutral as possible. The students tend to react to the old
  "we against they" tradition toward adults, and we
  found in some cases the students found it a real threat,
  banded together, and ended up debating with us instead
  of each other.

Our best class noted that girls knew more about boys'
interests than the boys knew about theirs. When we asked them
to explain that, one girl replied, "When a girl has a boyfriend
interested in motorcycles, she learns about motorcycles. But a
guy with a girlfriend doesn't learn how to bake."

Class meeting:
Meetings are good opportunities for focusing on particular problems in your classroom involving conflicts (e.g., "Why is it

always the boys that get to do _____, etc.), or more general issues (what it means to be a boy or a girl, or a man or a woman). A good example of this is reported by Griffith, a third-grade teacher in San Francisco.

Class meetings to discuss:

- Women in leadership roles.

- Do you think a woman could be president?

- What can women do that men cannot do?

- What can men do that women cannot do?

- Should a woman get paid as much as a man?

- Children sit on chairs in a circle and record the discussion.

Purpose:

- To encourage children to listen to each other on a question that requires thinking.

- To encourage children to verbalize their ideas on this subject.

- To learn what ideas they have about the subject.

- To give them a chance to hear themselves in the discussion.

- To give me a chance to hear my role in the discussion.

Twenty-minute meetings were held. Both boys and girls argued for and against the stereotypes. Children expressed the opinion that they could accept a woman president and that women should receive the same pay as men, but they thought that "other people" would not agree.

My facilitating was reasonably neutral (my goal), except when I asked about a woman president. I think my voice was more animated, suggesting perhaps an important question.

Interesting remarks:

> Most women would not want to be president.

> Men make better rules than girls.

> Girls are smart.

> Women are too emotional to be president, they cry too much.

> If a woman ran a fork lift where my father works there would be a walkout.

> Men cannot be pom-pom girls. (He was told there are pom-pom boys.)

> A woman president would make you get your hair cut.

> Some laws stop women from doing some things, like being drafted.

> Women could probably fight better than men.

> I know a man who cooks better than women.

> My cousin is a girl and she fixes her own car.

Talking to the tape as a group generated more discussion. The tape has been placed in the classroom recording center and is available to the children in their free time.

CHAPTER
SIX

Resources
For Teachers

Teachers' Perspectives

This section provides resources for the teachers interested in implementing nonsexist materials in classrooms. Background articles which explain how sex-role stereotyping is perpetuated in unexamined activities and policies in the school structure are included. Critical articles about children's literature are supplemented by bibliographies for the different ages which indicate high-quality nonsexist books for children. Lists of the major agencies and publishers of nonsexist materials are provided as possible sources of more complete and specific information. Since the best evaluators of an experimental curriculum are the teachers who attempt to use it, a section of this chapter describes how the teachers in the intervention study responded to particular pieces in this selected nonsexist curriculum.

General Recommendations for Initiating Programs to Assess and Reduce Sex-Role Stereotyping in Schools

1. Initial contacts should be made with central school administrators, curriculum directors, pupil personnel supervisors, and any other officials who are involved in the decision-making process in the school.

2. Clear and relevant research material should be presented, suggesting the need for schoolwide efforts to determine whether sex-role stereotyping exists, to what

extent, in what areas, and in what ways. The approach should be vertical as well as horizontal, i.e., grade by grade and subject by subject, spanning kindergarten through grade 12.

3. University personnel or researchers may serve most effectively as consultants. Major responsibility for assessment and implementation of any changes in programs or materials should lie with administrators, curriculum directors, and teachers. Initially they need to critically examine their own content areas, curricular units, textbooks, classroom practices, etc., for sex bias. Take care to determine whether there was equal opportunity in facilities (e.g., athletic department) and equal availability and encouragement in all courses (e.g., carpentry, cooking, etc.) for all students.

4. Optimum results could be obtained by the development of summer workshops or in-service training programs, with teachers and curriculum directors working out approaches and materials that are suitable and relevant to their specific grade level or course.

5. Teachers must be fully involved in creating and understanding the materials they will use in their own classrooms; they will be most aware of their students' needs and interests and be more sensitive to the nature of the community they work in.

6. The general approach toward sex-role discussion should involve no didacticism or propaganda. Information should be presented impartially, with ample opportunity for students to discuss all aspects and points of view. It is important to stress the need for equal educational opportunity for social, emotional, and cognitive development. Activities or curricular units adopted for use should have substantial academic content and provide sufficient opportunity for further development of traditional language arts skills.

7. Community resources (e.g., elected or volunteer government officials of both sexes) outside of the school should be identified for possible use as guest speakers or models.

8. Careful attention should be paid to the appropriateness and variety of the materials developed in reference to the age and ability levels of the students.

SEXUAL STEREOTYPES START EARLY*

by Florence Howe

"I remember quite clearly a day in sixth grade," a college freshman told me a year ago, "when the class was discussing an article from a weekly supplementary reader. The story was about a chef, and someone in the class ventured the opinion that cooking was women's work, that a man was a 'sissy' to work in the kitchen. The teacher's response surprised us all. She informed us calmly that men make the best cooks, just as they make the best dress designers, singers, and laundry workers. 'Yes,' she said, 'anything a woman can do a man can do better.' There were no male students present; my teacher was a woman."

Children learn about sex roles very early in their lives, probably before they are eighteen months old, certainly long before they enter school. They learn these roles through relatively simple patterns that most of us take for granted. We throw boy-babies up in the air and roughhouse with them. We coo over girl-babies and handle them delicately. We choose sex-related colors and toys for our children from their earliest days. We encourage the energy and physical activity of our sons, just as we expect girls to be quieter and more docile. We love both our sons and daughters with equal fervor, we protest, and yet we are disappointed when there is no male child to carry on the family name.

---

*Reprinted with permission from *Saturday Review*, Oct. 16, 1971.

A hundred fifty years ago, Elizabeth Cady Stanton learned to master a horse and the Greek language in an attempt to comfort her father who had lost his only son and heir. No matter what evidence of brilliance Cady Stanton displayed, her father could only shake his head and murmur, "If only you were a boy, Elizabeth," much to the bafflement of the girl who had discerned that riding horses and studying Greek were the activities that had distinguished her dead brother from her living sisters. Only thirty years ago, at family gatherings, I remember hearing whispers directed at my brother and me: "Isn't it a pity that he has all the looks while she has all the brains." Others could contribute similar anecdotes today.

The truth of it is that while we in the West have professed to believe in "liberty, equality, and fraternity," we have also taken quite literally the term "fraternity." We have continued to maintain, relatively undisturbed, all the ancient edicts about the superiority of males, the inferiority of females. Assumptions current today about woman's alleged "nature" are disguised psychological versions of physiological premises in the Old Testament, in the doctrines of the early church fathers, and in the thinking of male philosophers, writers, educators—including some who founded women's colleges or opened men's colleges to women. In short, what we today call the "women's liberation movement" is only the most recent aspect of the struggle that began with Mary Wollstonecraft's *Vindication of the Rights of Women* in 1795—a piece of theory that drew for courage and example on the fathers of the French and American revolutions. It is, of course, only one hundred years since higher education was really opened up to women in this country, and many people know how dismal is the record of progress for professional women, especially during the past fifty years.

How much blame should be placed on public education? A substantial portion, although it is true that schools reflect the society they serve. Indeed, schools function to reinforce the sexual stereotypes that children have been taught by their parents, friends, and the mass culture we live in. It is also perfectly understandable that sexual stereotypes demeaning to women are also perpetuated by women—mother in the first place, and teachers in the second—as well as by men—fathers, the few male teachers in elementary schools, high school teachers, and many male administrators and educators at the top of the school's hierarchy.

Sexual stereotypes are not to be identified with sexual or innate differences, for we know nothing about these matters. John Stuart Mill was the first man (since Plato) to affirm that we could know nothing about innate sexual differences, since we have never known of a society in which either men or women lived wholly separately. Therefore, he reasoned, we can't "know" what the pure "nature" of either sex might be: What we see as female behavior, he maintained, is the result of what he called the education of "willing slaves." There is still no "hard" scientific evidence of innate sexual differences, though there are new experiments in progress on male hormones of mice and monkeys. Other hormonal experiments, especially those using adrenaline, have indicated that, for human beings at least, social factors and pressures are more important than physiological ones.

Sexual stereotypes are assumed differences, social conventions or norms, learned behavior, attitudes, and expectations. Most stereotypes are well-known to all of us, for they are simple—not to say simple-minded. Men are smart, women are dumb but beautiful, etc. A recent annotated catalogue of children's books (distributed by the National Council of Teachers of English to thousands of teachers and used for ordering books with federal funds) lists titles under the headings "Especially for Girls" and "Especially for Boys." Verbs and adjectives are remarkably predictable through the listings. Boys "decipher and discover," "earn and train," or "foil" someone; girls "struggle," "overcome difficulties," "feel lost," "help solve," or "help [someone] out." One boy's story has "strange power," another moves "from truancy to triumph." A girl, on the other hand, "learns to face the real world" or makes a "difficult adjustment." Late or early, in catalogues or on shelves, the boys of children's books are active and capable, the girls passive and in trouble. All studies of children's literature—and there have been many besides my own—support this conclusion.

Ask yourself whether you would be surprised to find the following social contexts in a fifth-grade arithmetic textbook:

1. Girls playing marbles; boys sewing;

2. Girls earning money, building things, and going places; boys buying ribbons for a sewing project;

3. Girls working at physical activities; boys babysitting and, you guessed it, sewing.

Of course you would be surprised—so would I. What I have done here is to reverse the sexes as found in a fifth-grade arithmetic text. I was not surprised, since several years ago an intrepid freshman offered to report on third-grade arithmetic texts for me and found similar types of sexual roles prescribed: Boys were generally making things or earning money; girls were cooking or spending money on such things as sewing equipment.

The verification of sexual stereotypes is a special area of interest to psychologists and sociologists. An important series of studies was done in 1968 by Inge K. Broverman and others at Worcester State Hospital in Massachusetts. These scientists established a "sex-stereotype questionnaire" consisting of "122 bipolar items"—characteristics socially known or socially tested as male or female. Studies by these scientists and others established what common sense will verify: that those traits "stereotypically masculine . . . are more often perceived as socially desirable" than those known to be feminine. Here are some "male-valued items" as listed on the questionnaire:

> very aggressive
> very independent
> not at all emotional
> very logical
> very direct
> very adventurous
> very self-confident
> very ambitious

These and other characteristics describe the stereotypic

male. To describe the female, you need only reverse those traits and add "female-valued" ones, some of which follow:

    very talkative
    very tactful
    very gentle
    very aware of feelings of others
    very religious
    very quiet
    very strong need for security

and the one I am particularly fond of citing to men who control my field—"enjoys art and literature very much."

The Worcester scientists used their 122 items to test the assumptions of clinical psychologists about mental health. Three matched groups of male and female clinical psychologists were given three identical lists of the 122 items unlabeled and printed in random order. Each group was given a different set of instructions: One was told to choose those traits that characterize the healthy adult male; another to choose those of the healthy adult female; the third, to choose those of the healthy adult—a person. The result: The clinically healthy male and the clinically healthy adult were identical—and totally divergent from the clinically healthy female. The authors of the study concluded that "a double standard of health exists for men and women." That is, the general standard of health applies only to men. Women are perceived as "less healthy" by those standards called "adult." At the same time, however, if a woman deviates from the sexual stereotypes prescribed for her—if she grows more "active" or "aggressive," for example—she doesn't grow healthier; she may, in fact, if her psychiatrist is a Freudian, be perceived as "sicker." Either way, therefore, women lose or fail, and so it is not surprising to find psychologist Phyllis Chesler reporting that proportionately many more women than men are declared "sick" by psychologists and psychiatrists.

The idea of a "double standard" for men and women is a familiar one and helps to clarify how severely sexual stereotypes constrict the personal and social development of women. Studies by child psychologists reveal that while boys of all ages clearly identify with male figures and activities, girls are less likely to make the same sort of identification with female stereotypes. With whom do girls and women identify? My guess is that there is a good deal of confusion in their heads and hearts in this respect, and that what develops is a pattern that might be compared to schizophrenia: The schoolgirl knows that, for her, life is one thing, learning another. This is like the Worcester study's "double standard"—the schoolgirl cannot find herself in history texts or as she would like to see herself in literature; yet she knows she is not a male. Many women may ultimately discount the question of female identity as unimportant, claiming other descriptions preferable—as a parent, for example, or a black person, or a college professor.

Children learn sexual stereotypes at an early age, and, by the time they get to fifth grade, it may be terribly difficult, perhaps hardly possible by traditional means, to change their attitudes about sex roles—whether they are male or female. For more than a decade, Paul Torrance, a psychologist particularly interested in creativity, has been conducting interesting and useful experiments with young children. Using a Products Improvement Test, for example, Torrance asked first-grade boys and girls to "make toys more fun to play with." Many six-year-old boys refused to try the nurse's kit, "protesting," Torrance reports, "I'm a boy! I don't play with things like that." Several creative boys turned the nurse's kit into a doctor's kit and were then "quite free to think of improvements." By the third grade, however, "boys excelled girls even on the nurse's kit, probably because," Torrance explains, "girls have been conditioned by this time to accept toys as they are and not to manipulate or change them."

Later experiments with third, fourth, and fifth-graders using science toys further verify what Torrance calls "the inhibiting effects of sex-role conditioning." "Girls were quite reluctant," he reports, "to work with these science toys and frequently protested: 'I'm a girl; I'm not supposed to know anything about things like that!'" Boys, even in these early grades, were about twice as good as girls at explaining ideas about toys. In 1959, Torrance reported his findings to parents and teachers in one school and asked for their cooperation in attempting to change the attitudes of the girls. In 1960, when he retested them, using similar science toys, the girls participated willingly and even with apparent enjoyment. And they performed as well as the boys. But in one significant respect nothing had changed: The boys' contributions were more highly valued—both by other boys and by girls—than the girls' contributions, regardless of the fact that, in terms of sex, boys and girls had scored equally. "Apparently," Torrance writes, "the school climate has helped to make it more acceptable for girls to play around with science things, but boys' ideas about science things are still supposed to be better than those of girls."

Torrance's experiments tell us both how useful and how limited education may be for women in a culture in which assumptions about their inferiority run deep in their own consciousness as well as in the consciousness of men. While it is encouraging to note that a year's effort had changed behavior patterns significantly, it is also clear that attitudes of nine-, ten-, and eleven-year-olds are not so easily modifiable, at least not through the means Torrance used.

Torrance's experiments also make clear that, whatever most of us have hitherto assumed, boys and girls are *not* treated alike in elementary school. If we consider those non-curricular aspects of the school environment that the late anthropologist Jules Henry labeled the "noise" of schools, chief among them is the general attitude of teachers, whatever their sex, that girls are likely to "love" reading and to "hate" mathematics and science. As we know from the Rosenthal study of teacher expectations, *Pygmalion in the Classroom,* such expectations significantly determine student behavior and attitudes. Girls are not expected to think logically or to understand scientific principles; they accept that estimate internally and give up on mathematics and science relatively early. And what encouragement awaits the interested few in high school? For example, in six high school science texts published since 1966 and used in the Baltimore city public schools—all of the books rich in illustrations— I found photographs of one female lab assistant, one woman doctor, one woman scientist, and Rachel Carson. It is no won-

der that the percentage of women doctors and engineers in the
United States has remained constant at 6 per cent and 1 per cent
respectively for the past fifty years.

Though there is no evidence that their early physical needs
are different from or less than boys', girls are offered fewer
activities even in kindergarten. They may sit and watch while
boys, at the request of the female teacher, change the seating
arrangement in the room. Of course, it's not simply a matter of
physical exercise or ability: Boys are learning how to behave as
males, and girls are learning to be "ladies" who enjoy being
"waited on." If there are student-organized activities to be
arranged, boys are typically in charge, with girls assisting,
perhaps in the stereotyped role of secretary. Boys are allowed
and expected to be noisy and aggressive, even on occasion to
express anger; girls must learn "to control themselves" and
behave like "young ladies." On the other hand, boys are
expected not to cry, though there are perfectly good reasons
why children of both sexes ought to be allowed that avenue of
expression. Surprisingly early, boys and girls are separated for
physical education and hygiene, and all the reports now being
published indicate preferential treatment for boys and nearly
total neglect of girls.

In junior high schools, sexual stereotyping becomes, if
anything, more overt. Curricular sex-typing continues and is
extended to such "shop" subjects as cooking and sewing, on
the one hand, and metal- and woodworking, printing, ceramics,
on the other. In vocational high schools, the stereotyping
becomes outright channeling, and here the legal battles have
begun for equality of opportunity. Recently, the testimony of
junior high and high school girls in New York has become
available in a pamphlet prepared by the New York City chapter
of NOW (*Report on Sex Bias in the Public Schools,* available
from Anne Grant West, 453 Seventh St., Brooklyn, N.Y.
11215). Here are a few items:

- Well, within my physics class last year, our teacher
  asked if there was anybody interested in being a lab
  assistant in the physics lab, and when I raised my hand,

he told all the girls to put their hands down because he was only interested in working with boys.

- There is an Honor Guard . . . students who, instead of participating in gym for the term, are monitors in the hall, and I asked my gym teacher if I could be on the Honor Guard Squad. She said it was only open to boys. I then went to the head of the Honor Guard . . . who said that he thought girls were much too nasty to be Honor Guards. He thought they would be too mean in working on the job, and I left it at that.

- We asked for basketball. They said there wasn't enough equipment. The boys prefer to have it first. Then we will have what is left over. We haven't really gotten anywhere.

Finally, I quote more extensively from one case:

Mother: I asked Miss Jonas if my daughter could take metal-working or mechanics, and she said there is no freedom of choice. That is what she said.

The Court: That is it?

Answer: I also asked her whose decision this was, that there was no freedom of choice. And she told me it was the decision of the board of education. I didn't ask her anything else because she clearly showed me that it was against the school policy for girls to be in the class. She said it was a board of education decision.

Question: Did she use that phrase, "no freedom of choice"?

Answer: Exactly that phrase—no freedom of choice. That is what made me so angry that I wanted to start this whole thing.

The Court: Now, after this lawsuit was filed, they then permitted you to take the course; is that correct?

Daughter: No, we had to fight about it for quite a while.

Question: But eventually they did let you in the second semester?

Answer: They only let me in there.

Q: You are the only girl?

A: Yes.

Q: How did you do in the course?

A: I got the medal for it from all the boys there.

Q: Will you show the court?

A: Yes (indicating).

Q: And what does the medal say?

A: Mctal 1970 Van Wyck.

Q: And why did they give you that medal?

A: Because I was the best one out of all the boys.

The Court: I do not want any giggling or noises in the courtroom. Just do the best you can to control yourself or else I
will have to ask you to leave the courtroom. This is no
picnic, you know. These are serious lawsuits.

Such "serious lawsuits" will, no doubt, continue, but they
are not the only routes to change. There are others to be
initiated by school systems themselves.

One route lies through the analysis of texts and attitudes.
So long as those responsible for the education of children
believe in the stereotypes as givens, rather than as hypothetical
constructs that a patriarchal society has established as desired
norms—so long as the belief continues, so will the condition.
These beliefs are transmitted in the forms we call literature and
history, either on the printed page or in other media.

Elementary school readers are meant for both sexes.
Primers used in the first three grades offer children a view of a
"typical" American family: a mother who does not work, a
father who does, two children—a brother who is always older
than a sister—and two pets—a dog and sometimes a cat—
whose sexes and ages mirror those of the brother and sister. In
these books, boys build or paint things; they also pull girls in
wagons and push merry-go-rounds. Girls carry purses when
they go shopping; they help mother cook or pretend that they
are cooking; and they play with their dolls. When they are not
making messes, they are cleaning up their rooms or other
people's messes. Plots in which girls are involved usually

depend on their inability to do something—to manage their own roller skates or to ride a pony. Or in another typical role, a girl named Sue admires a parachute jumper: "What a jump!" said Sue. "What a jump for a man to make!" When her brother puts on a show for the rest of the neighborhood, Sue, whose name appears as the title of the chapter, is part of his admiring audience.

The absence of adventurous heroines may shock the innocent; the absence of even a few stories about women doctors, lawyers, or professors thwarts reality; but the consistent presence of one female stereotype is the most troublesome matter:

> Primrose was playing house. Just as she finished pouring tea for her dolls she began to think. She thought and thought and she thought some more: "Whom shall I marry? Whomever shall I marry?
>
> "I think I shall marry a mailman. Then I could go over to everybody's house and give them their mail.
>
> "Or I might marry a policeman. I could help him take the children across the street."

Primrose thinks her way through ten more categories of employment and concludes, "But now that I think it over, maybe I'll just marry somebody I love." Love is the opiate designated to help Primrose forget to think about what she would like to do or be. With love as reinforcer, she can imagine herself helping some man in his work. In another children's book, Johnny says, "I think I will be a dentist when I grow up," and later, to Betsy, he offers generously, "You can be a dentist's nurse." And, of course, Betsy accepts gratefully, since girls are not expected to have work identity other than as servants or helpers. In short, the books that schoolgirls read prepare them early for the goal of marriage, hardly ever for work, and never for independence.

If a child's reader can be pardoned for stereotyping because it is "only" fiction, a social studies text has no excuse for denying reality to its readers. After all, social studies texts ought to describe "what is," if not "what should be." And yet, such texts for the youngest grades are no different from readers. They focus on families and hence on sex roles and work. Sisters are still younger than brothers; brothers remain the doers, questioners, and knowers who explain things to their poor, timid sisters. In a study of five widely used texts, Jamie Kelem Frisof finds that energetic boys think about "working on a train or in a broom factory" or about being President. They grow up to be doctors or factory workers or (in five texts combined) to do some hundred different jobs, as opposed to thirty for women.

Consider for a moment the real work world of women. Most women (at least for some portion of their lives) work, and if we include "token" women—the occasional engineer, for instance—they probably do as many different kinds of work as men. Even without improving the status of working women, the reality is distinctly different from the content of school texts and literature written for children. Schools usually at least reflect the society they serve; but the treatment of working women is one clear instance in which the reflection is distorted by a patriarchal attitude about who *should* work and the maleness of work. For example, there are women doctors—there have been women doctors in this country, in fact, for a hundred years or so. And yet, until the publication this month of two new children's books by the Feminist Press (Box 334, Old Westbury, N.Y. 11568), there were no children's books about women doctors.

In a novel experiment conducted recently by an undergraduate at Towson State College in Maryland, fourth-grade students answered "yes" or "no" to a series of twenty questions, eight of which asked, in various ways, whether "girls were smarter than boys" or whether "daddies were smarter than mommies." The results indicated that boys and girls were agreed that 1) boys were not smarter than girls, nor girls smarter than boys; but 2) that daddies were indeed smarter than mommies! One possible explanation of this finding depends on the knowledge that daddies, in school texts and on television (as well as in real life), work, and that people who work know things. Mommies, on the other hand, in books and on television, rarely stir out of the house except to go to the store—and how can someone like that know anything? Of course, *we* know that half of all mothers in the United States work at some kind of job, but children whose mommies do work can only assume—on the basis of evidence offered in school books and on television—that their mommies must be "different," perhaps even not quite "real" mommies.

If children's readers deny the reality of working women, high school history texts deny women their full historical role. A recent study by Janice Law Trecker of thirteen popular texts concludes with what by now must seem a refrain: Women in such texts are "passive, incapable of sustained organization or work, satisfied with [their] role in society, and well supplied with material blessings." Women, in the grip of economic and political forces, rarely fighting for anything, occasionally receive some "rights," especially suffrage in 1920, which, of course, solves all *their* problems. There is no discussion of the struggle by women to gain entrance into higher education, of their efforts to organize or join labor unions, of other battles for working rights, or of the many different aspects of the hundred-year-long multi-issue effort that ended, temporarily, in the suffrage act of 1920. Here is Dr. Trecker's summary of the history and contributions of American women as garnered from the thirteen texts combined:

> Women arrived in 1619 (a curious choice if meant to be their first acquaintance with the New World). They held the Seneca Falls Convention on Women's Rights in 1848. During the rest of the nineteenth century, they participated in reform movements, chiefly temperance, and were exploited in factories. In 1920, they were given the vote. They joined the armed forces for the first time during the Second World War and thereafter have enjoyed the good life in America. Add the names of the women who are invariably mentioned: Harriet Beecher Stowe, Jane Addams, Dorothea Dix, and Frances Perkins, with perhaps Susan B. Anthony, Elizabeth Cady Stanton . . . [and you have the story].

Where efforts have been made in recent years to incorporate black history, again it is without attention to black women, either with respect to their role in abolitionist or civil rights movements, for example, or with respect to intellectual or cultural achievements.

Just as high school history texts rely on male spokesmen and rarely quote female leaders of the feminist movement— even when they were also articulate writers such as Charlotte Perkins Gilman, or speakers such as Sojourner Truth—so, too, literary anthologies will include Henry James or Stephen Crane rather than Edith Wharton or Kate Chopin. Students are offered James Joyce's *Portrait of the Artist as a Young Man* or the *Autobiography of Malcolm X*, rather than Doris Lessing's *Martha Quest* or Anne Moody's *Coming of Age in Mississippi*. As a number of studies have indicated, the literary curriculum, both in high school and college, is a male-centered one. That is, either male authors dominate the syllabus or the central characters of the books are consistently male. There is also usually no compensating effort to test the fictional portraits—of women and men—against the reality of life experience. Allegedly "relevant" textbooks for senior high school or freshman college composition courses continue to appear, such as Macmillan's *Representative Men: Heroes of Our Time*. There are two women featured in this book: Elizabeth Taylor, the actress, and Jacqueline Onassis, the Existential Heroine. Thirty-five or forty men—representing a range of racial, political, occupational, and intellectual interests—fill the bulk of a book meant, of course, for both men and women. And some teachers are still ordering such texts.

It's not a question of malice, I assume, but of thoughtlessness or ignorance. Six or seven years ago I too was teaching from a standard male-dominated curriculum—and at a women's college at that. But I speak from more than my own experience. Last fall at this time I knew of some fifty college courses in what has come to be known as women's studies. This fall, I know of more than 500, about half of which are in literature and history. I know also of many high school teachers who have already begun to invent comparable courses.

School systems can and should begin to encourage new curricular developments, especially in literature and social studies, and at the elementary as well as the high school level. Such changes, of course, must include the education and re-education of teachers, and I know of no better way to re-educate them than to ask for analyses of the texts they use, as well as of their assumptions and attitudes. The images we pick up, consciously or unconsciously, from literature and history significantly control our sense of identity, and our identity—our sense of ourselves as powerful or powerless, for example—controls our behavior. As teachers read new materials and organize and teach new courses, they will change their views. That is the story of most of the women I know who, like me, have become involved in women's studies. The images we have in our heads about ourselves come out of literature and history; before we can change those images, we must see them clearly enough to exorcise them and, in the process, to raise others from the past we are learning to see.

That is why black educators have grown insistent upon their students' learning black history—slave history, in fact. That is also why some religious groups, Jews for example, emphasize their history as a people, even though part of that history is also slave history. For slave history has two virtues: Not only does it offer a picture of servitude against which one can measure the present; it offers also a vision of struggle and courage. When I asked a group of young women at the University of Pittsburgh last year whether they were depressed by the early nineteenth-century women's history they were studying, their replies were instructive: "Certainly not," one woman said, "we're angry that we had to wait until now—after so many years of U.S. history in high school—to learn the truth about some things." And another added, "But it makes you feel good to read about those tremendous women way back then. They felt some of the same things we do now."

Will public education begin to change the images of women in texts and the lives of women students in schools? There will probably be some movement in this direction, at least in response to the pressures from students, parents, and individual teachers. I expect that parents, for example, will continue to win legal battles for their daughters' equal rights and opportunities. I expect that individual teachers will alter their courses and texts and grow more sensitive to stereotypic expectations and behavior in the classroom. But so far there are no signs of larger, more inclusive reforms: no remedial program for counselors, no major effort to destereotype vocational programs or kindergarten classrooms, no centers for curricular reform. Frankly, I don't expect this to happen without a struggle. I don't expect that public school systems will take the initiative here. There is too much at stake in a society as patriarchal as this one. And schools, after all, tend to follow society, not lead it.

WOMEN IN CHILDREN'S LITERATURE*

By Alleen Pace Nilsen

Some of my best and most adventurous girl friends are between the covers of books. They range from *Alice in Wonderland* to *Harriet the Spy*. In between are *Caddie Woodlawn, Heidi,* Laura of *The Little House* books, and Arriety of *The Borrowers*. Because of these friends, I was shocked last May to read Elizabeth Fisher's article in the *New York Times* which charged that children's books were unfair to girls. Her strongest claim was that books for our youngest and therefore most impressionable children not only fail to represent the real world of today, but also combine into "an almost incredible conspiracy of conditioning. Boys' achievement drive is encouraged; girls' is cut off. Boys are brought up to express themselves; girls to please. The general image of the female ranges from dull to degrading to invisible."

As I said, my first reaction was shock. This was followed by skepticism and finally by reluctant agreement. I took my first step between skepticism and agreement when I remembered some advice I received in a course entitled "Writing for Children." The instructor told us that the wise author writes about boys, thereby insuring himself a maximum audience, since only girls will read a book about a girl, but both boys and girls will read about a boy. At the time that I heard this, I felt nothing but

---

gratitude for being let in on a trade secret. Since then, I have heard that Scott O'Dell, who wrote the prize-winning *Island of the Blue Dolphins,* tells how the book was initially rejected by a publisher who wanted him to rewrite it, changing the heroine to a hero.

I took my second step when I sat down in front of the fifty-eight picture books which happened to be on the display cart for use by the children's literature teachers at Eastern Michigan University. As I thumbed through the books looking specifically at the way women and girls were pictured, I was struck first by what appears to be a cult of the apron. Of the fifty-eight books, twenty-five had a picture of a woman somewhere in them. And of these twenty-five books, all but four had a picture of a woman wearing an apron. Ets and Labastida showed women wearing their aprons to the public market in Mexico, and Robert McCloskey had a woman wearing an apron to the public gardens in Boston. Within these fifty-eight books, I also found a mother alligator, a mother rabbit, a mother donkey, and a mother cat all wearing aprons. In the four books which showed women without aprons, the leading characters included a teaching sister whose habit had a long white frontispiece, a queen who was knitting, an Indian squaw who was stirring a pot of food, and a mother who was taking her children on an outing.

This was enough to convince me that the matter was worthy of additional study. Knowing that I could never look at all children's books, I decided on a rather modest sampling, the winners and runners-up of the Caldecott Award[1] during the last twenty years. These books are fairly representative of the best that we have in picture books, and once a book gets on this exclusive list it is ordered by practically every children's librarian in the country. Hence these are books that reflect our adult values and at the same time influence the formation of early child values. People have told me that if I had looked at books

---

[1]This award is presented annually by the Children's Service Committee of the American Library Association for the most distinguished picture book of the year. Including the runners-up, eighty books received citations within the last twenty years.

written for junior high school students my findings would have
been different. Perhaps so. It's certainly an area that needs
investigation. But my reason for concentrating on picture books
rather than on those for independent readers (children age eight
and above) is that the illustrated books are the ones influencing
children at the time they are in the process of developing their
own sexual identity. Children decide very early in life what roles
are appropriate to male and female. Last summer in our own
family, we had a striking example of this. My sister was
accepted into medical school. Naturally there were congratula-
tions and comments from neighbors, friends, and relatives.
After a few days of this, she found her son (age six) and her
daughter (age five) crying real tears for no apparent reason.
When she at last got to the cause of their grief, she found that
they thought if she were going to become a doctor, she would
first have to turn into a man and they wouldn't have a mother.

But on to the survey of the eighty books—I will start by
giving some very quick comparisons. First, just going through
the titles of the stories, I found fourteen males (thirteen boys
and one man), but only four females (two girls and two women)
listed by name. In counting the characters pictured in the illustrations, I found a total of 386 females and 579 males. Of the
eighty books, there was not a single one that did not have a male
(human or animal), but there were six books in which females
were completely absent. In a larger group of books—in fact,
one-fourth of the entire sample—there were only what I would
call token females. Seven of these token females were mothers
who sewed on the buttons and packed the lunches so that, for
example, "The Fool of the World" could go away in his "flying
ship," and Si could get a job as "Skipper John's Cook." I
expected this, but I was surprised to notice how often women
and girls were pictured looking out at the action. They stand in
doorways (*The Storm Book*), they look through windows (*The
Two Reds*), and they sit on the porch in rocking chairs (*The Day
We Saw the Sun Come Up*). Most of the token females were
very unobtrusive, such as the princess who is only mentioned as
a marriage objective in *The Fool of the World and the Flying
Ship* and *Puss In Boots*. In *Why the Sun and Moon Live in the*

Sky, we see the moon as the sun's wife who helps build the house, but says nothing. In *Alexander and the Wind-up Mouse* the male characters happen to be in Annie's room. We never see Annie, but she turns out to be the villain because she throws away the old toys. In *One Wide River to Cross,* we see male and female animals, but not male and female people. In *Wave,* the only mention of females is a statement that even the women and babies climbed the mountain. In *May I Bring a Friend,* the queen knits and is swung in a swing. She frowns when they all go fishing and she sits on a cushion in the background when a golden trumpet is brought and all the males take a turn playing. In *Judge,* one of the five prisoners is a woman who is declared a "nincompoop," and in *Mr. T. W. Anthony Woo,* the whole plot is how the lovable Mr. Woo can get rid of his meddlesome sister and her bothersome parrot, who is also female. There is one book in this group that I think is the epitome of male chauvinism. It is an alphabet book called *Ape in a Cape.* It is dedicated to Timmy and it pictures thirty-six male animals and two females. It begins with the ape who wears a definitely male military cape. When we come to the "Dove in Love" page, we see two identical doves so I assume that one is female. The only other female is a ridiculous "fat lady" hippopotamus in the background of a circus scene. When I came to the "M" page and read "Mouse in a Blouse," I was certain I would see a female animal, but no! The author-artist pictures a mouse in a middy blouse and to make sure there is no mistake he adds a sailor hat labelled U.S. Navy.

But even this book I would not make a special effort to keep away from my daughter. In fact, there was not a single book in the survey that I would want her not to read. On the other hand, I would be very distressed if these books were the only books available to her. If a girl is continually faced with books where the boy does all the explaining while the girl does all the listening, where the boy does all the travelling while the girl does all the waving, where the boy does all the complaining while the girl does all the smiling, and worst of all, where the boy does all of everything and the girl isn't even visible, then I think it reasonable to predict that the girl might have problems in finding her own identity. If she accepts the placid role of the female as shown in some recent picture books, then she runs the risk of becoming an anachronism as well as an unhappy person. I think what is more likely is that if she has a fair amount of energy, ambition, and intelligence, she will reject the placid female role and will instead identify with the male. This too—as most of us know—brings its share of frustration. Rather than dwelling on this point, I will assume that we are in agreement that there is a real need for books presenting models which show accurately and realistically ways in which women and girls can successfully function as individuals.

In the rest of my paper, then, I will change my focus and look behind the statistics to see if we can see the reasons for what truly does look like a prejudice against girls. I am in hopes that if we understand some of the reasons, then perhaps we can be more efficient as we go about trying to ameliorate the situation.

Some people have already suggested that publishers are plotting against women and girls. I find this highly unlikely—at least on a conscious level—because the field of children's literature is one in which women have at least a numerical majority in the control of children's books as they go about their roles of being mothers, teachers, librarians, book sellers, critics, and children's editors. And if the Caldecott books are typical, then women are at least equally represented among the authors, although they are in the minority among the artists. There were thirty-eight male authors or author-artists, as compared with forty women; however among the free lance artists there were twenty-five men as compared to twelve women. The other reason that I do not think that the publishers are intentionally ignoring girls, is that I can see no way in which it would profit either their businesses or society. Until only very recently, it may have been thought best for the world as a whole if girls were not encouraged to do other than focus their lives around being housewives and mothers. But with our longer life expectancies and with the biggest single problem in the world being that of the population explosion, this viewpoint can no longer go unchallenged. I am not saying that we should go about de-emphasizing the traditional female roles, but I am saying that we need to provide dozens or even hundreds of models for young girls so that there is room for selection and individual differences. If women are really going to have smaller families, then they must be allowed additional ways to fulfill themselves. It's because we have such a need for both quantity and quality, that I think we should do all we can to get the commercial publishers to see the possibilities for presenting many roles for children of both sexes. My second reason for feeling that we must work through the commercial publishers is that we must reach all children—not just our own daughters. For example, it isn't going to profit us very much if we convince a little girl that she should become a doctor if we do not also persuade her future husband, neighbors, friends, teachers, counselors, and admissions committee, as well as all the men in the world who now think it unmanly to go to a woman doctor.

When the creator of the Barbie Doll was questioned about the values being promoted through the doll, she stated flatly that her company was a reflection of the culture, not a maker of it. When the time comes that little girls will really grow up to be doctors, then she will manufacture Barbie doctor kits, in addition to Barbie boyfriends and Barbie fashion shows. I don't think that anyone in the field of children's literature would have answered a question about books in this way. People have always recognized that books set standards of behavior and publishers have looked on this as both an obligation and an opportunity—witness the recent flood of black books.

If it is not a purposeful plot, and if I am correct in assuming that people working with children's books are genuinely people of good will who desire to be fair and to promote honest values, then why do we have a problem?

One reason is the English language. As linguists point out, English is perhaps defective in not having singular pronouns equivalent to the plurals: *they, their,* and *them.* Having no neuter in the singular form means that any animate being must be referred to as either *he* or *she.* Many books, particularly those about animals,[2] are dominated by males simply because

---

[2] There were fifteen books in the survey which had animals as the characters. Not one of these had female animals as the main characters.

the author is forced to choose between masculine and feminine pronouns. An author usually chooses masculine because it is easy and he (or she) has been taught that masculine can stand for both men and women, although not the other way around. A book which illustrates this point is *Feather Mountain*. This is a make-believe story of how the birds of the world first got their feathers. None of the birds have names and the author refers to all of them with the masculine pronouns even though some of them look very feminine as they stitch, and sew, and ruffle and paint. We might compare this to Taro Yashima's treatment of a group of children in *Seashore Story*, where he uses such phrases as "One asked," "Another asked," and "A young teacher answered." For a writer to do what Yashima does rather than referring to everyone as *he*, takes both greater awareness and greater skill in writing. The unadorned indefinite pronoun *one* is too stiff and formal to be appropriate for the intimate style of most picture books. It is no more a part of children's language than is the concept that *he* can stand for girls as well as boys.

Also, children interpret language quite literally. When they hear such expressions as *chairman, brotherly love, ten-man team,* and *fellow-man,* they think of men, not of the whole human race. Another language related problem is that names are based on the male form and to show a relationship, we often take the male form and then add a feminine suffix, such as *-ess, -ine,* or *-ette*. The *-ette* suffix is what Eve Titus used in naming Anatol's children so that we have *Paul and Paulette, Claude and Claudette,* and *George and Georgette.* It is unfortunate that *-ette* not only indicates feminine, but also smallness and sometimes falseness or insignificance as in *cassette, cigarette,* or *leatherette.* This same linguistic principle applies not only to proper names, but also to other designations such as *god-goddess, host-hostess, major-majorette,* etc. In all these examples the second term simply does not seem as important as the first.

Another problem is related to the artists. Sometimes a book, such as *A Tree is Nice,* is slanted towards boys strictly by the artist. There is nothing in the text of this book to suggest that it is a boy's book, but the illustrator drew twenty-seven males compared to thirteen females. He put eleven of the boys and only three of the girls in the branches of trees. The three girls are on the very lowest branches. The other girls are pictured in such poses as waving to a boy who is high in a tree, dragging a little boy through the leaves, helping another little boy into a tree, standing with a sprinkling can, and standing dejectedly alone while the boys climb a magnificent tree. In spite of all this, I think a girl might have been able to identify with the story which is written in the second person and all the way through talks to *you*. But alas, on the final page, the artist shows that *you* is a boy who is pictured planting a tree.

As you perhaps remember, the only real difference between the ratio of male and female authors and artists was in the number of free-lance artists who illustrated books. If these figures are typical, then we can assume that free-lance artists are more than twice as likely to be men as women. And because of the living conditions of New York artists, I think the men are unlikely to have intimate acquaintance with children. They base their drawings on what they can remember from their own childhood, which naturally enough centered around boys.

Out of the eighty books, I found ten modern and original picture-book stories which had girls as the leading characters,[3] compared to twenty-four stories having boys as the leading characters. There were twelve individual authors and artists involved in the production of these ten books. Nine of these twelve were women. The three men were Ludwig Bemelmens with his *Madeline's Rescue,* Robert McCloskey with both *One Morning in Maine* and *Time of Wonder,* and Taro Yashima with *Umbrella.* I think it significant that all three of these men have daughters of their own and the Yashima and McCloskey books are specifically about the artists' own daughters. Perhaps this means that it takes a special acquaintance before a man feels

---

[3]*The Egg Tree*, 1951; *The Most Wonderful Doll in the World*, 1951; *One Morning in Maine*, 1953; *Madeline's Rescue*, 1954; *Play With Me*, 1956; *One is One*, 1957; *Time of Wonder*, 1958; *Umbrella*, 1959; *Nine Days to Christmas*, 1960; and *Sam, Bangs and Moonshine*, 1967.

comfortable in picturing girls. Even McCloskey seems shy about drawing girls other than his own. In his two books, the only females he drew were his wife and his two daughters, as compared to twenty-five different males. It is also interesting that in *Time of Wonder,* his two girls are tremendously adventurous, even sailing across the bay by themselves, but when they get in a crowd of six boys who are diving from rocks, and swimming and surfing, the girls suddenly become very feminine as they play in the sand and sunbathe. Among the authors and artists, I found thirteen women who did books specifically about boys. Perhaps this indicates that women, through being mothers, teachers, or librarians—all roles where they observe both boys and girls—feel perfectly at ease in writing about boys and in drawing their pictures.

Now by looking at footnote three, which lists ten books written especially for and about girls, and by noticing the dates (publication was one year prior to the given date of the award), we come to what I think is my most significant finding. If the Caldecott books are representative, then we can conclude that there has been a steady decrease of illustrated books written for, or about, girls. Nine of the ten "girl" books were written during the fifties. The only one written during the sixties is about a girl named Samantha and called Sam. I strongly suspect that the choice of her name was influenced by a desire to attract boys to the book which is entitled *Sam, Bangs and Moonshine.* Further evidence pointing to the fact that girls are losing, rather than gaining, a place in books for the very young is a comparison of the number of girls and the number of boys pictured in the survey books calculated at five-year intervals.[4] From 1951 to

4

	BOYS	GIRLS
1951–55	273	228
1956–60	148	100
1961–65	66	29
1966–70	92	29

1955, the percentage of girls pictured in the books was forty-six. By 1956 to 1960, the percentage of girls had shrunk to forty-one, and by 1961 to 1965, it was down to thirty-five. In the most recent period, 1966 to 1970, only twenty-six percent of the characters were girls.

Why should girls be losing out? To answer this we have to go beyond the survey books and look at certain developments that I think have influenced all children's books in the last two decades. If publishers are guilty, I think it's not individually, but collectively. In striving to compete, they let themselves be pulled along in certain movements which in combination have served to harness some of the creative variety that is naturally present in authors and artists. These movements grew out of the placid fifties when the wars (including Korea) were over, the soldiers were home, and the women seemed perfectly happy to return to their kitchens and leave the working world to the veterans. Probably other factors also contributed to what was a general emphasis on motherhood and homemaking skills such as gourmet cooking and fancy needlework. Anyway, during the fifties, the feeling was very strong that "A Woman's Place is in the Home!" Suddenly in the fall of 1957, the Russian's Sputnik burst into the picture and we were all caught up in the education explosion which followed. We became interested in science and math and foreign languages, and in 1961 Congress passed the National Defense Education Act which specified that federal funds could be used to purchase science books for school libraries. Publishers stumbled over each other in trying to fill their catalogues with books that would not only qualify for purchase under this Act, but would also excite children enough so that they would read them, and perhaps even purchase them, on their own. In the United States, science has always been thought of as a field appropriate to males. The producers of the new science books had their hands full in breaking new ground. Never before had anyone succeeded in writing informative books that great numbers of children would love to read. Writers could hardly be expected to compound their difficulties by attempting at the same time to break down centuries-old sex barriers. The science books proved to be so popular that publishers expanded into social studies books, mostly centering around great events and great people. This was another natural for male orientation since women have always been practically absent from history books. An example of this type are the Random House Landmark books which are described and advertised as "colorful and dramatic chapters in American history." However, of the 165 books now in print, there are only five of them about individual American women. Last month when I asked a Random House representative about this, he candidly said that they thought if they got the boys interested, the girls would follow. Even ten years ago, I doubt that he would have dared to say, "If we get the white kids interested, the blacks will follow."

The results of the National Defense Education Act might be summarized in Remy Charlip style: children can now go to the library and find a wealth of high quality informative books about every conceivable subject. What good luck! But these thousands of informative books are highly male orientated and male dominated. What bad luck!

Another significant part of the education explosion was that people began discovering and paying attention to a fact that we females—both teachers and students—had long known, but been too polite to mention. Little boys did not learn to read nearly as fast nor nearly as well as little girls did. Someone said that Johnny couldn't read because the textbooks were dull and were full of feminine values. This claim was widely publicized and Dr. Seuss started a new word game which turned the writer's craft inside out. The object was to find interesting and exciting situations to fit words from the basic reading lists, rather than the usual writing method of finding words to fit situations. This in itself is questionable. But the important point about these books as they relate to this paper is that they were written to answer a specific need. They were written to help *Johnny*—not Joanie, nor Janet, nor Jeannie—learn how to read. They were purposely and openly defeminized. Dick and Jane, Jack and Janet, Alice and Jerry, and Tom and Betty were replaced by Cowboy Sam, Sailor Jack, Dan Frontier, and such other males as Harold, Tom, Max, Bob, Mr. Pine, Morris, and the Binky brothers. Even the animals were made masculine.

Standing next to Little Bear, who is of course a male, we see
Chester the Horse, Harry the Dirty Dog, Sam the Firefly, Zeke
the Raccoon, Julius the Gorilla, and Albert the Albatross. Many
of these books turned out to be delightfully creative and children
of both sexes are reading and enjoying them. What good luck!
But they are equally, or even more, male-oriented than the
science and social studies books. What bad luck!

It is ironic that in recent years, little girls lost out in two
different ways. Boys are the dominant figures in the non-fiction
section of the library because they are thought to be *more* able
than girls in such fields as math, science, and statesmanship.
Then they are the dominant figures in the beginning-to-read
books for just the opposite reason. They are thought to be *less*
able than girls in the field of language arts.

Once the producers of children's books began thinking in
terms of boys, nothing happened in the sixties to make them
think otherwise. Probably the most significant development of
the sixties was the large number of books about black children,
but here again, we see mostly boys. Going back to the survey, in
Lion, William Pène du Bois pictured the 104 artists who
designed the earth. There was one with dark skin, but there was
not a single female. In Leo Lionni's *Swimmy,* I'm sure children
are quick to see that Swimmy is brave and bright and black, but
they are probably just as quick to see that he is a *he.* The
hundreds of other fish are given no sex distinction. Ezra Jack
Keats, who was one of the first to produce really quality picture
books about black children, has created a charming and very
modern individual named Peter. But in *The Snowy Day,* Peter's
mother is seen only as a stereotype Negro "mammy." In *Goggles,* the only female is Peter's sister who sits on the sidewalk
with a baby, drawing pictures while all the excitement of a
miniature gang war rages around her.

Another development in the sixties is related to inflation
and spiraling production costs. As publishers seek ways to cut
their expenses, they look increasingly to the world's folktales
where there is no need to pay an author's royalty or double
copyright. Perhaps my sampling was weighted in this direction,
since the Caldecott Award is given mainly on the basis of the

illustrations, and folktales are a favorite with many artists. Out
of the eighty Caldecott books, nineteen were based on folktales.
Folktales are set several hundred, or even thousand, years ago
when almost any activity required brute strength. Hence it was
by necessity that the men were the doers and the women were
the on-lookers.

In summary, what is it that I'm asking for? Certainly not
that we involve children in our adult male-female quarrels or
that we take from the library shelves any of the books that I've
talked about. But I am asking for fair play. If we have an
alphabet book strictly for boys, let's recognize it as a book
teaching male roles rather than the alphabet, and then let's
provide something equally interesting which teaches female
roles.

I doubt that we can add a new pronoun to the English
language, but with a little bit of effort, a good writer can avoid
referring to every animal or every character as *he*. And when a
book is addressed to the second person *you*, artists can be
careful that their illustrations do not restrict this nondefinite
pronoun to one sex or the other. Artists can also take a second
look at their crowd scenes. What earthly purpose does it serve
to draw seven males for every female, which is the ratio that one
of my students found in Dr. Seuss's books? I have nothing
against artists looking for folktales to illustrate, but I hope that
in the future they will look a little deeper. The theme of many
folktales is the triumph of the small and the weak through
cleverness or perseverance. This was often a female. I am
making a plea that we look for some of the most interesting of
these stories, and reproduce them to serve as a balance to the
many male-oriented folktales now in print. And in the field of
social studies and biography, we must also look a little deeper.
Surely a firm with all of the resources of Random House can find
more than five interesting women in the history of America. And
can't we be more realistic when we draw pictures of mothers?
Let's show them driving cars, playing guitars, typing letters, and
even going to work. When over forty percent of the mothers in
the United States hold jobs I think we should do what we can to
help children develop pride in their mother's accomplishments,

rather than a sense of shame or embarrassment in feeling that their mothers *have* to work.

In the easy-to-read books I am all for keeping a low vocabulary combined with action and a high interest level. But I think we are obligated to remember that little girls still read faster and better than little boys, and it is very likely that the easy-to-read books are read by many more girls than boys. Girls like action too. Let's not stop it; let's just include the girls as part of it.

I guess that what I'm asking for is that we stop accepting as a fact the idea that boys will not read books about girls. I think that many of us have been guilty of playing both sides of this coin because at the same time that we were lamenting and prophesying that boys shouldn't read books about girls, we were taking many unnecessary steps to see that they never got the chance. I want a *Harriet the Spy* for pre-school and primary age children. This is a book "discovered" by sixth grade boys. The sex of the leading character is immaterial. What is important is the action and the humor. I think we can have books like this for younger children just as soon as we quit predicting their failure, which in the past has served to frighten away much of the best talent, and start producing books about real little girls— not the stiff, stilted, and placid creatures that we see in so many picture books. The lesson that we should have learned when we began looking at the elementary reading texts in the fifties was that boys wouldn't read books about dull children—male or female.

IT'S NEVER TOO EARLY: SEX-ROLE STEREOTYPING IN THE PRESCHOOL YEARS*

By Merle Froschl

We live in a world filled with preconceived concepts of masculinity and femininity. "Why not?" we are asked. Why not let boys be boys and girls be girls? *Vive la difference!*

*Reprinted with permission from *Colloquy*, 6, no. 9, 1973. Copyright © 1973 by The Feminist Press.

Would—given the choice—*all* "boys be boys" and *all* "girls be girls"? Are we not setting the stage with sex-role stereotypes and assigning the parts before we even know who's to play them? What happens when the effort to fit the role—to strive for approval as a boy or as a girl—distorts the individual's natural proclivities? What happens when it limits the individual's growth potential, affects the outlook for his or her happiness? How many effective human beings can we sacrifice in the name of traditional role-playing?

All these questions have arisen in my mind as a result of trying to raise my consciousness and two children at the same time. I have seen a son through second grade and a daughter into nursery school. The more I read and think about sex stereotyping, the more I realize how much I still have to learn.

It is some comfort to discover that this is true no matter how sophisticated or learned is one's point of view. When I spoke to Dr. Selma Greenberg of Hofstra University, she freely admitted that when she began her research in 1971, even she didn't fully realize the significance and extent of sex-role stereotyping in the preschool years. "It's not that children are assimilating these messages from the world around them—the concepts of masculinity and femininity are being driven into their heads! The nursery school years are crucial," she avers. "Those are the learning years, and the affectively oriented early childhood educators, in particular, are delivering stereotypic messages and driving them home to stay."

Reinforcements of this prejudicial attitude are clearly evident in the homes, social structures, and schools of most prekindergarteners. As Professors Selma Greenberg and Lucy Peck state in the introduction to their Basic Human Needs Curriculum: "Children's aspiration levels . . . are developed at a very early age. . . . Through the visual stimuli of mass communication, through their interaction with role models, and through the direct and indirect verbal messages they receive children learn . . . who is smart . . . who is powerful . . . who can be creative . . . who can be assertive . . . who can be independent . . . who will be successful . . . and WHO WILL FAIL."

"IT'S SO EASY EVEN A CHILD CAN DO IT!"

For many preschool educators, this statement exemplifies a kind of early childhood stereotyping all its own and is the base for all future role stereotyping (whether sexual, racial, or ethnic). Elspeth MacDonald, a Montessori-trained teacher of three- and four-year-olds in New York City, consciously calls all the children in her class "people." To her, it is absurd for anyone to think that anything a child does is "easy." "On the contrary," she says, "the concepts and ideas the three-year-old deals with would boggle an adult mind. And to instill the concept that only if it's easy can you do it in the mind of a three-year-old is to instill a lack of self-worth that is almost criminal." So we can easily see how limiting notions such as "It's so easy even a *girl* can do it" must be.

THE EARLY SIGNS OF SEX-ROLE STEREOTYPING

I recently observed a preschool class's dramatic skit about the circus. A girl in the class wanted to play the role of a tiger. She was firmly told by the teacher that only boys could be lions and tigers. In other classrooms boys are asked to carry books and move chairs; girls are asked to water plants and wash the sink. One popular set of Community Helper figures not only has the males and females in traditional role models (i.e. seven men— fireman, policeman, etc.—and a nurse), but in the family situation literally has the child glued (and thus immovable forevermore) to the mother-figure!

Selma Greenberg has observed, "In classrooms where there is a head teacher and an assistant, the head teacher tends to work with the boys while the assistant, who is less experienced, is relegated to the girls." She has also found that when teachers suggest initiating an activity, "It is almost always directed to the boys in the class."

As we also know, one of the most effective peddlers of sexist views is children's picture books. Boys in books build and create things, use their intelligence and wit, show initiative, are strong and brave. Girls rarely are depicted as having these characteristics. When a girl masters a skill, it's usually a domestic one.

Is it any wonder, then, that children are already locked into conventional roles when they arrive in kindergarten? And the older they are, the harder it is to get them thinking differently.

AN OPPORTUNITY FOR CHANGE

With more and more children attending nursery schools and child-care programs *before* kindergarten, educators have a better chance than ever before to insure the freedom for all children to develop their full individuality.

In general, nursery schools offer a kind of mobility and sense of independence for the child within the classroom. They therefore seem to offer particularly promising possibilities for breaking down sex stereotypes. A well-run classroom stresses maximum freedom of choice for *all* children. In Elspeth MacDonald's Montessori classroom, there is no noticeable division of sex roles. Children of both sexes cook, sew, saw wood, take care of animals, clean up the room.

However, an open classroom per se is not enough. There must be constant consciousness-raising—that is, continual awareness on the part of teacher, parent, and child—to combat the constant messages children receive. The Woodward School in Brooklyn acted after a committee of mothers complained to teachers about sex-role limitations. The school used to have two playrooms, one with dolls for the girls and one with blocks for the boys. The standard arrangement began to change only when teachers started to *encourage* girls to take part in building cities and to *tell* boys that there was nothing "sissy" in liking dolls.

BLUEPRINT FOR CHANGE—A CURRICULUM THAT WORKS

Selma Greenberg also cautions against mistaking the open classroom for a panacea to sex-typing ills. "What is not considered," she explains, "is that in 'free' nursery schools the choices presented to the child already have built-in role stereotyping. When left alone, a child will probably choose a role-stereotyped activity." Examples of this are the boy who heads for the hammer and nails or the climbing equipment, and the girl who sits quietly in the reading corner or dress-up area. Is this really "freedom of choice"?

That is why Dr. Greenberg feels there is a need for affirmative programming and a structured curriculum that deals directly with sex-role stereotyping. And that is why she and Professor Peck developed a curriculum which focused on men and women as they relate to basic human needs. Rather than looking toward the home for reinforcement ("Most likely children would find the wrong kind of sex-role reinforcing," says Dr. Greenberg), they structured their curriculum units with an occupation orientation.

During 1972 and 1973 this curriculum was introduced into the ongoing program of the Hofstra Child Development Center. With children in the nursery and kindergarten classes of the Westbury (Long Island) Friends School as the control group, a Caldwell preschool inventory was administered to both groups as well as a picture-reaction test to assess the children's present level of aspirations and their perceptions of sex-role behavior. For each two weeks thereafter, class activities covered a different basic human need, including shelter, clothing, food, health and recreation, love and affection, and community. Initially, there would be discussion and then various activities on: What is this need? Why do we need it? How do we use it? How do people get it? How do they take care of it? For example, in the clothing unit the children—in Dr. Greenberg's words—"created their own sweat shop." They made cobbler's aprons, plastic ponchos, and fur dance slippers. During the health and recreation unit, the children set up a medical center and a health spa. The unit on community had the class holding an election for mayor, building roads, taping interviews, writing and producing a newspaper. During the week classes were filmed and at the end of each week there were Friday Flicks. For these popular events children popped corn and made and sold tickets. The rate of activity and creativity seems amazing. *Child's* play indeed!

I asked Dr. Greenberg about some of the results of the experiment. "The kids had a good time and learned a lot," she answered. "We released their activity—girls and boys alike. We originally said the experiment was going to free their intelligence—and it did. The Hofstra kids did far better than the control group on the Caldwell preschool inventory test. The children's perceptions of role behavior did not significantly change, however. That won't happen overnight. But when we put a hard hat on a young girl during the shelter unit and told her she was a builder of cities, she went right ahead and built tall buildings from blocks (contrary to the theory that she should have been building "womb-like" structures)! The teachers? Well, in the short time we worked with them we managed to move them from denial to defense!"

This last statement may sound cynical, but in reality it is a positive stage of consciousness-raising that everyone goes through at some point. We are, after all, just human. And change is never easy.

CREATING THE NECESSARY MATERIALS

Another group researching sex stereotyping in child care is The Women's Action Alliance, a nonprofit national organization with headquarters in New York. I spoke with Barbara Sprung and Carol Shapiro. They ask, "How can a child care center offer the greatest possibility for a child's growth and development *without* dealing with the sex stereotyping that restricts a child to a traditional role model?" The answer? "It can't."

The Women's Action Alliance, in developing a nonsexist approach to early childhood teaching, includes extensive consciousness-raising work with parents through questionnaires and discussion groups. But as open classrooms are not sufficient without awareness, consciousness-raising without materials can go just so far.

The materials now available are far from abundant (see bibliography), but Barbara Sprung and Carol Shapiro have been developing nonsexist lotto games, flannel boards, and puzzles.

They are also currently working on sets of Community Helper figures for block accessories that are a long way from the role-model mold. They stress the endless possibilities of teacher-made materials: "Lotto and sorting games can be made with pictures of mothers as professional women or in community jobs, and fathers in the nurturing role. Nonstereotyped photographs can be mounted on board and cut up for effective puzzles."

With a little imagination, teachers can also turn the liabilities of currently available materials into assets. For example, there can be supportive discussion while watching TV to point out the distortion in role models being presented. The same kind of conversation (as well as on-the-spot editing) should take place during story hour or song time. The Alliance also suggests making use of the "natural resources" of the classroom. During a scheduled talk about Mommies-as-Experts, they invited mothers involved in nonstereotypic behavior to share their experiences with the class.

GIVING CHILDREN ROOM TO GROW

It is important to provide true freedom—the freedom to learn and grow with no preconceived boundaries—for every child beginning with the earliest educational experiences. This is our responsibility. Dealing with sexism in the nursery classroom is much the same as on all other levels of education. *The key is awareness.* And since a nursery school experience is a family experience, it is awareness on the part of parent, teacher, and administrator. Basic questions must be asked: Do we have different expectations for boys than for girls? Do we expect boys to be more aggressive and active? Do we ever say (or even think) "It isn't ladylike to do that" or "Boys don't cry"?

Whatever the curriculum in a given classroom, children should be provided with room to grow, with opportunities to express their feelings and thoughts. As a result of research for this article as well as observing and working in my daughter's nursery school, I have devised a checklist (below) for observation in any preschool classroom. If, after observation, you cannot say "yes" to each item listed, then it's time for some classroom consciousness-raising.

Ages three through five, in many ways, are the significant growing years. *And it's never too early to start growing up equal.*

A VIEW OF A NONSEXIST CLASSROOM: CHECKLIST FOR OBSERVATION IN A PRESCHOOL

- Classroom has both male and female teachers.

- Both teachers share jobs equally (i.e., male does not teach while female serves juice and cookies).

- Teachers greet boys and girls equally (i.e., teacher does not shake hands with boys while telling girls "how pretty they look").

- Block area accessories include doll furniture as well as trucks, animals, etc.

- Community Helper figures are interracial.

- Community Helper figures are not sex-role stereotyped.

- Dress-up area includes hard hats, police badges, and firefighters' hats as well as crinolines and lace scarves.

- Boys and girls are encouraged to use housekeeping and/ or dress-up area.

- Books and records are strongly nonsexist in title selection.

- Girls and boys are encouraged to use climbing equipment.

- Musical instruments are not sex-typed in usage (i.e., girls play the bells while boys get the drums).

- All children use carpentry equipment equally.

- Teacher-made equipment, such as lotto games and puzzles, are not role stereotyped.

- Pictures on walls are interracial and depict women and men in nonstereotypic roles.

- Art materials are used equally.

- Toilets are coeducational.

- All children are allowed to express affection physically.

- All children are allowed (if not encouraged) to get messy.

- Teachers approach all noise, fights, emotional outbursts of anger or crying the same, regardless of sex involved.

- Teachers value and encourage independent and assertive behavior.

MATERIALS NOW AVAILABLE

Puzzles:
"Dressing and Undressing"—A boy and girl of the same size are holding fishing nets and fish. The clothes come off revealing the biological sex differences. Galt Toys.

"School Crossing Guard"—An occupation puzzle shows a Black policewoman crossing a child (Black) with an Oriental and a white child in the background. Judy Puzzles.

Both puzzles are available through Childcraft and Education Corporation, 967 Third Avenue, New York, N.Y. 10022.

Pictures:
Set of eight photographs of professional women.

Set of eight photographs of women in community jobs.

Both sets of photographs are available through Feminist Resources for Equal Education, P.O. Box 185, Saxonville Station, Framingham, Mass. 01701.

Mutual Benefit Life Insurance Company will be glad to send you reprints of its advertisements featuring fathers in the nurturing role. The address is 520 Broad Street, Newark, N.J. 07101, attention Mr. Atno.

Your local hospital will probably be glad to send you photographs of female doctors from their files.

Record:

A delightful nonsexist record called "Free to Be . . . You and Me" may be ordered through *Ms. Magazine.*

Books:

Reading resources are discussed in "The Dilemma of Dick and Jane" appearing on page 12.

A LINGUIST GATHERS THE EVIDENCE: THE ROLE OF MALE AND FEMALE IN CHILDREN'S BOOKS—DISPELLING ALL DOUBT*

By Mary Ritchie Key[1]

. . . Bill said, "I will sit in front and steer the sled, Joan. You sit in the back so that you can hold on to me." [2]

Textbooks and children's literature are under scrutiny these days by persons interested in the full potential of both male and female. It is being discovered that the above quote appears to be typical of the general atmosphere in children's literature today: *Boys do; girls are.*

In general, children's books show that boys: climb, dig, build, fight, fall down, get dirty, ride bikes, and have many adventures, while girls sit quietly and watch. Boys are taught to express themselves; girls to please. According to an infamous little book called *I'm glad I'm a boy! I'm glad I'm a girl* (Windmill, 1970), "Boys invent things," and "Girls use what boys invent." Illustrations showing a little boy inventing a reading lamp and a little girl in an easy chair reading under his lamp are captioned by these phrases.

The theoretical basis behind this is, of course, Freud's

---

*Reprinted by permission from the October 1971 issue of the Wilson Library Bulletin. Copyright © 1971 by the H. W. Wilson Company.

hackneyed "biology is destiny," without regard for a balanced consideration that "psychology can also be destiny."

At this point it is difficult to judge how much influence children's books have in shaping the child's life. One cannot be certain whether the structure of society is simply reflected in the books, or whether the books are further determining the structure of society. Leah Heyn, for one, speaks of the role in child growth that children's books have and feels that books do, indeed, have an influence in terms of the development of the senses, idea reinforcement, knowledge expansion, and the liberation from the child's born-into environment.

In any case, it is clear that the prejudices and myths held by the majority of the members of society are perpetuated in children's literature. For example, John P. Shepard's study[3] in 1962 showed that the characters "strongly tend to be clean, white, healthy, handsome, Protestant Christian, middle-class people. Villains much more often turn out to be ugly, physically undesirable persons of non-Caucasian races, often either very poor or of the wealthy classes." In this study however, the categories investigated did not include the sex variable which is under investigation today.

One of the earliest statements in the recent acknowledgment of sex prejudice in children's books was made by the well known anthropologist, John Honigmann, in *Personality in Culture* (1967):

Reflecting a poorly concealed bias in American society, central characters in the stories are male more than twice as often as they are female. Surely this confirms the reader's belief that one sex is more important than the other, even if that isn't the only way he finds it out. Stories frequently differentiate male and female roles, just as our culture does. They generally leave female characters to display affiliation and nurturance and to flee danger; rarely do girls display traits of activity, aggression, achievement, or construction; seldom do they win recognition. In other words, girls are pictured as kind, timid, inactive, unambitious, and uncreative. Furthermore, characters in the story who are nurtured by a central character are mostly female, suggesting that females are

likely to be in a helpless position. . . . The school readers portray
males as bearers of knowledge and wisdom, and also as the
persons through whom knowledge reaches a child (pp. 203–4).

This statement was, in part, based on a 1946 study by Irwin
Child and others.[4]

The idea that sex prejudice is the only prejudice now
considered socially acceptable seems remarkably applicable to
the books found in the field of education, one of our most
respected institutions. One writer, Marjorie U'Ren, notes that
textbooks written for co-education early in this century present
a much more favorable picture of women and girls than do
textbooks written from 1930 on. The atmosphere has changed
since then. In 1946 Child did a content analysis and concluded
that "the most striking single fact of all . . . about the differences between the sexes is that the female characters do simply
tend to be neglected."

STUDYING THE STUDIES

During the last two years over a dozen different studies have
been made on children's books: picture books, early childhood
books, teen-age books, general library books, a series for minority groups, and California textbooks, which *every* child in California is exposed to. The remarkable thing about these studies is
that, although they often make statements which are identical or
similar and they reinforce the conclusions of one another, there
appears to be no awareness between them of the other studies.
They seem to have sprung up spontaneously across the nation,
from student, mother, writer, professor, administrator, teacher,
and librarian. The studies overwhelmingly document discrimination and prejudice against females in children's books.

Before proceeding further to the focus of our statement, let
us stop here to evaluate other recent studies which seem to
indicate opposite conclusions, namely the studies of first-grade
reading books by Blom, *et al;* Waite, *et al;* Wiberg and Trost[5];
and others which these articles quote. For example, the Wiberg
and Trost article concludes that children's books have "a ten-

dency to denigrate the masculine role." Blom, Waite, and Zimet show that "A large number of stories were in the boy-girl activity category (46 percent) as compared to boy activity (26 percent), and girl activity (28 percent) . . ." "Active Play, Outings, Pranks, and Work Projects were related to boy activity. Quiet Activities, School, Folk Tales, and Real Life with Positive Emotions were related to girl activity." Such statements are somewhat misleading and must be tempered with other facts and other perspectives. In addition, the terminology of studies such as these obfuscates. What is meant by "ambiguity in sex role, sex role appropriateness, oedipal conflict, sex of activity, sex preference"?

Other facts to be considered, for example, are how many boys and how many girls figure as the central character of those so-called "boy-girl activities" comprising 46 percent of the studies mentioned above. Worley counterbalances with other facts:

> In most of the stories examined, the central character was a boy and the plot development reflected male circumstances . . . there were twice as many stories reflecting male story situations as there were stories reflecting female story situations.

He suggests that:

> A larger proportion of basal reader stories should involve a female as the central character. The heavy emphasis given male figures creates a distorted and perhaps harmful sex role image for all readers. (p. 148)

Other perspectives to be considered concern the judgments made about what, indeed, is a girl-activity and what is a boy-activity. It is highly possible that *all* activities that six-year olds participate in could be either boy or girl activities, if the youngsters weren't socialized to what adults *think* they should do. There don't seem to be great differences in muscular ability, and this age is still a long way from child-bearing functions—two activities which are, indeed, not culturally learned. It would appear from the evidence presented in the studies I am summarizing that a significant number of scholars, persons in education, and lay people disagree with the stereotyped roles assigned to boys and girls in the foregoing studies. Apparently females also like to climb trees, explore caves, go fishing; feel invigorated with accepting responsibility; and can accept leadership with equanimity.

WE NEEDN'T HAVE FEARED!

This present paper is a result of a two-fold approach: a survey of studies already made, and an analysis of some actual books to confirm statements made. In our committee discussions while formulating plans for the project, we were concerned about how one would come to conclusions as to whether or not the text or pictures showed discrimination. How would one avoid subjective, biased statements? We needn't have feared! In many cases, there was no analysis to do because of the absence or the paucity of females either as protagonists or supporting characters. It would appear that modern children's literature follows true to the tradition of early English literature. George K. Anderson commented on the place of women in Old and Middle English literature:

> Indeed, the relative insignificance of women in the social scene marks the Old English period as different even from the Middle English. Women had a hard enough time of it at best in the Middle Ages, partly because they had no opportunity to do much of anything except in the domestic sphere and partly because Christian tradition traced the fall of man to a woman. . . . If we were to judge by Old English literature alone, we would conclude that only queens, princesses, abbesses, a few wives, and a scattering of mistresses comprised the female population of England at that time.[6]

In the *Be a Better Reader* series for the 7th grade, story after story unfolds without any female in existence. It is the exception when a female is a real part of any scene, such as in a

farm story in which the mother and daughter are depicted as
more thoughtful and intelligent than the boy and husband.

The absence or almost absence of females is also typical of
The Roberts English Series: A Linguistics Program, (Books 3 to
8), especially the later books. In Book 6, out of 30 main sections, only two focus on the female. One section discusses a
poem of comparison between the jaded and weary hill-country
wife (not woman, but *wife*) and the prairie wife who owns "one
last year's dress" and whose life is a series of long, dull, lonely
hours (pp. 132–133). The other section treats a humorous (?)
poem about a remarkable (neurotic?) little girl "who didn't let
things bother her very much." The "things" she deals with are
an enormous bear, a wicked old witch, a hideous giant, and a
troublesome doctor (Ogden Nash, in Book 6, pp. 262–264).
Book 8 has three sections out of 30 in which females dominate
the scene. One is "The Solitary Reaper," another is a story
about a crotchety old aunt. The book, and the series, end with
the third and final piece about a female, "The Hag," a witch
who rides off with the Devil to do their mischief.

Some of the other recent textbooks adopted or recommended for second through sixth grade in California were analyzed by U'Ren, Gail Ann Vincent, and our committee. In these
books at least 75 percent of the main characters are male. The
stories about females are not as lengthy. Often the stories about
males include no mention of a female, although the stories about
females include males with whom the females interact. The
mother figure is typically presented as a pleasant, hardworking,
but basically uninteresting person:

> . . . she has no effect upon the world beyond her family, and
> even within the family her contribution is limited to that of
> housekeeper and cook. . . . She enters a scene only to place a
> cake on the table and then disappears. Or she plays foil to her
> husband by setting him up for his line. It is mother who asks,
> "What shall we do?" and by doing so invites a speech from
> father. (U'Ren, p. 7)

Librarian Marjorie Taylor confirms this: "Daddy is the

predominant character. His are the ideas, the main portions of the conversations, 'where the action is'."

Vincent's study concentrates on the socialization of the female in the California textbook series. References are made to previous studies on sex-role concepts. Lawrence Kohlberg's[7] study, for example, is said to show that children age five to eight "award greater value or prestige to the male role." "He also finds that identification with the father and other male figures increases dramatically for boys during these years, whereas preferential orientation to the mother in girls declines." Females are not seen interacting together as are males. In the one instance where girls are grouping together and excluding boys ("I *never* play with boys"), they are ridiculed by the boys. Vincent observes that the reverse, i.e., girls ridiculing boys for similar behavior, never occurs. Taylor also documented stories where high value is put on all male activity. In *All Through the Year* by Mabel O'Donnell (Harper & Row, 1969), when the children are going to play detective, Mark shouts, "Boy, this is going to be fun. . . . No girls can be in on this. Just boys. . . ."

With regard to physical tasks, Vincent observes that boys are more competent than girls in the California textbooks: the boy fixes his bike and rides it while the kneeling girl admires him; the boy shoots a basket, while the girl tries and misses.

In creative activities the males also excel: A boy is the best painter; a boy is the best story teller; father is the best at riddles; a boy wins a contest in snow-sculpting.

In children's books, females do not have the freedom to inquire, explore, and achieve. Margaret Mead is quoted as saying, "man is unsexed by failure, women by success." This indoctrination starts early. Vincent analyzes the repeated theme of a female not succeeding and notes that when a girl does initiate a tree-climbing episode, punishment is the result (a broken leg for one boy), and a grandmotherly character scolds her for shameful behavior: "What's wrong with you?"

With regard to pictures and illustrations, U'Ren found that many California textbooks included females in only about 15 percent of the illustrations. In group scenes, invariably the males dominate. In *The Roberts English Series: A Linguistics*

Program, which includes a great deal of poetry, many of the poems are written with pronoun referent unspecified as to sex, e.g., "I, me, we, they." The pictures accompanying the poems, however, with the exception of Book 3, are almost all male-dominated. In Book 4, eleven poems are illustrated thus, with none illustrated by a female or female-dominated picture. The prose story of Daphne (p. 65) is illustrated by three pictures in which Apollo and Cupid hold the scenes. Daphne is shown only as the transformed laurel tree. In the text, which is presented in three sections, Daphne doesn't enter the story until the second section. Thus, even when a story is supposed to be about a female, the actual pictorial and textual presentation may diminish the female.

THE AWARD WINNERS

Alleen Nilsen analyzed the winners and runners-up of the Caldecott Award during the last twenty years. Presented annually by the Children's Service Committee of the American Library Association for the most distinguished picture book of the year, this exclusive award makes for wide distribution of these books across the country. Of the eighty books analyzed, Nilsen found that the titles included names of males over three times as often as names of females. One fourth of the books had only token females. In the last twenty years, the presence of females in the Caldecott books is steadily decreasing. This statistic parallels other statistics which are commonplace today, such as the percentage of women in administrative positions in education and the percentage of women professors, which is less now than it was in the 1930s. Among the forty-nine Newberry Award winners of 1969, books about boys outnumbered books about girls some three to one.

Elizabeth Fisher studied books for young children found in bookstores and libraries. There were five times as many males in the titles as there were females. The fantasy worlds of Maurice Sendak and Dr. Seuss are almost all male.

In children's books, there is a significant reversal of the usual use of "she/her" for animals and inanimate objects. I have discussed pronoun referents in another study of the linguistic behavior of male and female.[8] Grammar rules and usage indicate, among other things, that large animals are "he," small animals are "she," and other inanimate objects are usually "she." Admittedly there is a great deal of confusion and inconsistency in rules and usage, which I point out in the paper. Storybook animals in our children's books, however, are almost all male, and female animals tend to carry names of derogation or are objects of derision: Petunia the Goose, Frances the Badger, and the sow who entered the Fat Pigs contest (Wodehouse, in *The Roberts English Series 8*). Personifications of the inanimate are invariably male; for example, in *The Roberts English Series*. While no sailor worth his salt in real life would refer to a ship as "he," our children's books have boats, machines, trains, and automobiles which carry only male names and gender. This contradicts T. Hilding Svartengren's study[9] where he showed that these items were referred to in literature by the referents "she/her."

The Butt of the Joke

The treatment of females in comedy is another area of concern in children's books. Too often the butt of the joke in poems and stories is a female. *The Roberts English Series: A Linguistics Program* is chock full of such "funny" poetry by writers such as Belloc, Nash, and Thurber.

As far as role identity is concerned, when women are mentioned or pictured, they are usually shown in relation to men or as accouterments to men. Virginia Woolf pointed out that in literature as a whole this is the situation. In one of the Newberry Award winners, our next generation was advised, "Accept the fact that this is a man's world and learn how to play the game gracefully."

Books written for teen-age boys often tell them that females do not exist; life moves on without girls or women. The worlds of Mark Twain *(The Roberts English Series 7)* and Robert Louis Stevenson *(The Roberts English Series 8)*, without a single mention of a female, are being reiterated in contemporary literature. The *Field Educational Checkered Flag Series,* written for boys, is such an example (Henry A. Bamman and Robert Whitehead, California State Text, 1969). When females do occur in books written for young people approaching adulthood, the girls and women are not like the people whom young men will meet in real life.

What Do Big Girls Do?

The following list, compiled from one of *The Roberts English Series,* written for Junior High students, gives a comprehensive covering of what females do in Book 8:

- Count votes for males who were nominated;

- Accompany men to the hunt;

- Find their beauty is shortlived;

- Sit with their fans in their hands and gold combs in their hair;

- Put cream on their faces and "lie in bed staring at the ceiling and wishing [they] had some decent jewelry to wear at the . . . Ball";

- Poison their husbands;

- Die because they "never knew those simple little rules . . .";

- Get eaten up by alligators;

- Cut and gather grain and sing to no one;

- Listen to men give speeches;

- Rear children;

- Do silly, ridiculous things (James Thurber);

- Ride with the Devil.

Diane Stavn analyzed for attitudes about girls and women novels which are known to be popular with boys. She made two observations: " . . . the sweeping, sometimes contradictory" incidental comments about the female sex, and "the fact that the girlfriends and mothers are almost always unrealized or unpleasant characters—one-dimensional, idealized, insipid, bitchy, or castrating—while sexually neutral characters, such as little sisters and old ladies, are most often well conceived and likable." For example, the girlfriend of jazz freak Tom Curtis turns out to be "merely a mouthpiece to relate information about other characters in the book and a sounding board for their ideas and problems." In general, the girls accompanying these teenage boys are inadequately fleshed out, tinny, paper thin, made of the stuff of angels, gentle, feminine, fairly quiet, doomed to be unreal. Good old Mom, on the other hand, often is depicted as "an insipid lady who flutters around chronically worrying and inanely commenting."

Stavn does discuss a few books where boys can come away with pretty good feelings about girls and women. The following quotes, however, seem to outweigh the good attitudes:

> Women in the States . . . have forgotten how to be women; but they haven't yet learned how to be men. They've turned into harpies, and their men into zombies. God, it's pitiful!

> Remember—she's a female, and full of tricks.

> Men . . . liked to talk about women as though they had some sort of special malignant power, a witch-like ability to control men.

> Polly . . . says 'I'm a witch . . . I *was* being nasty . . . Girls just do those things, I guess . . .'

> Even old girls like my mother. If she hadn't torpedoed my father's idea to buy a garage, he might not have taken off.

> [Polly]. . . began to think she should run the show. That's where I had to straighten her out. And after I got her straightened out she seemed happier.

Boys and young men are reading quotes such as these at the time of their lives when their thoughts of female relationships are predominant, and they are formulating ideas about the kind of woman they want as a partner—or are developing patterns of rejection altogether.

After reviewing the current lists of girls' books, one anonymous observer noted that a preponderance of stories about love, dating, and romance occurred among the themes identified. According to her literature, a female has no alternate life styles, but lives in a limited world with no control over her future. Nilsen calls this the "cult of the apron" and notes that this conditioning starts early. Of fifty-eight picture books which happened to be on a display cart of children's literature at Eastern Michigan University last year, twenty-one had pictures of women wearing aprons. Even the animals wore aprons!—the mother alligator, mother rabbit, mother donkey, and mother cat.

It is well known nowadays that 40 percent of all mothers work, and yet many studies indicate that there is not one mention of a working mother in the particular group of books reviewed. A notable exception is Eve Merriam's *Mommies at Work* (Knopf, 1961). And a notable discrepancy is the *Bank Street Readers,* a series designed for the inner-city child. In the three books, only one mother is shown as a working mother, a woman who serves in a cafeteria.

Social Studies Texts

In Jamie Frisof's analysis of social studies textbooks, men are shown in or described in over one hundred different jobs and women in less than thirty, and in these thirty jobs, women serve people or help men to do more important work. Men's work requires more training; men direct people and plan things; men go places and make decisions; at meetings men are always the speakers; men make the money and are the most important members of families. The pictures in these social studies books show men or boys more than seven times as often as women or girls. Rarely are men and women working together or seen in equally competent roles. In short, these socializing books "do their part in preparing girls to accept unquestioningly their future as unimportant, nonproductive, nonadventurous, and unintelligent beings."

Regarding professional persons depicted in children's books, Heyn points out that among the several books in the field of health and medicine, without exception the doctor is portrayed as a white male—nurses and receptionists as female.

U'Ren and Vincent report that one of the California textbooks gave an account of Madame Curie, where she appears to be little more than a helpmate for her husband's projects (Eldonna L. Evertts and Byron H. Van Roekel, *Crossroads,* Harper and Row Basic Reading Program, Sacramento: California State Department of Education, 1969). "The illustration which accompanies this section reinforces that view of her. It portrays Madame Curie peering mildly from around her husband's shoulder while he and another distinguished gentleman loom in the foreground engaged in serious dialogue."

Dialogue

It might be well at this point to examine other examples of dialogue which occur in children's literature. Linguistic behavior is culturally taught, as are other expressions of behavior. In surveying the dialogues which occur in these books, one notes a pathetic lack of conversation with bright, adventurous females of any age. Rarely is there a give-and-take dialogue in which a female is shown to be capable of making a decision or where the input of the female is intelligent and useful information. The things which girls and women say in these books too often reflect the stereotypes of society: "Women are emotional."

In *The Story of Mulberry Bend* (William Wise, Scott Foresman, 1965), we read, "One little girl thought they were so beautiful she began to cry."

During a scene about fishing and baiting the hook, the girl says, "I can't . . . I don't want to touch those things." "Of course you don't, here I'll do it for you." And then she would have lost the pole but Johnny grabbed it in time (Nila Banton Smith, "Cowboys and Ranches" *Be a Better Reader Series,* Foundation A, Prentice Hall, 1968).

Peter said, "You can't do it, Babs. You will get scared if you do." "No I won't," said Babs. "Yes, you will. You will get scared and cry," said Peter (Mae Knight Clark, *Lands of Pleasure*, Macmillan, California State Department of Education, 1969).

The Little Miss Muffet syndrome, which depicts females as helpless, easily frightened, and dreadfully dull, occurs over and over again in the literature. If one compares this image, which crystallizes in the formative years of child development, with the potential of women in adulthood, it becomes apparent that both male and female have difficulty in participating in equal sharing dialogues at the professional level. Males who have grown up learning dialogues such as are in children's books today are not able to listen to a female in adult life. Males paralyze when a rare female makes a constructive suggestion. Likewise females are trained not to take their share, or hold their own in decision-making interchange. There are no linguistic models in this early literature for females to take active parts in the dialogue nor for males to respond with dignified acceptance and a willingness to listen. With such indoctrination as this, is it any wonder then, that doctors don't permit women on the surgical team and women scientists are excluded from projects and from the laboratory where a female is thought to be useless or a nuisance?

It must also be realized that in some sense male stereotypes are also projected in these books. Future research could be undertaken on these aspects: Is a male permitted to be a whole person? Is he permitted the whole range of emotions that all human beings should have in their repertoire? Must he always be aggressive? Must he always be taller than the females in his circle? Is he allowed to make mistakes and still be accepted?

It is likely that the discrimination and obtrusive imbalance which occurs in the books is unintentional for the most part. But, as Vincent says, this does not mitigate its destructiveness. The results may be of much wider consequence than one might imagine. One of the studies (Anon, "A Feminist Look . . .") asks, "Is depression in the adult woman perhaps linked to the painful suppression of so many sparks of life?" It cannot be said, moreover, that all this treatment is out-of-awareness. For example, Nilsen reports that in a course entitled "Writing for

Children" the instructor advised: "The wise author writes about boys, thereby insuring himself a maximum audience, since only girls will read a book about a girl, but both boys and girls will read about a boy." And Nilsen reports that the prize-winning *Island of the Blue Dolphins* was initially rejected by a publisher who wanted the heroine changed to a hero.

In order not to end on a blue note, it might be well to point out that remedies are in the offing. The National Organization for Women (NOW) initiated a bibliography[10] of children's books showing females in nonstereotyped roles—females "who assume a balanced role during the growing-up process. Traits such as physical capability, resourcefulness, creativity, assertiveness, ingenuity, adventuresomeness, and leadership are emphasized, in addition to literary quality." Thousands of copies of this bibliography have been sold, and authors are already writing material which is more equitable to both male and female. We might expect then, that the new dialogues will take other forms and that "A Ride on a Sled," the story of Joan and Bill, might sound something like this:

> . . . *Joan then spoke up, "It's my turn to steer, Bill. Hang on, 'cause we're going a new way!"*

REFERENCES

1. The Research Committee of the Gamma Epsilon Chapter of Delta Kappa Gamma took the topic expressed in the title as a study project. Members of the committee collected materials and made analyses of several series of books. As chairman of the committee, I compiled the reports and worked them into this larger study. References to these analyses will be made by name only, since none of this was previously published. The contributions were from the following members: Marguerite Pinson, coordinator of bilingual education; Marguerite Sharpe; Marjorie Taylor, coordinator of library services; and Laura Wright.

2. Glenn McCracken & Charles E. Walcutt. *Basic reading,* Philadelphia: Lippincott, 1963, California State Department of Education, 1969, 41.

3. John P. Shepard, The treatment of characters in popular children's fiction. *Elementary English,* November 1962, *39,* 672–676.

4. Irvin L. Child, Elmer H. Potter, & Estelle M. Levine. Children's textbooks and personality development. *Psychological Monographs,* 1946, *60,* no. 3, 1–7, 45–53.

5. Gaston E. Blom, Richard R. Waite, & Sara Zimet. Content of first grade reading books. *The Reading Teacher,* January 1968, *21,* no. 4, 317–323.

   Richard R. Waite, Gaston E. Blom, Sara F. Zimet, & Stella Edge. First-grade reading textbooks. *The Elementary School Journal,* April 1967, *67,* 366–374.

   John L. Wiberg and Marion Trost. A comparison between the content of first grade primers and the free choice library selections made by first grade students. *Elementary English,* October 1970, 792–798.

6. George K. Anderson. *Old and middle English literature from the beginnings to 1485.* Vol. I, *A History of English Literature.* New York: Collier, 1962.

7. Lawrence Kohlberg. A cognitive-developmental analysis of children's sex-role concepts and attitudes. In Eleanor Maccoby (Ed.). *The development of sex differences.* Stanford, Calif.: Stanford University Press, 1966.

8. Mary Ritchie Key. Linguistic behavior of male and female. To be published in *Linguistics: an international review.*

9. T. Hilding Svartengren. The use of the personal gender for inanimate things. *Dialect Notes* [1925] 1928–1939, *6,* 7–56.

10. *Little Miss Muffet fights back.* Feminists on Children's Media (P.O. Box 4315, Grand Central Station, New York 10017), p. 48.

SOURCES AND SELECTED BIBLIOGRAPHY

(Anon) A feminist look at children's books. Feminists on children's literature. *School Library Journal,* January 1971, 19–24.

(Anon) Little Miss Muffet fights back. *School Library Journal,* November 1970, 11, 14.

(Anon) *Little Miss Muffet fights back.* Feminists on Children's Media (P.O. Box 4315, Grand Central Station, New York, N.Y. 10017).

(Anon) *Report of the Advisory Commission on the Status of Women, California Women.* "Textbooks," 1971, 16.

(Anon) Sex role stereotyping in elementary school readers. *Report on sex bias in the public schools.* New York: NOW, 1971, 13–18.

(Anon) Sugar and spice. Editorial, *School Library Journal,* January 1971, 5.

Child, Irwin L., Potter, Elmer H., & Levine, Estelle M. Children's textbooks and personality development. *Psychological Monographs,* 1946, *60,* no. 3, 54.

Eliasberg, Ann. Are you hurting your daughter without knowing it? *Family Circle,* February 1971, 38, 76–77.

Fisher, Elizabeth. Children's books: The second sex, junior division. *The New York Times Book Review,* Part II, May 24, 1970, 6, 44.

Frisof, Jamie Kelem. Textbooks and channeling. *Women: A Journal of Liberation,* Fall 1969, *1,* no. 1, 26–28.

Heyn, Leah. Children's books. *Women: A Journal of Liberation,* Fall 1969, *1:*1, 22–25.

Honigmann, John J. *Personality in culture.* New York: Harper & Row, 1967, 203–205.

Howe, Florence. Liberated Chinese primers: (let's write some too). *Women: A Journal of Liberation,* Fall 1970, *2,* no. 1, 33–34.

Meade, Marion. Miss Muffet must go: a mother fights back. *Woman's Day,* March 1971, 64–65, 85–86.

Miles, Betty. Harmful lessons little girls learn in school. *Redbook,* March 1971, 86, 168–69.

Nilsen, Alleen Pace. Women in children's literature. *College English,* May 1971, *32,* no. 8, 918–926.

Schlaffer, Maria. Sexual politics: Junior division. *All you can eat.* Reprinted in *Sherwood Forest: Orange County People's Press,* October 1970, *1,* no. 20, 10.

Stavn, Diane Gersoni. The skirts in fiction about boys: a maxi mess. *School Library Journal,* January 1971, 66–70.

Steffire, Buford. Run, Mama, run: women workers in elementary readers. *Vocational Guidance Quarterly* December 1969, *18,* no. 2, 99–102.

U'Ren, Marjorie. Sexual discrimination in the elementary textbooks. Unpublished manuscript. To be published in *51%: The case for women's liberation*. New York: Basic Books.

Vincent, Gail Ann. Sex differences in children's textbooks: a study in the socialization of the female. Unpublished manuscript, 1970.

Worley, Stinson E. Developmental task situations in stories. *The Reading Teacher*, November 1967, *21*, no. 2, 145–148.

About TV:

Gardner, Jo Ann. Sesame Street and sex-role stereotypes. *Women: A Journal of Liberation, 1,*3, Spring 1970,

THE CONTRIBUTIONS OF WOMEN: AUTOBIOGRAPHIES, BIOGRAPHIES, AND HISTORICAL FICTION*

This section has been designed to supplement regular classroom units. The books show the role or contributions of actual women, or present in fictional form the lives of women in a historical period. Many of the biographies are not written from a feminist perspective, but are included here anyway because they are about women who made important contributions and are not normally included in textbooks. These books should be used with study questions, keeping in mind that the students have to *learn* how to recognize and question the portrayal of women in books. (Books which should be supplemented with study questions are noted in the annotation.) Several of the books on this list have been considered sexist because the characters succumb to pressures to become "a lady," succumb to stereotypical ideals, or because their marriage spells the end of their careers. However, they are valuable books as reflections of a historical time. For example, a book such as *Caddie Woodlawn* is important for students to read to understand the pressures on a young pioneer girl to give up her independence and freedom and conform to the roles of a pioneer woman. It is a book which

---

*Reprinted with permission from The Feminist Press. Copyrighted © 1974 by Laurie Olsen Johnson.

deals directly with a woman's struggle with sex-role expectations, and does so within the context of historical accuracy. Because it reflects the actual experiences of so many women of that time, it is a feminist book, and an important supplement to the stories of women who *did* manage to remain independent or achieve.

As this bibliography was being compiled, it became painfully clear (as it will become in reading it) how many individual women, classes, and kinds of women simply do not appear at all in the available literature. This list is barely a beginning. *Most* of our history still needs to be written.

EARLY SETTLERS AND THE REVOLUTIONARY PERIOD

Cheney, Cora. *The Incredible Deborah*. New York: Scribner, 1967. The story of Deborah Sampson who, disguised as a man, fought in the Revolutionary War. Grade 5+

Clarke, Mary Stetson, *Petticoat rebel*. New York: Viking, 1964. Novel set in the revolutionary era. About sixteen-year-old Candace who, when the schoolmaster goes off to fight in the war, takes over the school and insists on allowing girls to attend classes. Strong fighter for the education of women. Grade 6+

Crawford, Deborah. *Four women in a violent time*. New York: Crown, 1970. Includes stories of Anne Hutchinson, Mary Dyer, Deborah Moody, and Penelope Stout. Grade 5+

Dalgliesh, Alice. *The courage of Sarah Noble*. New York: Scribner, 1954. Set in Connecticut in the 1700s. Grade 3+

Petry, Ann. *Tituba of Salem Village*. New York: Thomas Y. Crowell, 1964. The story of a Barbados slave who was accused of being a witch in Salem. Excellent. Grade 6+

Speare, Elizabeth George. *The witch of Blackbird Pond*. Boston: Houghton Mifflin, 1958. Set in colonial Connecticut in the 1680s, this Newberry Award winner deals with a young girl whose rebellion against the solemn strict Puritan life leads to a terrifying witch hunt. Good for a discussion of the hysteria and fear behind the witch trials. Grade 6+

PIONEERS AND THE MOVE WEST

Bond, Gladys Baker. *A head on her shoulders.* New York: Abelard-Shuman, 1963. When the father of a family of four children breaks his leg, the eldest daughters sets out to take the younger children to Idaho Territory. Grade 6+

Brink, Carol Ryrie. *Caddie Woodlawn.* New York: Macmillan, 1935. A book to be used with study questions: see discussion in the introduction to the bibliography. Grade 4+

Casell, Maryanne. *Pioneer girl.* New York: McGraw Hill, 1964. The collected letters of a fourteen-year-old pioneer girl in the late 1800s. Grade 6+

Cook, Olive Rambo. *Serilda's star.* New York: McKay, 1959. Pioneer girl in Missouri whose quick thinking and sympathetic heart create both problems and unexpected joys. Nice relationship between brother and sister. Grade 3+

Lenski, Lois. *Indian captive.* Philadelphia: Lippincott, 1941. A fictional account of the true story of Mary Jemison, who was captured by the Indians and chose to remain with them for the rest of her life. Grade 6+

Markley Miller, Helen. *Woman doctor of the West: Bethenia Owens-Adair.* New York: Messner, 1960. The first graduate woman doctor in the West. She divorced her husband, and with a child to support alone, went to school to become first a teacher and later a doctor. She fought prejudice and ridicule to become a great physician, brilliant surgeon, and a fighter for women's rights. Grade 6+

Seymour, Flora. *Sacajawea: bird girl.* New York: Bobbs-Merrill, 1957. A warmly written account of Sacajawea's girlhood and her trip as Lewis and Clark's guide across western territory to Oregon. Grade 3+

Wilder, Laura Ingalls Wilder. *Little house in the big woods* (and series). New York: Harcourt, Brace, 1953. The entire series is excellent for portraying the life of the pioneer family in America. Offers a human and realistic picture of the pioneer woman and children. The series is graduated in reading ability, the earlier books being suitable for Grade 2 and the latter books being suitable for 5+.

ABOLITIONIST MOVEMENT AND CIVIL WAR

Alcott, Louisa May. *Little women.* New York: World Publishing, 1946. This classic story of a family of four girls set in Civil War times is one of the few books which reflects the experience of women and children during a war. Grade 7+

Epstein, Sam, and Epstein, Beryl. *Harriet Tubman: guide to freedom.* Champaign, Ill.: Garrard, 1968. Black leader on the underground railroad. Grade 3+

Hoehling, Mary. *Girl soldier and spy: Sarah Emma Edmundson.* New York: Messner, 1959. Wonderfully written story of a girl's determination to make it up to her father for not having been born a boy, her rebellion against settling down to a life of marriage, and her bravery as a soldier and spy during the Civil War disguised as a boy. Grade 6+

McGovern, Ann. *Runaway slave: story of Harriet Tubman.* New York: Four Winds, 1965. Story of Harriet Tubman for young readers. Grade 1–4

Meltzer, Milton. *Tongue of flame: the life of Lydia-Maria Child.* New York: Thomas Y. Crowell, 1965. Political writer and author of the first anti-slavery book in America. Grade 6+

Petry, Ann. *Harriet Tubman: conductor on underground railroad.* New York: Thomas Y. Crowell, 1955. Another child's biography of Harriet Tubman. Good account. Grade 6+

Rushmore, Robert. *Fanny Kemble.* New York: Macmillan, 1970. An actress ends her marriage to a southern plantation owner because of her conviction that slavery must be abolished. She published the diary she had kept while living on the plantation, exposing to the British public the evils of slavery. Grade 5+

Sterling, Phillip. *Four took freedom.* New York: Doubleday, 1967. Includes Harriet Tubman and Blanche K. Bruce. Grade 6+

Wise, Winifred. *Fanny Kemble: Actress, author and abolitionist.* New York: Putnam, 1966. Story of the actress' fight to end slavery. Grade 6+

BLACK WOMEN: BLACK HISTORY

Starred items listed in other categories should also be included in this section.

Brownmiller, Susan. *Shirley Chisolm*. New York: Archway, 1972. Excellent biography of a black, female member of the U.S. Congress. Grade 7+

Carruth, Ella Kaiser. *She wanted to read: the story of Mary McLeod Bethune*. Nashville, Tenn.: Abingdon, 1966. The story of a black woman educator who founded a school. Grade 3+

Fitzgerald, Edward. *I always wanted to be somebody: the story of Althea Gibson*. New York: Harper & Row, 1973. A famous female tennis player. Grade 5+

Jordan, June. *Fanny Lou Hamer*. New York: Thomas Y. Crowell, 1973. Wonderful book for young readers about Fanny Lou Hamer's strong fight for the rights and dignity of Black people. Grade 3+

Meriwether, Louise. *Don't ride the bus on Mondays*. Englewood Cliffs, N.J.: Prentice-Hall, 1973. The story of Rosa Parks and the beginnings of the bus boycott in the 60s. Grade 4+

Newman, Shrilee. *Marian Anderson: lady from Philadelphia*. Philadelphia: Westminster, 1966. Photos plus narrative covering this black singer's career from high school days to her farewell concert at Carnegie Hall. Grade 5+

Peare, Catherine. *Mary McLeod Bethune*. New York: Vanguard, 1951. Black educator who opened a school in the 1800s. Grade 6+

Yates, Elizabeth. *Prudence Crandall: woman of courage*. New York: Dutton, 1955. Opened and reopened the first school for Negro girls in the North. Grade 6+

TURN OF THE CENTURY: SOCIAL CHANGE

Hay, Ella. *A child's life of Mary Baker Eddy*. Boston: Christian Science Press, 1942. Founder of the Christian Science Church. Biography suitable for preschool through Grade 4.

Lavine, Sigmund. *Evangeline Booth: daughter of salvation*. New York: Dodd, Mead, 1970. Leader and general in the Salvation Army in the early 1900s. Grade 7+

Lader, Lawrence, and Meltzer, Milton. *Margaret Sanger: pioneer of birth control*. New York: Thomas Y. Crowell, 1969. Staunch fighter for the rights of women to birth control information. Grade 5+

Meggs, Cornelia. *Jane Addams: pioneer for social justice.* Boston: Little, Brown, 1970. Founder of Hull House, a settlement house in Chicago, and winner of the Nobel Peace Prize. Jane Addams was also a feminist. Grade 6+

Pace, Mildred, *Juliette Low.* New York: Scribner, 1947. The founder of the Girl Scouts. Grade 4+

Shulman, Alix. *To the barricades: the anarchist life of Emma Goldman.* New York: Thomas Y. Crowell, 1971. Feminist biography of the anarchist and Wobblie leader. Grade 5+

LITERATURE

Aldis, Dorothy. *Nothing is impossible: the story of Beatrix Potter.* Boston, Atheneum, 1969. The lonely childhood and later life of the naturalist and writer of the Peter Rabbit stories. Grade 4+

Barth, Edna. *I'm nobody, who are you?* New York: Seabury, 1971. Life of Emily Dickinson, poet. Grade 3+

Franchere, Ruth. *Willa: story of Willa Cather's growing up.* New York: Thomas Y. Crowell, 1972. Easy reading. Book focuses on childhood of this Midwestern writer, author of *My Antonia.* Grade 3–6.

Kyle, Elisabeth. *Girl with a pen: Charlotte Bronte.* New York: Holt, 1964. Grade 5+

Longsworth, Polly. *Emily Dickinson: her letter to the world.* New York: Thomas Y. Crowell, 1965. The life and poetry of Emily Dickinson. Grade 6+

Meigs, Cornelia. *Invincible Louisa.* Boston: Little, Brown, 1968. Story of Louisa May Alcott, author of *Little Women.* Grade 6+

Muir, Jane. *Famous modern American women writers.* New York: Dodd, Mead, 1959. Includes Emily Dickinson, Laura Ingalls Wilder, Willa Cather, Eudora Welty, Jessamyn West, Pearl Buck, Amy Lowell, Gertrude Stein. Grade 6+

Vipont, Elfrida. *Weaver of dreams: girlhood of Charlotte Bronte.* New York: Walck, 1966.

Vipont, Elfrida. *Towards a high attic: George Eliot.* New York: Holt, 1971.

WOMEN IN SCIENCE AND MEDICINE

Baker, Rachel. *First woman doctor: the story of Elizabeth Blackwell.* New York: Messner, 1946. Grade 6+

Baker, Rachel, and Merlen, Joanna Baker. *America's first woman astronomer: Maria Mitchell.* New York: Messner, 1960. Maria Mitchell fought prejudice to become the first woman elected to the American Academy of Arts and Sciences. She discovered an unknown comet, and in her later years joined the struggle for women's rights (written by a mother and daughter team). Grade 6+

Crawford, Deborah, *Lise Meithner: atomic pioneer.* New York: Crown, 1969. Grade 6

deLeeuw, Adele. *Marie Curie, woman of genius.* Champaign, Ill.: Garrard, 1970. Grade 5

Douty, Esther M. *America's first woman chemist: Ellen Richards.* New York: Messner, 1961. Ellen Richards was a student of Maria Mitchell's and the first woman student at MIT. Grade 6+

Fleming, Alice. *Doctors in petticoats.* Philadelphia: Lippincott, 1964. Collection of short biographies of women doctors. Grade 6+

Grant, Madeleine. *Alice Hamilton: pioneer doctor in industrial medicine.* New York: Abelard-Schuman, 1968. Grade 6+

Harmelink, Barbara. *Florence Nightingale: founder of modern nursing.* New York: F. Watts, 1969. Grade 6+

Heyn, Leah Lurie. *Challenge to become a doctor: the story of Elizabeth Blackwell.* Old Westbury, N.Y.: Feminist Press, 1971. Grade 3+

Hume, Ruth. *Great women of medicine.* New York: Random House, 1964. Grade 6+

Markley Miller, Helen. *Woman doctor of the west: Bethenia Owens-Adair.* New York: Messner, 1960. (See description under Pioneers and Move West.)

Riedman, Sarah. *Men and women behind the atom.* New York: Abelard-Schuman, 1958. Grade 6+

Sterling, Phillip. *Sea and earth: the life of Rachel Carson.* New York: Thomas Y. Crowell, 1970. Grade 5+

Thorne, Alice. *Story of Madame Curie*. New York: Grosset & Dunlap, 1959. Excellent biography of Marie Curie, discoverer of radium, as a scientist, professor, wife, and mother. Shows a good working relationship between husband and wife. Illustrates Marie Curie's determination to become a scientist.

Yost, Edna. *Women of modern science*. New York: Dodd, Mead, 1959. Grade 6+

AVIATORS, REPORTERS

Auriol, Jacqueline. *I live to fly*. New York: Dutton, 1970. About a female test pilot.

de Leeuw, Adele. *The story of Amelia Earhart*. New York: Grosset & Dunlap, 1955. Good biographical account showing Amelia Earhart's extraordinary courage, her unusual relationship with her husband George Putnam, her belief that women must try things "as men have tried. When they fail, that failure must be but a challenge to others." Grade 4+

Graves, Charles. *Nellie Bly*. Champaign, Ill.: Garrard, 1971. About Nellie Bly, a woman reporter who traveled around the world in less than 80 days.

Hahn, Emily. *Around the world with Nellie Bly*. Boston: Houghton Mifflin, 1959. Another biography of Nellie Bly, reporter. Grade 4+

COLLECTIONS

Nathan, Dorothy. *Women of courage*. New York: Random House, 1964. Well-written biographical accounts of the lives of Amelia Earhart, Margaret Mead, and others. Grade 5+

Ross, Pat. *Young and female*. New York: Random House, 1972. Turning points in the lives of Shirley MacLaine, Shirley Chisholm, Dorothy Day, Emily Hahn, Margaret Sanger, Althea Gibson, Edna Ferber, Margaret Bourke White. Grade 6+

POLITICS

Brownmiller, Susan. *Shirley Chisholm*. New York: Archway, 1972. Biography, with photos, of Shirley Chisholm's early involvement in politics, culminating with her election to the U.S. Congress. Grade 4+

Davidson, Margaret. *Story of Eleanor Roosevelt.* New York: Four Winds, 1969. Written for young readers, this biography covers the emergence of Eleanor Roosevelt from the President's wife to a political force in her own right. Grade 3+

Garnett, Emmeline. *Madame Prime Minister: the story of Indira Gandhi.* New York: Farrar, Straus & Giroux, 1967. Biography of the female leader of India. Grade 6+

Graves, Charles. *Eleanor Roosevelt.* Champaign, Ill.: Garrard, 1966. Another young people's biography of Eleanor Roosevelt. Grade 3+

Lawson, Don. *Frances Perkins: first lady of the Cabinet.* New York: Abelard-Schuman, 1973. First female Secretary of Labor, under the Roosevelt Administration.

SINGLE STRONG VOICES

Brown, Marion and Ruth Crone. *The silent storm.* Nashville, Tenn.: Abingdon, 1970. The story of Annie Sullivan, teacher of Helen Keller. Grade 6+

Frank, Anne. *The diary of a young girl.* New York: Doubleday, 1967. Autobiography of a young Jewish girl in hiding with her family from the Nazis during World War II. Grade 6+

Graff, Polly Anne, and Graff, Stewart. *Helen Keller: toward the light.* Champaign, Ill.: Garrard, 1963. Story of Helen Keller's remarkable struggle as a deaf, blind, and mute child to communicate with the world. Grade 2

Hickok, Lorena. *The story of Helen Keller.* New York: Grosset & Dunlap, 1958. Another biography of Helen Keller. Grade 4+

Kosterina, Nina. *The diary of Nina Kosterina.* Translated by Mirra Ginsburg. New York: Crown, 1968. Diary of a Russian girl during Stalin's reign, suggested for *better* readers.

Nakamoto, Hiroko, and Pace, Mildred. *My Japan, 1930–1951.* New York: McGraw Hill, 1970. Story of a young girl from a wealthy family growing up in Japan and the effects of war on her life. Grade 5+

THE ARTS

Cavanah, Frances. *Jenny Lind and her listening cat.* New York: Vanguard, 1961. Jenny Lind's struggle to become a singer. Set in her childhood. Grade 3+

Kyle, Elizabeth. *Duet: the story of Clara and Robert Schumann.* New York: Holt, 1968. A marriage between two great musicians. Grade 5+

Malvern, Gladys. *Dancing star: the story of Anna Pavlova.* New York: Messner, 1942. Famous Russian prima ballerina. The story of her dedication, and hard work in becoming one of the greatest dancers. Grade 6+

Neilson, Frances, and Neilson, Winthrop. *Seven women: great painters.* Philadelphia: Chilton, 1969. Collection of biographies of seven women artists. Grade 6+

Tobias, Tobi. *Maria Tallchief.* New York: Thomas Y. Crowell, 1972. Native American girl who became a great dancer. Grade 3

SUFFRAGE

Beatty, Patricia. *Hail Columbia.* New York: Morrow, 1970. A suffragist aunt deals with narrow-minded people in the 19th century. Fiction.

Bernard, Jacqueline. *Journey toward freedom: life of Sojourner Truth.* New York: Norton, 1967.

Bryan, Florence. *Susan B. Anthony: champion of women's rights.* New York: Messner, 1947. Story of Susan B. Anthony, fighter for women's rights.

Faber, Doris. *Lucretia Mott: foe of slavery.* Champaign, Ill.: Garrard, 1971. Grade 3

Faber, Doris. *Oh, Lizzie! the life of Elizabeth Cady Stanton.* New York: Lothrop, 1972. Story of the childhood and adult life of this fighter for the rights of women. Grade 5+

Faber, Doris. *Petticoat politics: how American women won the right to vote.* New York: Lothrop, 1967. The history of how the suffrage movement began, developed. Focus on the leaders of the movement. Grade 5+

Hall, Elizabeth. *Stand up, Lucy.* Boston: Houghton Mifflin, 1971. A novel set in the early 1900s of Lucy's fight against the prejudice of her father and school, and her fight for women's rights. Grade 3

Peterson, Helen Stone. *Susan B. Anthony: pioneer in women's rights.* Champaign, Ill.: Garrard, 1971. Encompasses the life and fights of Susan B. Anthony. Easy reading. Grade 3+

FICTION: BOOKS FOR LIBERATED READING

Amerman, Lockhart. *Cape Cod casket.* New York: Harcourt, Brace, 1964. Jonathan Flower baby-sits two precocious children during a summer full of mystery. Lucy, an intelligent girl, saves the day at the crucial moment by firing a cannon. Grade 7+

Bacon, Martha. *Sophia Scrooby preserved.* Boston: Little, Brown, 1968. Pansy, a bright, courageous and talented African slave girl is sold to a family in New Haven in the 1700s, and goes through many adventures before winning fame as a singer at Covent Gardens in England. Not to be read for historical accuracy because of the unusual circumstances of her slavery and escape, but a good novel of a strong female. Grade 6+

Bagnold, Enid. *National Velvet.* New York: Morrow, 1949. A young girl who loves horses enters a race disguised as a boy and wins. Grade 6+

Baum, Frank. *The Wizard of Oz.* Chicago: Reilly & Lee, 1908. Courageous, intelligent, and loving Dorothy's adventures. Grade 4

Bawden, Nina. *Squib.* Philadelphia: Lippincott, 1971. Characters fall into fairly typical roles, but the story depicts a friendship between a boy and a girl and a child being raised by a single working mother. The main character, a girl, deals with the death of a father and younger brother. Grade 4+

Boston, Lucy. *Treasure of Green Knowe.* New York: Harcourt, Brace, 1958. A blind girl in 18th-century England learns to be independent, her ghost still haunts the house. Grade 6+

Brink, Carol Ryrie. *Caddie Woodlawn.* New York: Macmillan, 1935. A book to be used with study questions; see discussion in introduction to the bibliography. Grade 4+

Bruckner, Karl. *Day of the bomb.* New York: Van Nostrand, 1963.

Fictionalized story of the life of Sadako Sasaki, the "Anne Frank of Hiroshima," first person to die of radiation sickness more than ten years after the bombing. There is a statue erected in her memory at the Peace Park in Hiroshima. Grade 6+

Burch, Robert. *Queenie Peavy.* New York: Viking, 1966. The school tomboy, whose father is in prison. Queenie is a girl who grapples with the difficulties of a father in prison by becoming the school smart aleck and bully. Good book with minor cop-out ending. Use with study questions. Grade 4+

Burnett, Frances. *Secret garden.* New York: Lippincott, 1911. Mary, an ill-tempered orphan, discovers a garden and a friend. Good nonstereotypic portrayal of a boy and of a friendship between a boy and a girl. Grade 6+

Byars, Betsy. *Go and hush the baby.* New York: Viking, 1971. A big brother has fun babysitting. Grade 3+

Cameron, Eleanor. *A room made of windows.* New York: Little, Brown and Company, 1971. The struggle of a young girl to become a writer and to accept her mother's wish to get remarried. Grade 4+

Carpenter, Frances. *Tales of a Chinese grandmother.* New York: Doubleday, 1937. Tales told by a grandmother.

Carroll, Lewis. *Alice in wonderland.* New York: F. Watts, 1907.

Cleaver, Vera, and Cleaver, Bill. *Where the lilies bloom.* Philadelphia: Lippincott, 1969. Young Appalachian girl's desperate, resourceful attempt to keep her family together after their father's death. Grade 6+

Constant, Alberta. *The motoring Millers.* New York: Thomas Y. Crowell, 1969. A young girl wins an automobile race. Grade 4+

Daringer, Helen Fern. *Stepsister Sally.* New York: Harcourt, Brace, 1966. A young girl adjusts to life with her remarried father, her new stepbrother and stepsister. Grade 4+

DeJong, Meindert. *Tower by the sea.* New York: Harper & Row, 1950. The villagers set out to burn the wise woman who keeps an odd-eyed cat, as a witch. Study of prejudice and fear. Grade 6+

Engdahl, Sylvia. *Enchantress from the stars.* New York: Atheneum, 1970. A young girl becomes involved in an inter-planetary intrigue. Grade 6+

Enright, Elizabeth. *The Saturdays.* New York: Dell, 1966. A motherless family of boys and girls who enjoy each other's company. Grade 4+

Eyerly, Jeanette. *A girl like me.* Philadelphia: Lippincott, 1966. Problems of unwed motherhood. Grade 6+

Fitzhugh, Louise. *Harriet the spy.* New York: Harper & Row, 1964. Harriet stops at nothing in collecting data for her spy notebook. Grade 4+

Forbes, Kathryn. *Mama's bank account.* New York: Harcourt, Brace, 1943. A strong mother guides her Norwegian family through the painful and gradual process of Americanization. Working class family. Grade 6+

Faulkner, Georgene, and Becker, John. *Melindy's medal.* New York: Messner, 1945. An eight-year-old black girl earns a medal for bravery. Story includes unusual family situation (family of Melindy, her father and her grandmother) and bits of black history. Grade 4+

Fisher, Dorothy Canfield. *Understood Betsy.* New York: Avon, 1973. A pale and frightened little girl becomes rosy, strong and capable under the influence of two aunts and an uncle who take her in. Unusual adult role models and good strong female character. Grade 4+

Gates, Doris. *Blue willow.* New York: Viking, 1948. Realistic and strong portrayal of a young girl in a migrant family. Grade 4+

Gripe, Maria. *The night daddy.* New York: Delacorte, 1971. A young girl whose mother works nights has an eccentric male babysitter.

Gripe, Maria. *Hugo and Josephine.* New York: Dell, 1969. In spite of the protector role which Hugo plays for Josephine, this is a lovely story of a friendship between a boy and a girl. Grade 3+

Hautzig, Esther. *The endless steppe: growing up in Siberia.* New York: Thomas Y. Crowell, 1968. True story of the author's childhood as a prisoner of the Russians during World War II. Large print, but complex style. Grade 6+

Hunter, Kristin. *The soul brothers and sister Lou.* New York: Scribner, 1967. Contemporary story about a black girl and her friends in an urban ghetto. Grade 6+

Jackson, Jesse. *Tessie.* New York: Harper & Row, 1968. A bright black girl faces an exclusive all white private school. Grade 6+

Klein, Norma. *Mom, the wolf man and me.* New York: Pantheon,

1972. An independent, illegitimate child doesn't think her mother ought to get married. Grade 7+

Konigsburg, Elaine. *George*. New York: Atheneum, 1970. George is a little man who lives inside the hero's head, and makes it impossible for the boy to pursue a purely intellectual approach to life. George keeps telling him feelings are also important. Grade 4+

Konigsburg, Elaine. *Jennifer, Hecate, Macbeth, William McKinley and me, Elizabeth*. New York: Atheneum, 1967. A black girl and a white girl share adventure and friendship. Grade 4+

Lansing, Elizabeth Hubbard. *Liza of the hundredfold*. New York: Archway, 1969. A pioneer girl's struggle with expected sex-role behavior and her chance to prove herself.

Lenski, Lois. *Judy's journey*. Philadelphia: Lippincott, 1947. A young girl in a migrant family. Grade 4+

Lenski, Lois. *Strawberry girl*. Philadelphia: Lippincott, 1945. In the language of a Florida strawberry family, this book tells the story of a young girl's desire for an education and an organ. Grade 4+

Lindgren, Astrid. *Pippi Longstocking*. New York: Viking, 1950. A series about an adventurous ten-year-old girl on her own. Grade 4+

Matsutani, Miyoko. *Witches' magic cloth*. New York: Parents Magazine Press, 1969. Japanese folk tale with strong female characters and beautiful illustrations. Grade 3+

Minsky, Reba. *Thirty-one brothers and sisters*. New York: Dell, 1973. Books about the daughter of a Zulu chief. With a strong female character, this book excitingly and sensitively deals with issues such as the conflict between Western medicine and traditional African healers. This entire series is useful. Grade 5+

Murray, Michele. *Nellie Cameron*. New York: Seabury, 1971. A wonderful story about a young black girl growing up in Washington, D.C., her struggle to learn to read. Grade 4+

Nevin, Evelyn. *The extraordinary adventures of Chee Chee McNerney*. New York: Four Winds, 1971. A girl and her hunting party search for gold in Alaska. Grade 4+

Neville, Emily. *The Seventeenth Street gang*. New York: Harper & Row, 1966. The story of a neighborhood gang of both boys and girls, set in New York City, light and humourous. Grade 4+

O'Dell, Scott. *Island of the blue dolphins*. Boston: Houghton Mifflin, 1960. A strong Indian girl survives 18 years alone on an island. Grade 6+

O'Dell, Scott. *Sing down the moon*. Boston: Houghton Mifflin, 1970. A Navajo woman defies the white man by living with her husband and son on land taken from her people. Grade 6+

Rankin, Louise. *Daughter of the mountains*. New York: Viking, 1948. Momo walks from the high mountains of Tibet to Calcutta, in search of her dog which was sold against her wishes by her father. Grade 6+

Sawyer, Ruth. *Roller skates*. New York: Viking, 1936. A young girl's roller skate adventures in New York in the 1890s. Quick-tempered, stubborn, astute and sympathetic all at once. Grade 6+

Seredy, Kate. *The good master*. New York: Viking, 1935. Although the characters fall into stereotyped roles, this book set in Hungary, shows truly human, sensitive relationships and characters. About Jancsi, a young boy, and his mischievous cousin Kate. Grade 4+

Snyder, Zilpha Keatley. *The changeling*. New York: Atheneum, 1970. Excellent story of the friendship between two girls, their struggle between wanting to conform and fit in, and yet feeling that inside they were really different. Grade 4+

Sterling, Dorothy. *Mary Jane*. New York: Scholastic Books, 1959. Excellent, fictional account of one of the first black students attending a white junior high school. Grade 6+

Stolz, Mary. *A wonderful, terrible time*. New York: Harper & Row, 1967. The experience of two black girls in summer camp. Sensitive portrayal of the different feelings and reactions of the two girls. Grade 4+

Stramm, Claus. *Three strong women: a tall tale from Japan*. New York: Viking, 1962. Three women teach a man how to become wealthy by wrestling in public. Grade 4+

Streatfield, Noel. *Ballet shoes*. New York: Random House, 1950. Story of three orphan girls in a stage academy. Pauline becomes an actress, Posy becomes a dancer, but Petrova is only interested in motors and takes up flying as soon as she can. Grade 4+

Taylor, Sydney. *All of a kind family*. Chicago: Follett, 1951. A series about a Jewish family on the Lower East Side of New York City. Five girls in the family. Good portrayal of Jewish culture, warm treatment of family relationships. Should be used with study questions about the role of women, for example, when the father is praying that the new child be born a boy. Grade 4+

Watson, Sally. *Other sandals*. New York: Holt, 1966. Wild Devra from the Kibbutz and self-pitying Etyan from Tel Aviv change places for the summer. Etyan learns to get along with other people and Devra helps an Arab girl become a nurse. Interesting view of a country where equality of the sexes is written into law. Grade 6+

Wilder, Laura Ingalls. *Little house in the big woods* (and series). New York: Harper & Row, 1953. Entire series is excellent for portraying the life of the pioneer family in America. Offers a human and realistic picture of the pioneer woman and the female children. Grade 2+ Series is progressively more difficult: last book suitable for Grade 5+

White, E. B. *Charlotte's web*. New York: Harper & Row, 1952. Grade 4+

HISTORY

GENERAL HISTORY

Barney, Laura. *Women in a changing world: The story of the International Council of Women since 1888*. Atlantic Highlands, N.J.: Fernhill, 1966.

Beard, Mary. *Women as force in history*. New York: Macmillan, 1946.

Beard, Mary. *Force of women in Japanese history*. Washington, D.C.: Public Affairs Press, 1953.

Beard, Mary. *On understanding women*. Westport, Conn.: Greenwood, 1968.

Borer, Mary. *Women who made history*. New York: Warne, 1963. Grades 7–11

Bradford, Gamaliel. *Elizabethan women*. Plainview, N.Y.: Books for Libraries, 1936.

Buckmaster, Henrietta. *Women who shaped history*. New York: Macmillan, 1966.

Clark, Alice. *Working life of women in the 17th century.* A. M. Kelley, Publishers, 1919.

Cleverdon, Catherine L. *The woman suffrage movement in Canada.* Toronto: University of Toronto Press, 1950.

Cuddeford, Gladys. *Women and society from Victorian times to the present day.* Atlantic Highlands, N.J.: Fernhill, 1967.

Culvert, Elsie Thomas. *Women in the world of religion.*

Forfreedom, Ann (Ed.). *Women out of history: a herstory anthology.* Venice, Calif.: Everywoman, 1972.

Fuller, Margaret. *Nineteenth century woman.* New York: Norton, 1971.

Hughes, Muriel. *Women healers in medieval life and literature.* Plainview, N.Y.: Books for Libraries, 1943.

Kirkpatrick. *Nazi Germany: its women and family life.* 1939.

Morton, Ward M. *Women suffrage in Mexico.* Gainesville, Fla.: University of Florida Press, 1962.

O'Connor, Lillian. *Pioneer women orators.* New York: Columbia University Press, 1954.

Putnam, Emily James. *The lady: studies of certain significant phases of her history.* Chicago: University of Chicago Press, 1910.

Reynolds, Myra. *Learned lady in England (1650–1760).* New York: Smith, 1920.

Rover, Constance. *The punch book of women's rights.* Cranbury, N.J.: A. S. Barnes, 1970.

Schneir, Miriam (Ed.). *Feminism: the essential historical writings.* New York: Vintage, 1972.

Sichel, Edith. *Women and men of the French Renaissance.* Port Washington, N.Y.: Kennikat, 1970.

Seltman, Charles. *Women in antiquity.* New York: St. Martin's, 1957.

Stenton, Doris. *English woman in history.* Atlantic Highland, N.J.: Fernhill, 1957.

Thomas, Edith. *The women incendiaries.* New York: George Braziller, Inc., 1966. Role of women in revolutions.

Vicinus, Martha (Ed.). *Suffer and be still: women in the Victorian age.*

Bloomington, Ind.: Indiana University Press, 1972. Collection of essays describing the plight of women in the last century.

Wilson, R. McNair. *Women of the French Revolution*. Port Washington, N.Y.: Kennikat, 1970.

AMERICAN HISTORY

Abbott, Edith. *Women in industry*. New York: Arno, 1969.

Beard, Mary (Ed.). *America through women's eyes*. Westport, Conn.: Greenwood, 1968.

Benson, Mary S. *Women in 18th century America*. Port Washington, N.Y.: Kennikat, 1935.

Brandeis, Louis D., and Goldmark, Josephine. *Women in industry*. New York: Arno, 1969. $5.00.

Brown, A. *Women of colonial and revolutionary times*. Spartanburg, S.C.: Reprint 1968.

Butler, Elizabeth. *Women and the trades*. New York: Arno, 1969.

Clarke, I. Wood. *Emigres in the wilderness*. Port Washington, N.Y.: Friedman, 1941.

Commetti, Elizabeth. Women in the American Revolution. *New England Quarterly*. September 1947, *20*, 329–346.

Courtney, Janet. *Adventurous thirties, a chapter in the women's movement*. Plainview, N.Y.: Books for Libraries, 1933.

Earle, Alice M. *Colonial dames and goodwives*. New York: Ungar, 1962.

Ets, Marie Hall. *Rosa*. Minneapolis: University of Minnesota Press, 1970. Italian immigrant.

Flexner, Eleanor. *Century of struggle*. New York: Atheneum, 1968.

Gruber, Martin. *Women in American politics: an assessment and source book*. Oshkosh, Wisc.: Academa, 1968.

Humphrey, Grace. *Women in American history, 1919*. Plainview, N.Y.: Books for Libraries.

Josephson, Hannah. *Golden threads: New England's mill girls and magnates, 1949*. Russell Reprints, 1967.

Kaur, M. *Roll of women in the freedom movement 1857–1947*. Mystic, Conn.: Verry, 1968. Concerning India.

Kraditor, Aileen. *The ideas of the woman suffrage movement 1880–1920*. New York: Columbia University Press, 1965.

Kraditor, Aileen. *Up from the pedestal: selected writings in the history of American feminism*. Chicago: Quadrangle, 1968.

Lerner, Gerda. *The woman in American history*. Reading, Mass.: Addison-Wesley, 1971.

Lutz, Alma. *Crusade for freedom: women of the anti-slavery movement*. Boston: Beacon Press, 1968.

Massey, Mary Elizabeth. *Bonnet brigades*. New York: Knopf, 1966. Women in the Civil War.

O'Neill, William L. *Everyone was brave: the rise and fall of feminism in America*. Chicago: Quadrangle, 1968.

Ozer, Jerome (Ed.). *Women suffrage in America*. 13 volume series. New York: Arno, 1969.

Ross, Isabel. *Sons of Adam, daughters of Eve. The role of women in American history*. Harper & Row, 1969.

Scott, Anne Firor. *The southern lady: from pedestal to politics 1830–1930*. Chicago: University of Chicago Press, 1970.

Simkins, Francis, and Patton, J. W. *The women of the Confederacy*. Reprint House International, 1936.

Sinclair, Andres. *The better half*. New York: Harper, 1965. Shows a condescending attitude toward 19th century feminists.

Smith, Page, *Daughters of the promised land: women in American history*. Boston: Little, Brown, 1970.

Sourcebook Press, 185 Madison Avenue, New York 10016, has announced a series of 40 reprints on the history of woman's rights.

Stanton, E. C., Anthony, S. B., Gage, M. J., and Harper, I. H. (Eds.). *The history of woman suffrage, 1881–1922*. New York: Arno, 1969.

Stern, Madeline. *We the women: career firsts of the 19th century America*. Schulte, 1963.

Trecker, Janice Law. Women in U.S. history high school textbooks. *Social Education,* March 1971.

Woody, Thomas W. *A history of women's education in the U.S.* 2 volumes. New York: Octagon, 1966.

HISTORY FOR CHILDREN

Coigney, Virginia. *Margaret Sanger: rebel with a cause.* New York: Doubleday, 1969. Ages 10 to 15

Coolidge, Olivia. *Women's rights: the suffrage movement in America, 1848–1920.* New York: Dutton. Grade 7+

Faber, Doris. *Petticoat politics: how American women won the right to vote.* New York: Lothrop, Grade 7+

Foster, G. Allen. *Votes for women.* New York: Criterion Books, 1966. Grades 6–10

Gersh, Harry. *Women who made America great.* Philadelphia: Lippincott, 1962. Grades 7–11

Johnson, Dorothy. *Some went West.* New York: Dodd, Mead, 1965. Grades 7–10

Swern, Bill. *Free but not equal: how women won the right to vote.* New York: Messner, 1967. Grades 7–12

BOOKS FOR LIBERATING YOUNG READERS*

By Pamela R. Giller

Children's books are one of the major written ways we transmit our culture to our young. If our goal is to move toward full equality for females and males, then children's books must reflect this thinking.

Since females have been so underrepresented and misrepresented in literature, there is a current tendency (a kind of overcompensation) to concentrate on books featuring strong females. This list includes a fair sprinkling of such books as well as some emphasizing three-dimensional males. However, the

---

*Reprinted with permission from Pamela R. Giller.

focus in this list is on books that portray fully developed females and males relating as equals.

Nonsexist books emphasize a positive, nonstereotyped portrayal of females and males. The following criteria were used in designating a book nonsexist:

- A full participation by females in physical and intellectual activities

- Female characters leading active, independent lives

- Girls dealing with a variety of choices and aspiring to diverse goals

- Male characters respecting female characters and relating to them as equals

- Male characters exhibiting a wide range of interests and emotions

Books included reflect personal choice as well as recommendations in *Little Miss Muffet Fights Back* (Feminists on Children's Media), *Your Child's Reading Today* by Josette Frank, and *Good Books for Children,* edited by Mary K. Eakin.

The inclusion of a number of books that, while popular with children, either have sexist overtones or are quite stereotyped offers a broad, realistic range of children's books of literary merit. Also, in the attempt to emphasize books of literary merit, nonsexist books that feature propaganda rather than literature are not included.

Assigning this wide range of books to categories of sexism (numbers in parentheses after publishing data) was far from a cut-and-dried procedure.

- Books in category 1 are nonsexist.

- Books in category 2 present a basically three-dimensional view of either females or males, but slip in the overall presentation.

- Books in category 3 are otherwise fine books that have the deadly flaw of sexism.

Hopefully, indications of minor (category 2) or major (category 3) sexism will sharpen student and teacher awareness of this aspect of books, while they are in the process of developing their own perceptions of sexism. Hopefully, also, the labeling of these books will provide the basis for healthy discussion of the limitations and biases of even good literature.

Books in category 1 will help children think positively and encourage them in the development of their own identities as full human beings. Used unthinkingly, books in category 2 and especially those in category 3 can negatively affect children's self-images and aspirations. Used with insight and full knowledge of their limitations, however, these books can help children think and grow.

5-YEAR-OLDS

ANIMALS

Hoban, Russell. Illustrated by Lillian Hoban. Bread and jam for Frances. New York: Harper, 1964. (2) One in a series about a young female badger who humorously survives typical childhood problems, but in a stereotyped family.

Katz, Bobbie. Illustrated by Esther Gilman. Nothing but a dog. Old Westbury, N.Y.: Feminist Press, 1972. (1) Active and full of initiative, this girl's longing for a dog can only be cured by a dog!

McCloskey, Robert. Make way for ducklings. New York: Viking, 1941. (2)

Minarik, Else. Illustrated by Maurice Sendak. Little bear. New York: Harper, 1957. (2) One in a series about Little Bear, whose mother, while loving and sensitive, is always aproned and domestic.

Mizmurma, Kazue. If I were a mother. New York: Crowell-Collier 1968. (3)

Wells, Rosemary. Noisy Nora. New York: Dial, 1973. (1)

CHILDREN AND THEIR FAMILIES

Baldwin, Anne Norris. Illustrated by Ann Grifalconi. Sunflowers for Tina. New York: Four Winds, 1970. (1)

Felt, Sue. Rosa-too-little. New York: Doubleday, 1950. (1) Good feelings follow when a little girl grows big enough for her own library card.

Gaeddert, Lou Ann. Noisy Nancy Norris and Nick. New York: Doubleday, 1970. (1)

Goffstein, M. B. Two piano tuners. New York: Farrar, Straus, Giroux 1970. (1) Debbie decides to become a piano tuner like her grandfather.

Krasilovsky, Phyllis. Illustrated by Ninon. The very little girl. New York: Doubleday, 1963. (3) The theme of growing and mastering new skills has great appeal; unfortunately, the little girl's interests and aspirations are narrow and stereotyped.

McCloskey, Robert. One morning in Maine. New York: Viking, 1952. (1)

Merriam, Eve. Illustrated by Beni Montressor. Mommies at work. New York: Knopf, 1961. (1)

Welber, Robert. Illustrated by Deborah Ray. The train. New York: Pantheon, 1972. (1) A young girl conquers her fear of crossing the meadow to see the train she listens for so eagerly.

Zolotow, Charlotte. Illustrated by Ben Shecter. The hating book. New York: Harper & Row, 1969. (?)

Zolotow, Charlotte. Illustrated by William Pene DuBois. William's doll. New York: Harper & Row, 1972. (1)

CONCEPTS, NONFICTION

Baum, Arline, and Baum, Joseph. One bright Monday morning. New York: Random House, 1962. (1) A gay counting book that features an observant girl and boy.

Burton, Virginia Lee. The little house. Boston: Houghton Mifflin, 1942. (2)

Lawrence, Jacob. Harriet and the promised land. Windmill, 1968. (1)

McLeod, Emilie. Illustrated by W. Lorraine. One snail and me. Boston: Little, Brown, 1961. (1)

Tresselt, Alvin. Illustrated by Roger Duvoisin. White snow, bright snow. New York: Lothrop, 1947. (2)

Udry, Janice. Illustrated by Marc Simont. A tree is nice. New York: Harper & Row, 1956. (2)

Gross, Ruth. Illustrated by John Hawkinson. What is that alligator saying: a beginning book on animal communication. New York: Hastings House, 1972. (1) Refreshing in dealing with animals and their parents (not only mothers); noncoy explanations of mating communication. Simple references to scientists includes women.

FANTASY, HUMOR, AND FOLKTALES

Duvoisin, Roger. Petunia's Christmas. New York: Knopf, 1952. (2)

Krasilovsky, Phyllis. The man who didn't wash his dishes. New York: Doubleday, 1950. (1)

Marshall, James. George and Martha. New York: Houghton Mifflin, 1974. (2) Funny portrayal of friendship between a male and female hippo, but weighed down with sex stereotyping.

Ness, Evaline. Sam, Bangs and Moonshine. New York: Holt, 1966. (2)

Segal, Lore. Illustrated by Harriet Pincus. Tell me a Mitzi. New York: Farrar, Straus, & Giroux, 1970. (1)

Seuss, Dr. Horton hatches the egg. New York: Random House, 1940. (2) One of the few classic Dr. Seuss that even mentions a female, and she is lazy and selfish.

Wahl, Jan. Illustrated by Lillian Hoban. A wolf of my own. New York: Macmillan, 1970. (1)

Wiesner, William. Turnabout. New York: Seabury, 1972. (1) A Norwegian folktale about a housekeeping wife and a farmer husband who change places; unusual for folktales in presenting woman as strong but not nagging or witchlike.

Williams, Jay. Illustrated by Friso Henstra. The practical princess. New York: Parents Magazine Press, 1969. (1)

Young, Miriam. Illustrated by Beverly Komoda. Jellybeans for breakfast. New York: Parents Magazine Press, 1968. (1) About two girls, inventive and fun-loving; good also because of the relative scarcity of friendship between girls.

10-YEAR-OLDS

REALISTIC FICTION—CONTEMPORARY

Byars, Betsy. The 18th emergency. New York: Viking, 1973. (2)

Byars, Betsy. The house of wings. New York: Viking, 1972. (1) An insightful and moving story of the development of a grandfather, grandson relationship.

Cleaver, Vera, and Cleaver, Bill. Ellen Grae. Philadelphia: Lippincott, 1968. (1)

Cleaver, Vera, and Cleaver, Bill. Where the lillies bloom. Philadelphia: Lippincott, 1969. (1)

Cretan, Gladys. All except Sammy. Boston: Little, Brown, 1966. (2) About a nonmusical boy in a very musical family; he loves baseball and finds his artistic place in painting. Almost (1) except for a few gratuitous stereotypes.

Fitzhugh, Louise. Harriet the spy. New York: Harper & Row, 1964. (1)

Greene, Constance. The unmaking of Rabbit. New York: Viking, 1972. (1) An 11-year-old boy, unpopular and unwanted by his parents, grows to value himself while living with a no-nonsense, loving, very real grandmother.

Konigsburg, E. L. From the mixed-up files of Mrs. Basil E. Frankweiler. New York: Atheneum, 1967. (1) A sister guides her younger brother in a running-away adventure in the Metropolitan Museum of Art in New York.

Konigsburg, E. L. Jennifer, Hecate, Macbeth, William McKinley, and me, Elizabeth. New York: Atheneum, 1967. (1) Two spunky girls hide their loneliness in witchcraft until they gradually and humorously develop a true friendship.

Neville, Emily. Berries Goodman. New York: Harper & Row, 1965. (2)

Sharmat, Marjorie. Getting something on Maggie Marmelstein. New York: Harper & Row: 1971. (1)

Snyder, Zelpha. The changeling. New York: Atheneum, 1970. (1)

REALISTIC FICTION—SET IN THE PAST

Burch, Robert. Queenie Peavy. New York: Viking, 1966. (1)

Constant, Alberta Wilson. The motoring Millers. New York: Crowell, 1969. (1) The delightful family includes a daughter who is victorious in Kansas' first auto race.

Krumgold, Joseph. And now Miguel. New York: Thomas Y. Crowell, 1953. (2)

Lenski, Lois. Strawberry girl. Philadelphia: Lippincott, 1949. (1)

Taylor, Sydney. All-of-a-kind family. Chicago: Follett, 1951. (2) A loving family full of individuals; however, ultimate happiness is reached when a son is born to join the five daughters.

FANTASY AND HUMOR

Atwater, Richard, and Atwater, Florence. Mr. Popper's penguins. Boston: Little, Brown, 1938. (3) A wonderfully humorous tale of an ordinary housepainter who accumulates a family of penguins, but his mate is an extremely stereotyped, nagging, unimaginative housewife.

Butterworth, Oliver. The enormous egg. Boston: Little, Brown, 1956. (3)

Butterworth, Oliver. The trouble with Jenny's ear. Boston: Little, Brown, 1960. (3)

Corbett, Scott. The lemonade trick. Boston: Atlantic Monthly, 1960. (2)

Farmer, Penelope. Charlotte sometimes. New York: Harcourt, Brace, 1969. (1)

Lindgren, Astrid. Pippi Longstocking. New York: Viking, 1950. (1) A female counterpart, thus a good balance for Homer Price.

McCloskey, Robert. Homer Price. New York: Viking, 1943. (2) Preposterous happenings in a small town full of characters, but almost no females; the few shown are exaggeratingly unpleasant.

Raskin, Ellen. The mysterious disappearance of Leon (I mean Noel). New York: Dutton, 1971. (1)

Robertson, Keith. Henry Reed's big show. New York: Viking, 1970. (2)

White, E. B. Charlotte's web. New York: Harper & Row, 1952. (1)

HISTORICAL FICTION

Brink, Carol Ryrie. Caddie Woodlawn. New York: Macmillan, 1958. (2) The story of a brave and resourceful frontier girl who is finally convinced that she must grow up and give up her "tomboy ways."

Canfield, Dorothy. Understood Betsy. New York: Holt, 1916. (1)

Dalgliesh, Alice. The courage of Sarah Noble. New York: Scribner, 1954. (1)

O'Dell, Scott. Island of the blue dolphins. Boston: Houghton Mifflin, 1960. (1)

BIOGRAPHY

Heyn, Leah Lurie. Challenge to become a doctor; the story of Elizabeth Blackwell. Old Westbury, N.Y.: Feminist Press, 1972. (1)

Judson, Clara. George Washington, leader of the people. Chicago: Follett, 1951. (2) One of the most favored biographies of one of the most favored historical figures (with young readers); females are shown as following submissively, dependent, and without much personality.

McKown, Robin. Marie Curie. New York: Putnam, 1971. (1)

14-YEAR-OLDS

FICTION—CONTEMPORARY

Green, Hannah. I never promised you a rose garden. New York: Holt, 1964. (1) Moving story of an adolescent girl who struggles to find her way out of her fantasy world.

Holland, Isabelle. The man without a face. Philadelphia: Lippincott, 1972. (1)

Jordan, June. His own where. New York: Thomas Y. Crowell. 1971. (1) A poetic, affecting story of love between two urban black teens.

Knowles, John. A separate peace. New York: Macmillan, 1960. (1)

Plath, Sylvia. The bell jar. New York: Harper & Row, 1971. (1) A creative and sensitive college girl moves into mental illness as she struggles to find herself.

Renvoize, Jean. A wild thing. Boston: Atlantic Monthly, 1971. (1) A British girl escapes to the wilderness to establish a new life.

Salinger, J. D. The catcher in the rye. Boston: Little, Brown, 1951. (1)

Walsh, Jill Paton. Fireweed. New York: Farrar, Straus, Giroux, 1969. (2) Beautifully written story of an adolescent boy and girl who survive together in the streets of World War II's bombed-out London. Julie is well drawn and strong, but there is unnecessary constant concern for protecting her by Bill.

Wojcieshowska, Maia. Don't play dead before you have to. New York: Harper & Row, 1971. (2) An unusual story—the relationship between 15-year-old boy and the 5-year-old boy he babysits for.

FICTION—SET IN THE PAST

Armstrong, William. Sounder. New York: Harper & Row, 1969. (1)

Bronte, Charlotte. Jane Eyre. New York: Macmillan, 1962. (Many other editions) (1) Reading between the lines reveals the real depth of Jane's strength and independent spirit.

Gilman, Charlotte Perkins. The yellow wallpaper. Old Westbury, N. Y.: Feminist Press, 1973. (1) Originally published in 1892, the book reveals the difficulties of a nineteenth-century woman who yearns for intellectual stimulation and work.

Seed, Suzanne. Saturday's child: 36 women talk about their jobs. Chicago: O'Hara, 1973. (1)

BIOGRAPHY

Chisholm, Shirley. Unbought and unbossed. Boston: Houghton Mifflin, 1971. (1)

Davis, Rebecca Harding. Life in the iron mills. Old Westbury, N.Y.: Feminist Press, 1973. (1)

Klein, Mina C. Kathe Kollwitz: life in art. New York: Holt, 1972. (1)

McKown, Robin. The world of Mary Cassat. New York: Thomas Y. Crowell, 1972. (1)

Shulman, Alix. To the barricades: the anarchist life of Emma Goldman. New York: Thomas Y. Crowell, 1971. (1)

Teachers' Evaluation of the Curriculum

The teacher's use of suggested ideas and materials in their curriculum notebooks varied widely from class to class and from grade to grade. The following section will describe grade by grade what the teachers chose to use and how they evaluated these individual activities or units.

EARLY CHILDHOOD: The kindergarten teachers especially enjoyed reading the library books provided by the program. Many of them were new and unfamiliar both to the teachers and to their students. With a new "angle" from which to approach discussion of a new story, teachers found class discussions stimulating and refreshing. One kindergarten teacher read *Mummies Are for Loving* by Ruth Bonn Penn and asked her class what else Mummies are good for or can do. She received highly imaginative, nonstereotypical replies, ranging from plumbers, truck drivers, doctors, zoo keepers, and storekeepers to artists. This was in sharp contrast to an assignment in which the same children were asked to draw what they wished to be as grown-ups. Boys' replies ranged from painters and barbers to police officers and working for the city to fix pipes; similarly affected by their concrete experiences, girls' replies ranged from teachers and nurses to cleaning women. One imaginative child wanted to be a queen!

Another kindergarten children's class, when given the same assignment, expressed a wider range of roles for both sexes. Boys tended to select a much greater repertory of occupations than girls, although a few girls could visualize themselves as engineers, lawyers, and farmers. Most girls, however, saw themselves in roles for which they undoubtedly had familiar models, such as nurse, teacher, and policewoman.

Since most primary school teachers have always tended to use storytelling hour as a springboard for class discussion, it was easy for the kindergarten teachers to simply extend their discussions along a new dimension. Books like *William's Doll* and *A Wolf of My Own* sparked lively exchanges on a topic that has not usually been suggested by the story line or illustrations of picture storybooks for young children. No firm resolution of the issue was necessary at the kindergarten level; children could expand their thinking by hearing each others' comments and by hearing them accepted by the teachers.

Following the reading of William's Doll:

Boy 1: Dolls aren't for boys, they're for girls.

Boy 2: I don't like dolls. I never play with them, but I wouldn't like to see a boy cry because he doesn't have a doll.

Boy 3: I really would like a doll to take care of.

Boy 4: I would play bank robbers and good guys if I had a doll.

Girl 1: I never saw boys play with dolls except in school when we play together.

Girl 2: Boys aren't allowed to have dolls, I don't like to see them have one.

Following the reading of A Wolf of My Own:

Question: Was the main character a boy or a girl?

Boy 1: I think it is a boy because it does not make sense for a girl to have a wolf pet. I couldn't picture Kristin having a wolf for a pet. She would scream and run.

Boy 2: I think it is a boy.

Boy 3: I think it is a boy because boys aren't afraid of wolves and girls are because when they see mouses, they scream.

Girl 1: I think it is a boy, too.

Girl 2: I think it is a girl because some girls like wild animals.

Girl 3: I would say it is a boy.

Boy 4: She is a girl because she has long hair. If boys have long hair, they would look like they are wearing a wig. I don't like boys to have long hair.

Girl 4: I think it is easier for a boy to have a wolf because girls can't take care of the wolves.

Girl 5: Girls can have wolves as long as the wolves are gentle.

The kindergarten teacher who followed most closely the activities suggested in the curriculum notebook found them excellent for "promoting expanded thinking and understanding of other roles." They stimulated verbalization and associative skills, major goals for language development in the primary grades. All teachers found the pictures of professional women and community workers a worthwhile supplement to their classrooms and were unanimous in conveying the children's enjoyment of the record *Free to Be . . . You and Me*. Once the novelty of the melodies and their lyrics wore off, teachers could use some of the material to open up class discussion.

Following the selection, "Dudley Pippin and the Principal":

Question: What is a sissy?

1. A girl.

2. Could be a boy or a girl.

3. Someone that cries.

Question: Why do we cry?

1. Because we hurt ourselves.

2. Because someone hurt us.

Question: If you fall and hurt yourself and begin to cry, does that make you a "sissy"?

1. No comments!

The kindergarten teachers who replied in the final overall evaluation form made the following judgments:

1. Adequate information about the project had been pro-

vided for them in their curriculum notebooks; more suggested activities would be desirable.

2. The children had thoroughly enjoyed all the manipulative materials. "The beauty of the whole project was to watch the children carry out their own role playing."

3. More visual aids (film loops, transparencies, tapes, color pictures, movies) would be desirable supplements.

4. Class discussion based on curricular materials proved stimulating and thought provoking.

Clearly, the curricular activities for the kindergarten program easily fell into the traditional categories of materials and modes utilized by most teachers. These simply provided a different focus to examine and discuss. The teachers all felt that the program was low-keyed and an unobtrusive part of the regular kindergarten program. The children, as indicated by artwork about occupational choices or categorization of familiar adult roles, easily verbalized their understanding of a wide variety of occupational and familial roles for themselves and the adults with whom they are familiar. For example, one boy drew a picture of his "favorite woman"—his mother—and said, "She is washing dishes and she goes to work." One girl, depicting both parents, said, "My mother is picking flowers. Mommy makes the beds, Daddy helps too. He is putting up wallpaper. Mommy doesn't help put up wallpaper."

MIDDLE GRADES: Grade 5 teachers were able to draw from a much greater variety of materials, and no two teachers used the same materials in exactly the same way. The activities grade 5 teachers engaged in with their classes appeared to fall into four main content areas of sex-role stereotyping: (1) sports, (2) literature, (3) occupational categories, and (4) personality attributes.

Several teachers found there was much class interest in the subject of sex discrimination in sports activities within and outside of the school. One teacher effectively used a local news item regarding the efforts of several local girls to join the city's Little League baseball team as a springboard for discussion and debating skill development. The teacher first used the newspaper clipping in a "manner similar to a TV news broadcast." He read the clipping and gave an analysis of it; he then threw open the issue to the class. The next day a more formal debate was organized, with all the students participating in one of three teams: (1) pro, (2) con, and (3) a panel of judges. The teacher listed on the chalkboard all the twenty reasons offered for and against girls' admittance into Little League. As pro and con teams debated each other on each item, the judges would decide upon the validity of the debaters' reasoning and strike out invalid reasons from the board. Interestingly, according to the teacher, "Only the boys produced reasons as to why the girls should be kept out and only the girls produced reasons as to why the girls should be allowed in. No one crossed the sex line."

A teacher in another school system similarly used several articles in *Scholastic Magazine,* one of which related the plight of a New Jersey girl who had been the subject of a court case involving admittance into the Little League. The class enjoyed discussing the articles; they reviewed the physical education programs in their own school, and questioned the possibility of girls being able to participate with boys in all sports. When mixed reactions occurred on the subject of girls on hockey teams, the class decided to investigate background materials and hold a debate. None of the students reacted negatively to the idea that women can be fine athletes. The teacher expressed a desire for more materials written about women as famous sports figures.

All grade 5 teachers were able to do a great deal with occupational choices and descriptions. Searching through the want ad section of the local newspaper proved to be a productive small-group activity; students were asked to collect job listings, note whether or not there were sex

restrictions, and discuss why or why not. One teacher
expected less participation from the boys but found "they
were eager to contribute"; the students "enjoyed scan-
ning the want ads and listing them." Another teacher
noted that her students disagreed with whatever restrictions they found in the want ads, feeling that training
oppportunities, not sex, made the difference. A third
teacher had his students choose five occupations that
interested them and then write their own want ads, listing
all necessary qualifications. The teacher expressed surprise at some of the students' stereotypes and their lack of
knowledge of qualifications needed for adult occupations.

Several teachers found the assignment of writing
about a future choice of career very popular and effective
with their students, especially if preceded by class discussion. One teacher followed up this writing assignment by
having boys and girls exchange papers with each other,
the boys reading out loud a career choice written by a girl
as if it were their own, and vice versa. "The class really
enjoyed this, and after a discussion, we concluded that
most of the occupations the girls had written about could
have been those written by boys and vice versa. Some
exceptions were football players, long-haul truck drivers,
etc." A third teacher found a wide variety of career
choices listed by both boys and girls, although the girls for
the most part "had typically 'female' desires with the
exception of electrician, spy, and doctor. The class as a
whole thought those were perfectly acceptable as
women's jobs."

The teachers also found the listing of occupations for
male, female, or both and the choosing of suitable descriptive adjectives a productive small-group or whole-class
activity. One class found that "with the exception of
cabdriver (some girls insisted men make better drivers),
all jobs on the list could be handled by men or women." A
similar conclusion was reached by another class which
saw "proper training" as the important and relevant variable. A third class, doing this activity solely as a whole-

class discussion, expressed stereotypes about some occupations that "amazed" the teacher. "Boys thought girls couldn't handle some jobs because they weren't strong enough. Girls thought some jobs were too easy for boys. After our discussion, however, some of the class reviewed their original opinions and decided that more jobs could be done by both men and women."

Several teachers found that the adjective game from the Karkau unit or the word association game on self-stereotyping provoked lively, even violent, discussions. Some students were surprised that the same adjectives could be on both a "masculine" and a "feminine" list; in fact, the terms "masculine" and "feminine" themselves produced much heated discussion. Several girls who had originally provided the adjective "dainty" became rather upset with their own choice in the ensuing discussions. They claimed it was what a woman "was supposed to be"; yet they didn't like the image.

The issue of women in leadership roles also provided good discussion material. The girls all felt that "a woman can do anything a man can do."

The reading materials were used in different ways by the grade 5 teachers. One teacher had small-group reading and discussion of several of the short biographies (Susan B. Anthony, Elizabeth Cady Stanton, and Sojourner Truth.) They were worthwhile not only for oral reading, vocabulary development, and discussion, but also for the interest they sparked in some of the children to read other nonfiction books on women. "Girls found the history of women's rights interesting"—a topic, one might add, not usually presented in grade 5 social studies material.

Two teachers used the Bement unit, one selecting *Caddie Woodlawn* and *On the Banks of Plum Creek* for her two reading groups, the other teacher using *Caddie Woodlawn, Journey to Topaz, Judy's Journey,* and *31 Brothers and Sisters.* The teachers found the unit very successful from the perspective of the literature the children were exposed to. The first teacher mentioned that "when I passed out the books, most of my boys were unhappy because they felt it was a girl's book. After they started reading it, however, they came up to me and told me how good it was." In fact, the only call from an irate parent during the entire intervention program was provoked by *Caddie Woodlawn!* One parent, a local police officer, called the teacher at home wanting to know why his son was reading a "girl's book." When he was assured his son could substitute another book for the class reading, the matter was smoothed over. Several days later, the boy, with his mother's encouragement, had begun to read the book and confessed to the teacher that it was a really good story—even if Caddie was a girl. The incident is an interesting commentary on the kind of unwitting bias in the literature that the school deliberately and selectively exposes students to. With just a little conscious effort on the part of curriculum makers, elementary school students could be exposed to much good children's literature that features strong, courageous, independent males *and* females in leading roles. As Beaven (1972) found, many older students have developed a fairly negative image of women in literature—as a result of the traditional literature program in the language arts.

Journey to Topaz proved an especially worthwhile story. It deals with the experiences of an eleven-year-old Japanese-American girl interned in a concentration camp in America during World War II—and was successfully integrated by the teacher with an ongoing social studies unit on Japan.

One teacher was also able to use the song "Free to Be . . . You and Me" as a successful stimulus for expository writing. The students were asked to interpret the lyrics in a short writing assignment.

In the overall evaluation of the program, grade 5 teachers indicated that:

1. Adequate information had been provided by the notebooks.

2. Directions in the use of curricular materials and the variety in structure of the materials were adequate.

3. The literature provided for the Bement unit was very worthwhile; the guides for this unit were "most helpful."

4. The individual library books sent to the classrooms were very much appreciated and enjoyed.

5. *Free to Be . . . You and Me* was enjoyed by all.

6. There was a need for more game-type activities, short biographies of famous women, and occupational pamphlets and brochures for boys and girls at this grade level.

An amusing reaction to the intervention program occurred in the essay writing of a rather precocious student. In an essay on *Alice in Wonderland,* this grade 5 student wrote:

> If she were around today, she'd be a woman's libber. Her dreams show this because in each situation the queen instead of the king is dominant. The king is a sort of yes-man.

JUNIOR HIGH SCHOOL: Grade 9 teachers had even more materials from which to choose than grade 5 teachers. Despite the fact that two of the grade 9 teachers were in social studies rather than in English, they all drew upon the materials originally provided for the English curriculum notebook. None, to our knowledge, used any of the material on the Susan B. Anthony Day Kit, the women's rights debate, the theme of women in politics, or the various texts and library books on the suffragette movement and women's rights that were provided in multiple copies for each of the social studies classrooms. It is not clear whether the teachers felt the topic was difficult to fit into the structure of their course or whether students simply would not have been interested at the grade 9 level.

Possibly, a more carefully delineated unit on the history of the women's rights unit, with a variety of resource materials and visual aids, would have been utilized more readily. In any event, it is not possible to offer any evaluation of the materials that might be more relevant to social studies.

All six teachers used the *Baby X* script,[1] finding it a popular unit with all their students. The general comment was that plays go over very well with students at this level; all enjoyed the role playing in class, and even the poorest readers wanted to read the play. Most teachers were able to follow up the reading of the play with lively discussions and a writing assignment. Many students took their copies of the play to other classes and shared it with their friends.

Conversational Clichés was also used by all the grade 9 teachers. These pages lent themselves easily to some vocabulary work, as many of the adjectives were unfamiliar to the students (e.g., charismatic, hysterical, articulate). Depending on the class, some teachers found it provocative, others less so. One teacher simplified the vocabulary altogether for her class. Another suggested that a follow-up exercise in which students create their own clichés would have been helpful.

Preferred Qualities of Male/Female was used by one teacher who thought "the discussion generated was beneficial and made them think in terms of values and value judgments." Clarification of vocabulary was also important here; e.g., did *"curious"* mean *"nosy"* or *"intellectually inquisitive"*? The project choices in The Socialization of Women and the Image of Women in the Media were judged "excellent, as [they] provided flexibility for long-term, at-home projects," although better directions

---

[1]This play was written by two elementary school children, Andrew Hoffman and Lucy Hull, adapted from a story by Lois Gould, "X, A Fabulous Child's Story," which appeared in *Ms.* magazine, December 1972, pp. 74–76, 105–6. The story and play deal with a fictional child whose sex is not revealed.

were needed and samples would have been helpful. The book report form was judged an "excellent book report form for a book of this type."

Teachers felt most of the activities aroused good discussion or lent themselves easily to short writing assignments. Several teachers, especially the social studies teachers, had their classes read the short biographies. They served as good springboards for discussing such related issues as racial discrimination, the civil rights movement, the problems of immigrants, and the abolition movement. Because they were written at a fairly low reading level, teachers found them very useful with less able readers. The fact sheets also proved of interest to several teachers who used them as a basis for class discussion.

Much more material has been made available within the past year and many of the teachers were able to use resources that came to their attention from other sources, e.g., their own audiovisual aids department, the magazine *Read*, published by the Xerox Company, and local news items or events within the junior or senior high school.

In their overall evaluation, grade 9 teachers made the following comments:

1. Several found the background information in the curriculum adequate; one thought it was vague and misleading. The general feeling was one of unclear expectations. The workshop helped, but some teachers felt that sample assignments might have been more useful.

2. Most teachers found sufficient materials and ideas offered in the notebooks. One teacher suggested that more short case histories, fictional or otherwise, dealing with the issue would have been useful. Another suggested more visual aids.

3. The teachers found the suggestions and directions adequate. They found the loose structure suitable for a short intervention program.

4. There was some feeling that the material in general appeared too one-sided, too female-oriented. Several teachers suggested use of "male lib" material as a supplementary counterpart. *Read* magazine provided this kind of supplement for two teachers.

5. All teachers felt that the program had made students more aware of the issue of sex-role stereotyping, but were skeptical as to its lasting effects on behavior or attitudes. As one teacher reported, "Perhaps the most enlightened remark made at the end of this project came from one boy who said, 'We all make the most liberal statements now, but we still act in the stereotyped fashion. Do you think it has made any difference?' And that—I guess—is the question. At least they are now aware that much of their thinking is conforming to stereotyped patterns."

In this chapter, we have described the formulation, preparation, conduct, and evaluation of a pilot curriculum program in sex-role stereotyping at three grade levels in three participating school systems. It should be noted that the objectives and the curricular activities were all conceived by individuals external to the schools in which the program was to be carried out. It was not possible to involve curriculum directors and teachers within the participating schools in the formulation of the objectives and the actual curriculum on an ongoing basis through workshops and numerous meetings as would normally be in the case for the introduction of any new curriculum in a school system. One condition insisted upon by school systems participating in the intervention program was a minimal demand on teacher time in advance of the program and in addition to their normal workload during the four to five weeks of the intervention period. It was therefore necessary to offer a complete curricular package to the participating teachers just before the onset of the program, with little opportunity for involvement and feedback on the part of the teachers. Ideally, teachers should always be involved to some extent in the preparation of a program they are to carry out. In this case, as it was not possible, the enthusiasm of teachers volunteering for an experimental program had to be relied upon in carrying out with some degree of fidelity a program conceived by those located in a more remote academic setting. It is not clear how strong an effect this organizational factor had in the overall implementation of the program.

In spite of this theoretical shortcoming, it was our judgment that most teachers implemented the suggested program with enthusiasm and interest. The programs appeared to be more fully carried out at the kindergarten and grade 5 levels. The ease with which a part-time intervention program can be integrated into the more flexible structure of the elementary school day may account to some extent for this subjective estimate. Moreover, the lesser degree of "sophistication" of elementary school children may make it easier for teachers to hold genuine, serious discussions of the issues. Teenagers are notoriously prone to a more skeptical or wise-cracking attitude. At the grade 9 level in some schools, there were inevitable conflicts with midsemester exams and the demands of secondary school subject matter skill work. Nevertheless, several grade 9 teachers were able to use a number of ideas offered in their notebooks. The teachers themselves were remarkably diverse in terms of age, years of teaching experience, and ethnic background. It would not be possible to consider any of these factors as relevant to the degree of success in implementing such a program at any grade level on the basis of this particular experiment.

The curricular programs at kindergarten and grade 5 seemed well balanced and fairly neutral in their overall construction and tone. At grade 9, there did appear to be some legitimate concern as to how comfortable male students would be with the program. Older students tended to see much of the curricular material as "women's lib" propaganda in a pejorative sense. Supplementary reading materials plus some carefully worked-out longer units with substantive content (similar to the Bement unit at grade 5) would be desirable additions to a grade 9 intervention program.

Resources for More Information

The addresses of groups, organizations, and publishers listed below provide more sources for nonsexist materials. These groups have provided bibliographies, graphics, critiques, films, articles, and books that can provide more material for the classroom. There is an ongoing effort to supply more and better nonsexist materials, and the places listed below are part of that extended information system. Inquire about the resources, reports, or catalogs they maintain about nonsexist issues and materials.

Change for Children, 2588 Mission Street, San Francisco, (415) 282-3142.

Clearinghouse on Women's Studies, State University of New York, College at Old Westbury, Old Westbury, N.Y.

Emma Willard Task Force on Education, 1520 West 27th Street, Minneapolis, Minn. 55408.

Feminist Book Mart, 162-11 9th Avenue, Whitestone, N.Y. 11357.

Feminists on Children's Media, P.O. Box 4315, Grand Central Station, New York, N.Y.

Feminist Press, State University of New York, College at Old Westbury, Old Westbury, N.Y. 11568.

Feminist Resources for Equal Education, P.O. Box 3185, Saxonville Station, Framingham, Mass. 01701.

Joyful World Press, 468 Belvedere Street, San Francisco, Calif. 94117.

Know, Inc., P.O. Box 86031, Pittsburgh, Pa. 15221.

Lollipop Power, Inc., P.O. Box 1171, Chapel Hill, N.C. 27514.

New England Free Press, 60 Union Square, Somerville, Mass. 02143.

Resource Center on Sex Roles in Education, 1156 15th Street, N.W., Washington, D.C. 20005.

Status of Women Committee, American Association of University Women, 36 Castle-down Road, Pleasanton, Calif. 94566.

Task Force on Sexism in Schools, Valley Women's Center, 200 Main Street, Northampton, Mass. 01060, (413) 586-2011.

Times Change Press, Penwell Road, Washington, N.J. 07882.

Women in Their Varied Occupations Series, Office of Human Relations, Berkeley Unified School District, Berkeley, Calif. 94709.

Women's Bureau, Employment Standards Administration, U.S. Department of Labor, Washington, D.C.

Women's History Research Center, Inc., 2325 Oak Street, Berkeley, Calif. 94708, (415) 524-7772.

Women's Work and Women's Studies, 1971 (Know, Inc.), Women's Center, Barnard College, New York, N.Y.

Nonsexist Multimedia Resources

Contemporary Films, McGraw Hill, 1221 Avenue of the Americas, New York, N.Y. 10020.

Downeck Films, 179 Van Buren Street, Newark, N.J. 07105.

Federal Women's Program Coordinator, Office of Civil Rights, Washington, D.C. 20405. Ask for bibliography of *Films on the Women's Movement.*

Feminist Resources for Equal Education, Box 185, Saxonville Station, Framingham, Mass. 01701.

Franciscan Communications Center, Teleketics Divisions, 1229 South Santee, Los Angeles, Calif. 90015.

Media Plus, Inc., 60 Riverside Drive, Suite 11D, New York, N.Y. 10024.

National Organization of Women, New York chapter, 28 E. 56th Street, New York, N.Y. 10022.

New Day Films, 267 West 25th Street, New York, N.Y. 10001.

Newsreel, 322 7th Avenue, New York, N.Y.

Women's Film Cooperative, Valley Women's Center, 200 Main Street, Northampton, Mass. 01060.

Women's Graphics Collective, Chicago Women's Liberation Union, 852 West Belmont Avenue, Chicago, Ill. 60657.

CHAPTER SEVEN

Changing Sex-Role Stereotypes: Before and After the Intervention

Kindergarten

PREINTERVENTION: It was difficult to measure the sex-role attitudes of kindergarten children. Although some children said a great deal in response to the measures, much of it had little to do with sex roles. Their stories naturally contained much irrelevant material, often given in a disconnected fashion.

Some kindergartners did tell stories with plots and coherent characters. Many of these fuller stories contained dramatic comments about social roles for men and women. Below is a story told by a precocious six-year-old girl.

> Once upon a time there was a man, and his wife cooked. One day his wife said, "I'm tired of cooking," so they switched jobs. She went out to his field to pick corn, and he cooked. He cooked some dough, the dough began to rise and rise and rise. It got on the babies. The babies cried so much that the china rattled. It broke. And when she came back it was a big mess. The end.

The same child parodying the man in the kitchen also had a story for the woman in the construction site.

Miss Jones worked for a building company; she worked very hard but she was careless. Every time she was in charge of a group, she was very strict to them. One day Miss Jones was working on a building. She said to her troopers, "If you don't work, I won't pay you one cent," and she started to work. She wanted to show the other workers how fast she was. So she took a gidder (girder?) and instead of screwing and bolting it in hardly, she just took a screw and stuck it in. When the building was done, she had forgotten she had done this and she decided to live in it. So one day in the middle of summer Miss Jones was having a nap. All of a sudden she felt there was an earthquake. She went downstairs and left the house. When she got out of the house it didn't shake any more. Then all of a sudden she remembered what she had done, and the building collapsed. Well, Miss Jones didn't get hurt but she had learned a lesson. The end.

The depth and intensity exhibited in these stories are not frequent on the kindergarten level. Some stories were too sparse to identify themes that would indicate specific sex-role attitudes. Interviewers often had to engage in extensive prompting to which the children responded with terse answers. For these reasons, generalizations about the opinions of the five-year-olds gleaned from the projective material must be tentative.

The objective testing measures did provide the opportunity to understand some of the kindergartners' attitudes. The job-list data was particularly useful since it was not a bipolar choice item. The children generated their *own* lists of ideas about jobs for men and women. Some qualities of the projective style of measurement were thus retained. Cognitively, the five-year-olds had difficulty with the distinctions between jobs, activities, and the purposes connected with both. Although they were asked for a list of jobs, the kindergartners also included leisure-time activities, social roles, and particular talents. Any activity they named that possibly could be full-time or of financial benefit as an occupation was coded, e.g., "plays golf," "counts money."

The data show that kindergartners show sex-role stereotyping about which sex does what kind of activity. Both boys and girls listed significantly more jobs for males (boys, 5.17; girls, 4.96) than for females (boys, 4.08; girls, 3.81). Stereotyping was stronger for male jobs for both boys and girls. Kindergartners apparently reported the jobs of people they knew or saw every day, e.g. crossing guards, firemen, window washers. Most of these jobs were stereotypically masculine. Many "feminine" jobs, like social worker, bank clerk, or hairdresser, were removed from the sphere of the five-year-old. The girls named significantly fewer male jobs as high status, undoubtedly because male workers with whom the children are familiar are relatively low in status. The five-year-olds seemed unaware of the power of status hierarchies in society. Both boys and girls listed significantly more interpersonal jobs for women than for men.

The listing tasks showed that kindergartners believe strongly that males and females do very different things. They believe that men and women seldom have the same job. The kindergartners presented the males in the traditional, time-worn jobs, many of them low in status. The women's jobs were notably interpersonal in nature. On personality characteristics, kindergartners were very clear about girls' stereotypes. Personality stereotypes for boys were not as strong. Girls at this age were confident that they are both as strong and as good-looking as the boys are.

POSTINTERVENTION: The kindergarten intervention was geared toward expanding the children's perception of possibilities for men and women, particularly in occupations. Postintervention effects were seen most clearly in the job-list data which are a direct index of the child's ideas about occupations. Job listing is a task which is fairly easy for the kindergarten children to handle, so that consistent and reliable results were possible. Results are summarized in the following table.

JOB-LIST DATA: KINDERGARTEN PRE- AND POSTINTERVENTION

	NUMBER FEMALE JOBS	NUMBER MALE JOBS	OVERLAP
Preintervention			
Girls	3.81	4.96	.11
Boys	4.08	5.17	.07
Postintervention			
Girls	7.0	7.1	.24
Boys	8.54	7.92	.17

Before the intervention, both boys and girls gave a significantly longer list of jobs for males than for females. The number of jobs which appeared on *both* lists (i.e., either a man or a woman could have them) was extremely low. After the intervention, the number of jobs the children named increased, perhaps because of the attention paid to alternative occupations in the classroom. Most importantly, the significant difference between the male and the female total list disappeared for both boys and girls. The number of jobs which both men and women could hold also increased dramatically. The original high level of stereotyping for female jobs, shown by both boys and girls, was greatly reduced after the intervention. The kindergarten children no longer mentioned just the traditional jobs like nurse, model, and housecleaner for women. Their lists broadened to include many jobs not traditionally held by women. The possibility of high-status jobs for women was readily absorbed by the kindergarten girls.

Before the intervention, both boys and girls maintained that women belonged in jobs which require social skills to a much higher degree than do males. This distinction faded after the intervention for the girls. Afterwards, girls were almost as likely to list an interpersonal job for a male as for a female. Boys, however, maintained their initial stereotypes. Even on the kindergarten level, girls were more interested in and affected by the intervention than were boys.

It was clear that kindergartners' attitudes were influenced by the ideas presented in the curriculum units. Images of women at work filtered into their play patterns and self-fantasies. The kindergarten girls did learn about occupational role flexibility for women, although they were less responsive to new socioemotional role possibilities.

Fifth Grade

PREINTERVENTION: Compared with the other ages in the study, the ten-year-olds were the least dogmatic about their sex-role attitudes. They showed considerable diversity of opinion about what is appropriately and inappropriately stereotypical for men and women. Boys and girls in this age group could be described as the least sexist since they seldom discriminated between men and women in societal or occupational roles. However, few children consistently showed nonsexist conviction; many children skirted the issue or made ambivalent or contradictory statements about sex roles. There was also little diversity in girls' attitudes as compared with boys' attitudes toward adult roles. Since individual scores were averaged, few noticeable sex differences appear between all the boys and all the girls. The children reported few differences between men and women. There was no general consensus about what is appropriate or inappropriate for men and women. Fifth graders do not support stereotyped notions, yet they do not unqualifiedly endorse nonstereotyped ideas. For instance, fifth graders would freely set women in nontraditional roles, but endow the "typical female" with overwhelming motherly or sisterly or popular qualities.

The intellectual issue of equality in occupations was easy for the fifth graders to accept. Many of them discerned and articulated issues of fairness and equality of opportunity and spoke with some personal knowledge about "women's libbers." However, the conventional socioemotional role of the sensitive, socially active, and nurturant female maintained its strength with these children. For example, in the Typical Day measure, the children usually gave Barbara Smith, the typical woman, an occupational role. After the child told the story, the interviewers tried some gentle probes to evaluate the boundaries of the children's attitudes. It became apparent from the probe that as soon as home, family, or husband were threatened by the woman's job, the job was no longer important for the woman. This pattern is illustrated in the story below. The child sets the woman in a nontraditional occupational setting, and then drops it during the probing.

> When she wakes up, she'll eat a good breakfast. Such a good breakfast that she's late for work, but not drowsy from eating so much. She'll be a school bus driver. She decided to go on a diet, so she went to the store after work and got a book about weight watching. She got a few phone calls. After she read the book, she decided to make supper from the book . . . salad and liver and cottage cheese. She watched TV and did exercises, then went to bed.

Probe responses:

> Yes, she might decide to do the opposite. Maybe she would get married and have kids. She would like to settle down. She might keep her job . . . depends on if he gets a job. Then she would quit her job, since her husband already has one.

Once again, the wife's job is just not as important as the man's job. The fifth grader tacitly assumes that the woman does not really *want* to work and worked in the past simply because she was not married.

The occupational pictures were designed to examine attitudes toward females and males in traditional and nontraditional jobs. Fifth graders stereotyped males in both traditional and nontraditional job roles. When they saw a picture of a male teacher, a traditionally nurturant role, they emphasized his power, control, and authority in the classroom. The following about a male teacher, given by a fifth grade boy, illustrates this tendency:

> Let's say he's a tutor. He came over to Glen's house and Glen has scarlet fever and now the tutor brings over this workbook and Glen don't want to do it. And then Glen ripped up the workbook and threw it up in the air. Now what are we going to do? I know one thing that's going to happen to him; he's going to get a couple of smashes. Then the teacher gave him a new workbook and he never ripped up a workbook again.

Whether a female was in a traditional or nontraditional job made a great difference to the children when they compared the female teacher with the female mechanic. The female mechanic was seen as in a less desirable occupational position than the female teacher, with lower status, less pay, and less ability. They believed the female mechanic encountered many more obstacles of all types and had less success in overcoming or resolving the problems that arose. The female teacher, who was in a traditional role, maintained respect and benefits from her occupational position, and received encouragement rather than suffering from obstacles.

Attitudes toward obstacles also showed significant differences on the male and female Typical Day stories. Fifth grade boys significantly more often said that men have no problems (men, 1.71; probability, .025), and no difficulty in being or doing what they want. This pattern recurs in many of the stories told by boys. Girls were much quicker to recognize the existence of obstacles in stories they told about both males (1.02, neutral) and females (1.09, neutral). This finding substantiates other research which has found that boys overestimate their own abilities while girls have a much lower expectancy of completing a task successfully (Stein et al., 1969). Neither sex is consistently accurate or realistic in assessing how one's own abilities will fare in relation to the requirements of the external environment. Thus these ten-year-old girls report all types of problems in the outside world, while boys deny any external difficulties.

On the level of societal roles, fifth graders show little unified or purposive discrimination between males and females. However, the children *do* stereotype activities which are not directly related to occupational roles. Leisure-time activities for men, men's routine activities, and the male's amount and type of problems were stereotyped. At fifth grade, boys and girls enter details into their Typical Day stories that are highly stereotypical for a male (boys, 1.79; girls, 1.83), such as jogging in the evening, picking up a date, and going out for a beer with the guys. Boys and girls seem to agree that there are a limited number of acceptable activities or leisure-time events for males. There are very few men in either boys' or girls' stories with strange hobbies or unique pastimes. The great majority of the male Typical Day stories ended with: "He read the newspaper. He watched TV. He went to bed." Fifth grade boys also stereotyped the activities of the typical female by emphasizing activities like coffee klatches, baking cakes, and talking on the telephone (boys, 1.49; probability, .001).

There was a clear tendency, which occurred across all grades, for each sex to stereotype the opposite sex to a greater degree than they did themselves. At the fifth grade level, this pattern occurred on the Semantic Differential measure, where children had to indicate what real and ideal boys and girls are like. On the lists of word pairs, the children frequently chose stereotyped personality characteristics for the opposite-sex children. Boys portrayed girls as more stereotypically feminine than did the girls. Boys thought girls were neat, sensitive, gentle, cautious, good-looking, obedient, quiet, apt to cry a lot, and weak. Girls' scores on these attributes were much closer to neutral.

Following the trend of sex stereotyping the opposite sex, girls' opinions on the Most Boys measure tended toward the masculine stereotype in eight out of twelve word pairs. Most children in the study felt that it was imperative for boys to have the masculine stereotyped qualities, even when at times these characteristics were not socially desirable. It was less essential for girls to have feminine qualities. They believed that men must be strong and must be the breadwinners, or at least must work at a money-making occupation to support the family. If a man fulfills these indispensable duties and has these necessary qualities, he may also be kind to children, be a gourmet cook, and be sensitive to other people's feelings. If he is not strong, he is a sissy or a homosexual. If he does not work, his wife gets angry with him, his children take advantage of him, and the neighbors gossip about him.

If this is what children believe is typical of boys—"the way most boys are"—do they believe it *should* be this way? Scores on the Semantic Differential What Boys Should Be and What Girls Should Be measures tap this question. An interesting boy-girl difference in attitudes emerged. Girls modified their scores on both the ideal girl and ideal boy measures toward characteristics which are desirable regardless of sex. Girls, more than boys, were tuned in to those qualities that are good for anyone, male or female, to have. They showed more androgynous attitudes toward what ideal boys and girls should be like. They believed being "sensitive" was important for either a man or woman who wants to be a totally fulfilled person. Girls appeared to be more aware of the artificiality of sex-typed characteristics, while boys continued to believe that current sex-typed personality characteristics reflect the way things should be.

The self-esteem measures (Typical Day, Self, and Semantic Differential, Self) showed the same trends in children's evaluation of their current and future sex roles. The boys expected to be occupationally satisfied and respected, and to have few problems of any kind. They intended to involve themselves only in proper masculine activities. Girls saw themselves as expressive, socially adept, and nurturant. Being good-looking was important even to preadolescent children. This concern about physical appearance grew in the next few years to become the single most important predictor of self-esteem in the early adolescent. From the Semantic Differential data, there was a significant sex difference on the "ugly–good-looking" items. Boys (3.8) portrayed themselves as good-looking, while girls (3.1) labeled themselves as neutral. These responses were consistent with self-image research which suggests that females have a generally more negative view of themselves than males. It is significant that this self-deprecatory trend for girls occurred even at ten years of age, although it was intensified at later ages.

It appeared that fifth graders were resolved that men and women should be treated equally in society, yet they maintained the more subtle masculine-feminine stereotypes about obstacles, time spending, and interpersonal concerns. Boys and girls were similar in many attitudes, yet boys appeared to be more rigid about the proper personality characteristics for the two sexes, especially girls.

POSTINTERVENTION: Most of the changes following the intervention in fifth grade occurred with the girls. Their attitudes about occupational roles changed sharply toward a nonstereotypical stance. The fifth grade boys, originally fairly neutral, changed little after the intervention. After the intervention, girls listed significantly more jobs for females. They also listed more interpersonal jobs for both men and women. Boys did not change. Girls maintained a similar pre- and postintervention proportion of jobs which both men and women could hold.

On the socioemotional role measure the girls changed, but again the boys did not. After the intervention, girls produced significantly longer lists of personality qualities for women than the boys did, suggesting that their views of role flexibility had expanded. After the intervention they showed a sharp increase in the proportion of interpersonal adjectives describing *both* men and women.

Before the intervention, girls stereotypically endowed women with social, interpersonal qualities and men with individualistic qualities. After the intervention, the girls dramatically increased the proportion of interpersonal words used to describe men and the number of individualistic words used by women. After the intervention, women were described as being intelligent and strong, rather than only in terms of personality characteristics which occur only in relationship to other people, e.g., affable and good-natured. Another preintervention/postintervention change occurred in beliefs about the qualities which both men and women can have (overlap measure). Girls' percentage of overlap increased from 27 percent (preintervention) to 56 percent (postintervention). Thus, girls began to understand that many personality qualities can belong to both men and women, and in fact *ought* to belong to both men and women. The girls' image of the ideal girl substantially changed—away from the stereotypical feminine (neat, obedient, gives in, etc.). Once again, it was the girls' conception of what is possible, particularly in roles for women, which was influenced by the intervention.

The Stein test, which measured children's preference for "masculine" and "feminine" activities, revealed strong sex typing. Girls preferred feminine hobbies, games, and activities. Boys preferred the masculine equivalents. Neither sex liked the other's traditional activities; they intensely valued their own. One experimental class in town C can be used as an example of how the intervention significantly changed these attitudes. In this class, the original divergence for the girls (male preference, 3.28; female preference, 4.06) was changed following the intervention to male preference, 3.42, and female preference, 3.85. Girls were more willing to express interest in "masculine" items and were less biased toward only "feminine" items. In this class, the teacher had organized the nonsexist intervention class activities to emphasize children's (rather than primarily adult's) involvement. The intervention was project-oriented, with children doing individualistic, goal-directed work as well as learning together cooperatively. Instead of lecturing, the teacher used class projects to direct students' attention to nonsexist issues. These served as a convenient topic for discussion and question. For example, why did Harry want to research dinosaurs while Lisa chose to classify flowers? Discussions of this type helped the children see that preferences for specific activities could easily overlap between boys and girls.

At fifth grade, following the intervention, girls were quicker than boys to reevaluate their attitudes when nonsexist materials were presented. Fifth grade girls' attitudes became less stereotyped in the occupational and socioemotional areas. The girls became considerably less stereotyped. In those classrooms where teachers actively and intensively engaged children in the nonsexist intervention materials, there were also scattered significant changes in boy's views. They too became less stereotyped.

Ninth Grade

PREINTERVENTION: Measures of the ninth grade provided a complex view of the attitudes of these early adolescents. The agreement between boys and girls which characterized fifth graders disappeared in the ninth grade. There were more instances of both definite stereotypy and definite nonstereotypy. Each sex tended to more strongly stereotype the opposite one; boys stereotyped females, girls stereotyped males. Leisure-time spending was stereotyped by both sexes for both the male and female stories.

Even a brief visit to a ninth grade classroom provides clear observations of the group dynamics, which are based on same-sex groups. In four of the six ninth grade classrooms observed for the study, teachers allowed some students to sit wherever they chose. Same-sex groups

clearly separated themselves physically from the opposite-sex group. Each group watched the other and com-
peted with each other. The girls often overtly flirted with
the boys, and the boys produced vignettes of bravery
(wise-guy remarks) in front of the teacher. These interactions received approval from the same-sex peer group.
The teacher also paid attention when the boys acted
aggressively and independently and the girls made socioemotional interpersonal overtures. Girls seemed to be
increasingly directed toward the expressive spheres.

Evidence for this increased admiration in girls of
socioemotional personality abilities came from five different measures in our study. On the adjective list data, the
ninth grade girls named many more interpersonal adjectives on the list which described females. These included
such adjectives as cheerful, friendly, shy, talkative, sexy,
and sociable. The Semantic Differential results show that
girls strongly supported socioemotional behaviors for girls
and believed it was important for the ideal girl to have
them. Although they believed that sensitivity was desirable for males, they did not think gentleness was as critical
for males as it is for females.

Both ninth grade boys and girls stressed stereotypically nurturant activities in stories about a typical day in
the life of an adult female. Girls were better able to
generate specific details about the routines in these stories
and ladened them with the facts of homemaking.

Both ninth grade boys and girls were more likely to
list jobs that were interpersonal in nature, like reception-
ist, waitress, and hairdresser, for females. If an occupation was considered feasible and acceptable for a female it
involved a prominent set of social skills and graces to
carry out the job, rather than problem-solving analytic
abilities. Even when occupational pictures were shown to
them the girls included more details from the socioemotional sphere in their stories of teachers and mechanics
than the boys did.

Nevertheless, ninth grade girls supported women in

occupations. The girls strongly valued occupational abilities as well as socioemotional skills. For example, on the female mechanic story, the girls showed less stereotyping on the affect score than the boys. Girls were sure about the woman's right to be a mechanic, while boys were concerned about how proper it was. The two stories below contrast the views of the ninth grade boys and girls about this picture.

From a ninth grade girl:

> This woman is working on a six-cylinder engine. She is skilled in her profession as a mechanic. She is what you call a liberated woman or Ms. for short. She has a family of two and has an equal partnership with her husband. They both split the duties of a man and woman. She is probably being discriminated upon.

From a ninth grade boy:

> She looks just like a man would fixing a car, but she doesn't look like a lady. She's fat and ugly and probably isn't married. She got to be a mechanic because no one else would let themselves get to the point where they would be as desperate as to take her, except in a dirty old garage. She will probably become a bum in the future.

In her story, the ninth grade girl shows a common pattern of legitimizing the woman's continuation of an occupation with a family. The heroine has both under control. The stereotyped perspective evident in the boy's interpretation presents the protagonist as incompetent at emotional tasks, and therefore forced into instrumental tasks. The ninth grade boys were able to handle an adult woman as either a homemaker, or, grudgingly, as an employed person, but they had difficulty combining the two roles.

Women in occupations are fairly well accepted by ninth graders. The teacher is described approvingly in her job. But children believed the female mechanic had a great many more obstacles than did the female teacher. The obstacles for the female teachers relate to the two themes: discipline in the classroom, and the decision about whether or not to give up the job to be a wife. Male teachers hardly ever had these problems. The basic issue for them was task-oriented—how to teach something to children who are mentally deficient, physically handicapped, or orphans.

On every measure males in occupations are consistently stereotyped as occupationally secure and satisfied by both boys and girls. Boys see themselves as having no problems, while girls are not as significantly optimistic about themselves. Girls acknowledge that women have social, internal, and societal problems. Girls, however, are quick to cast themselves in an occupational role. Ninth grade girls strongly believe that the typical woman can and should be in a job situation, as long as she also upholds her socioemotional responsibilities. Even more importantly, the girls describe a typical day in their own future as one which entails a job. The boys, on the other hand, do not depict the typical woman with a job. This is a crucial sex difference.

Ninth grade students seem especially concerned about their personality characteristics within the social context. Boys and girls share the perception of themselves as friendly, sensitive, and adventurous. Boys are especially concerned about two additional qualities: being strong and never crying. Of particular interest is their report of their own physical beauty or ugliness. Boys, as anticipated, claimed that they were above average (3.5) in their appearance. Girls assigned themselves a position (2.6) much closer to the direction of ugliness. This could be interpreted as an intensification of the negative self-image apparent at the fifth grade level. Attractiveness to girls in the ninth grade seems to be an exceptionally important attribute. They apparently believe that their social desirability hangs crucially on the dating game with its emphasis on clothing, cosmetics, and appearance. Girls Should Be scores reflect the desire to be beautiful

(4.4, very strong), and scores on that measure contrast sharply with the way many ninth grade girls believe most girls are (above average, 3.5), but most dramatically with the way girls see themselves (less than average, 2.6).

In summary, the ninth grade girls, in their stories about women, attempt to integrate both occupational roles and socioemotional abilities. Girls positively value both aspects of life. Boys cannot integrate the two roles for women and think of women either with jobs or in the home. Males are stereotyped by everyone, although there is some tolerance (especially by the girls) of nurturant qualities in males. Leisure and routine activities (family roles) are stereotyped by boys and girls for both men and women. Could a nonsexist intervention change these generalizations?

POSTINTERVENTION: The ninth graders were the most sensitive to the implications of the intervention. When positive changes in attitude occurred, they occurred among the girls. There were especially powerful changes following the intervention in one classroom in town A, which had the most active and enthusiastic teacher in the study. In general, the ninth grade boys showed stronger sex stereotyping about both occupational and personality roles following the intervention.

The task of listing jobs illustrated the ninth graders' lack of change. The boys did not change significantly on any item, although there was a trend toward more stereotyping of all occupational variables. Following the intervention, ninth grade boys showed a decrease in the number of jobs they thought of, an increase in the stereotyping of both male and female jobs, a slight increase in the proportion of high-status jobs for males, and an increase in the proportion of interpersonal jobs for females—all changes toward more stereotyping. The boys' overlap score for jobs which both men and women could hold decreased. These consistent variations by the boys showed an increased enhancement of the male's occupational situation and a depreciation of the female's job roles. Following the intervention, girls continued to maintain one significant occupational difference: they depicted women in more interpersonal jobs than men. However, the ninth grade girls, following the intervention, decreased their stereotyping of the type of and success in jobs for men and women.

Ninth graders were initially aware of the political issues of equality of opportunity and discrimination by sex, race, or age. They would seldom intimate that a woman could not have a job. Yet ninth graders, before the intervention, showed concern about subtle aspects of the desirability of a job in terms of how it related to issues of masculinity or femininity. For instance, how comfortable, they wondered, would a male feel in an untraditional job like airline steward? How possible is it for a woman to carry on a job as lab technician and also be a respectable homemaker? These socioemotional issues were more crucial to the ninth grader's inquiry about occupations than they were for the younger children.

Following the intervention, ninth grade boys and girls changed in opposite directions on the adjective list measure, which required them to describe socioemotional characteristics of men and women. Girls showed greater flexibility and expanded their ideas. Boys more rigidly enforced stereotyped limitations. After the intervention, boys decreased the number of adjectives which overlapped for men and women. They reemphasized stereotyped interpersonal roles for women, while deemphasizing even more any interpersonal role requirements for men.

The comparisons between ninth graders' ideas of what real boys and girls were like, and what ideal boys and girls should be like, following the intervention, showed similar trends. Ninth grade boys exhibited little change following the intervention. Girls, however, reduced the intensity of the "feminine" stereotype on what ideal girls should be like, following the intervention.

The ninth grade girls, who were convinced about the predominance of good-looking boys before the intervention, altered that view to a more realistic idea that boys were average in looks.

Although ninth grade boys did exhibit some nonpatterned changes in the direction of nonstereotyped concepts, they generally held on more firmly to many stereotypes. Perhaps the boys were more hesitant about supporting the equalization of roles because thcy currently felt in a position of power and may have believed they had more to lose in prestige and occupational advantages. Spending more time in family and socioemotional situations was not seen as an increase in role status for men, which is normally measured in terms of monetary or title advance. For the girls, however, an involvement in occupation and work outside the home enhanced their sense of worth in the society. Girls believed the woman in a career/marriage situation has the opportunity to maximize both the desires to be competent and to be nurturant. Generally, the ninth grade boys did not see analogous role advantages for men. Yet, all of the above generalizations about ninth graders must be qualified when we turn to classroom differences in the effects of the intervention. Situational effects related to the teacher's enthusiasm and use of the curriculum materials can be quite powerful in greatly modifying and making more flexible even the ninth grade boys' stereotyped views. The attitudes are not at all immutable, given strong situational influences.

Observational data from ninth grade classrooms clearly showed the power of peer-group pressures in the shaping of same-sex concepts and behaviors. The ninth graders banded together to decide, in the context of their peer group, whether the tasks were bothersome, and/or whether they need cooperate. Boys' peer groups devalued the intervention in some classrooms, and sometimes the girls' peer groups appeared to have taken up the tone of the boys' groups.

These results suggest that, following the intervention, there was a greater equalization of the relative social power of both sexes, especially in the eyes of ninth grade girls. They no longer felt so concerned about whether they would "make it" solely in terms of their physical attractiveness. The intervention apparently made them feel there were alternative routes to acceptability, and therefore the social power of the boys (expressed through beliefs about their greater attractiveness) was not as ominous. They were also less willing to excuse boys for sloppiness, etc., and less afraid to accept the good, human qualities (e.g., sensitiveness) from them that they believed *all* people should possess.

The ninth graders responded to the intervention in ways which were very different, depending on the characteristics of the different ninth grade classrooms. It was clear that there was a strong interaction between the social structural character of the classroom, the teacher's role, and the effects of peer groups in each classroom. In some ninth grade classrooms, for example, boys and girls engaged in easy dialogue about the various role positions of men and women. The key variable was the teacher, and the way he/she handled the classroom interactions. Attitudes of the ninth graders, both boys and girls, could be challenged and expanded if the teacher dealt with the subtle socioemotional aspects of stereotypes during the intervention. The observational results showed that effective nonsexist intervention depended not only on the curricular materials, but also on the conviction and skill with which the teacher implemented the nonsexist work.

EIGHT

Conclusions and Implications

The Nature of Sex-Role Stereotypy

Sex-role stereotyping exists across all ages. Our data show consistent trends across age which must be understood in order to design effective strategies to overcome sex-role stereotyping in schools. Teachers need to be aware of these age-specific content differences as they attempt to combat sex-role stereotypy within the classroom.

Children in all grades had a strong tendency to occupationally stereotype males. Generally, the occupational stories they told about males showed them as competent, happy with their tasks, and receiving good benefits from their jobs. Girls particularly emphasized stereotypical aspects of men's jobs. At the fifth grade, boys and girls had few definite convictions about women in occupations. Their scores clustered about the neutral categories which indicated neither approval nor dismay. The ninth grade girls fervently supported women in occupations. Boys were less enthusiastic. The overlap scores, which show jobs that *both* men and women could hold, illustrate these differences between grades

As expected, kindergartners originally had the lowest proportion of overlap since they tend to see things in an "all or none" manner. At first, they believed that a job was either for a woman or for a man. Following exposure to the intervention curriculum which showed males and females in multiple roles, both occupational and familial, the kindergarten children increased their overlap scores for jobs.

Fifth grade children began with a medium amount of overlap, and the intervention did not greatly change their opinions. The ninth graders, well aware of the issues of equality and discrimination, scored the highest in amount of overlap. Both fifth and ninth grade boys, however, lost some of their open-mindedness after the intervention.

Children in the study generally told happy, uncomplicated stories. Their characters were not overwhelmed with grief or trouble, unless it was for a humorous outcome. This lack of obstacles on projective materials was particularly noticeable in the fifth and ninth grade boys. If anyone was concerned about obstacles, it was the girls. They mentioned obstacles more often in stories about women. The obstacles they mentioned included fear, family disapproval, unpopularity, and outright societal prohibitions.

Ideas about how people spend their leisure time reflected stereotyping across all grades for both boys and girls. Although the children supported equal opportunity in occupations, they seldom used the same principle for family roles and personal activities. Occupations were treated in a deliberately nonsexist manner, but daily, home, and family routines were very stereotyped. Men and women were assigned highly stereotyped hobbies and daily routines. Women baked cakes for dinner; men read the newspaper. Scores on the activities preference measure reflect this stereotyping at both the fifth and ninth grade level. Every class in the program showed significant differences between their initial "masculine" and "feminine" activities. There was little androgynous liking of both types of activity at the same time.

Socioemotional aspects of the sex-role stereotypes showed considerable stereotyping of females before the intervention for both the fifth and ninth grade boys and girls. Girls, especially when speaking about themselves, gave socioemotional abilities and qualities a high priority. Yet, boys endowed the "typical women" with many more of the common stereotypes than girls did. When socio-emotional and occupational roles were in conflict, fifth graders did not show noticeable convictions about either extreme.

Ninth graders, however, gave both nonstereotypical responses and consistently stereotypical responses. They tolerated interpersonal and nurturant concerns in the occupational males, but these issues were emphasized for the females. Ninth grade girls described women as capable, pleased with the job they were doing, and generally single. The ninth grade girls described women who attempted to integrate occupational competency and socioemotional values. In contrast, fifth graders within one story might make internally contradictory statements, e.g., the hard-working female mechanic who wanted and needed to go home in the afternoon to pick up her children after school. Fifth graders seldom resolved the family versus occupation conflict in favor of either option.

A clear finding across age was that children were much less apt to stereotype themselves than they were to stereotype others of either the same or opposite sex. Boys' and girls' scores were extremely similar on the Semantic Differential measure when they reported their own personality characteristics. Children of both sexes, however, described themselves as having characteristics near the neutral score or slightly in the "masculine" direction. Children did not identify themselves with the same sex stereotypes. When they described jobs or personal qualities for themselves, they blended the two types of personality characteristics together and chose socially desirable feminine characteristics in balance with socially desirable masculine characteristics. This androgynous attitude for themselves did not, however, extend into family roles and leisure-time activities, or even into subtle aspects of occupational roles.

Children were also generally less stereotypical about

same-sex peers and adult roles than they were about
opposite-sex peers and roles. Girls stereotyped boys and
men, while boys stereotyped girls and women. These
trends were revealed in both the projective and objective
measures, and children's views of both future and current
adult roles. Consistent with research on prejudice and
stereotyping of any "out" group, the less familiar one is
with another group, the more easily that group is
described in stereotypical and biased fashion. This suggests that increased interaction between boys and girls is
one effective means of erasing the limitations that each
sex imposes on the other. Equal-status contact in the
classroom between children of both sexes is a necessity
for a diminution in stereotyping to occur.

Cross-sex stereotyping showed differential patterns
by sex and age when children gave their prescriptions for
ideal boys and girls. By the fifth grade, boys were more
stereotyped than girls about the ideal qualities of both
boys and girls. The fifth grade girls showed a greater
preference for the female stereotypes when asked about
the ideal girl than did the ninth grade girls. Boys at fifth
grade showed a strong trend to have both "real" and
"ideal" girls conform to the feminine affective stereotype.
This contrasted with the ninth grade boys, who were less
likely to stereotype Most Girls, but emphatically maintained feminine values in the Girls Should Be measure.

As we examined the nature and degree of stereotyping for adult roles, it became clear that although children
have different attitudes about women's roles which are
related to their age and sex, *all* children are certain about
the male role. In the projective material the men were
always placed in an occupational context, and described
as problem-free and generally successful. In all children
but those with strong nonsexist tendencies, men's leisure
time was strictly limited to golf, newspaper reading, and
other sports activities. This suggested that the male's role
in our society is much more tightly defined in terms of
economic success than the female's. In any effort to deal

with sex-role stereotyping, special attention should be given to explain the benefits for men which come from androgynous attitudes and roles.

Changing Stereotypical Attitudes

Our study showed that changing the content of children's sex-role concepts was not an easily accomplished task for the teacher. Children maintain strong convictions, sometimes overt but often subtle, about the appropriateness of certain activities, attitudes, or traits for the sexes. These deeply socialized stereotypes were difficult to neutralize. However the measures showed a number of attitudinal changes in children following the nonsexist intervention project. The items that showed significant postintervention changes and trends toward change across ages, and the changes which occurred at every grade level, were discussed in the preceding chapter.

It was clear that girls of all ages were more open to the adoption of nonsexist perspectives on roles for men and women. At every grade level the girls showed more attitude shifts and changed more strongly than their male counterparts. Girls were particularly ready to revise their concepts about options for women, both in familial and occupational capacities. Many of our test measures provided consistent evidence that boys were more eager than girls to maintain and enforce sex-role stereotypes. It was not surprising that males, who in our society generally hold more powerful positions, were more stereotyped about women. Higher-status groups, e.g., whites vis-à-vis minorities, tend to maintain more rigidly stereotyped views of lower-status groups. Since sex-role status has in the past been defined by typically masculine values, an expansion of sex roles (i.e., women in jobs, more men at home) may, to the males, appear to lead to a loss of status and power for them. Males may be less eager for androgynous societal roles, since they may lead to upward mobility for women and what may appear to be losses for men. For this reason, it is important, in the introduction of nonsexist educational materials, to emphasize the advantages to boys of androgynous role possibilities for both sexes.

Our data clearly indicate that the most powerful predictors of attitudinal change in students were the enthusiasm and convictions of the individual teacher. Teachers who were concerned about the limiting aspects of sex-role stereotypy, and reevaluations of sex-role stereotypes, were most successful in facilitating change. For instance, the classroom at the ninth grade level which showed the strongest shifts toward nonstereotyped attitudes on many issues for both boys and girls had the teacher who was independently ranked as most enthusiastic and consistent in her use of curriculum materials. This teacher was able to create new perspectives on roles for men and women, even among ninth grade boys.

Among the classrooms that were studied, there was a wide range of teaching and administrating styles. At the ninth grade level, for example, classes ranged from highly traditional (seats riveted in rows and students raising hands) to very open (pillows as informal seats and students talking spontaneously). In the traditional classrooms the most powerful and direct mediator of values was the teacher, particularly during the frequent and extended lecture times and during question and answer sessions. In open classrooms, the teacher indirectly attempted to channel discussion while permitting the students themselves to maintain the impetus, content, and direction of the exchanges. Peer-group status and popularity structures were clearly evident as students themselves initiated the decision making, evaluating, and general discussion in the open classrooms.

The different styles and atmospheres of the classrooms were supported by the formal observations. The preintervention classroom observations showed that boys initiated and responded more than girls. The Flanders observational analysis of classroom interactions after the intervention showed few overall behavioral changes on the part of students and teachers when the type of class-room was not taken into account. When, however, classes were divided into the traditional and open classroom types, teachers in traditional classrooms after the intervention had increased the number of questions they addressed to girls. Girls in these classrooms began to answer more questions because teachers provided them with more opportunities to respond. Yet, their initiation score did not change.

The opposite was true in the open classrooms. Teachers in open classrooms encourage the girls to initiate discussions of their own ideas more often. Posttest observations of open classrooms indicated a trend for girls to increase their spontaneous initiations during class, although they did not respond more frequently to questions. Teachers thus adopted a nonsexist mode of interaction in keeping with the classroom structure. Even more important, the girls responded by increasing the level of their contributions to the dominant mode of teacher-pupil interactions which characterized the classroom type.

Other variables were not predictive of stereotyping. Social class long has been suggested as a major predictor of the content of sex-role concepts. The three school systems which were studied were selected to include a range of different socioeconomic and ethnic groups. No differences in sex-role stereotyping were found in children from different socioeconomic or ethnic backgrounds. Individual classrooms in each school system accounted for more of the differences in sex-role stereotyping. These findings indicate that stereotypy is not a by-product of family patterns associated with particular educational and occupational positions. The results support a view that sex-role stereotypes are introduced and promulgated by the media and other institutions that cross social class. Mass media, peers, and schools are apparently more powerful in their influence on sex-role stereotypes than are families.

What about the presence of a working mother? Does

having a working mother influence sex-role stereotypes? Are children with working mothers more amenable to nonstereotypical occupational roles? The data on maternal employment in this study indicated that maternal employment did not significantly differentiate between the stereotyped and nonstereotyped children. Children with working mothers did not absorb the idea that occupations are valuable for women. In fact, there were slight indications that, at least for some boys, the opposite occurred. In the postintervention testing, a group of boys with working mothers developed more occupational stereotyping than their male counterparts with nonemployed mothers. It appeared that once these boys became aware of their peer-group's suspicion of changing occupational sex roles, boys with working mothers questioned even more strongly the appropriateness of women in nontraditional occupations.

In summary, such global factors as socioeconomic and ethnic background, maternal employment, and school system characteristics accounted for less of the pre- and postintervention differences in sex-role stereotyping than teacher enthusiasm and dynamic interactions in each classroom.

What These Findings Mean

This intervention into the sex-role stereotypes of children permits a new view of a change-oriented theory of sex-role learning. Sex-role stereotyping is not determined by biological drives or organ inferiorities. Nor is it a by-product of cognitive development. Sex-role stereotypes are not built into the process of establishing gender identity. An understanding of why or how a child stereotypes sex roles cannot be achieved by tracking down each and every reinforcing contingency in the child's environment. Sex-role stereotyping is the result of the dynamic socio-psychological situation of the child, who is surrounded by mediating forces of culture like schools, peers, and mass media. Stereotyping is self-perpetuating; it is not a developmental given nor is it the product of family influences or the socioeconomic status of the child. Because sex-role stereotyping is culturally induced, we can be optimistic about the possibility of changing and influencing it.

Data from this study do not support a cognitive-developmental view of sex-role concepts. From a cognitive-developmental perspective, sex-role attitudes and values are formed and reorganized as correlates of an invariant sequence of cognitive stages. This approach sees the locus of sex-role socialization as primarily internal, progressing toward a societally shared singular concept of appropriate sex roles. In Kohlberg's (1966) view, gender identity occurs very early, as a cognitive realization. The young child observes bodily differences between mother, father, friends, and self, and categorizes him- or herself as a male among males or a female among females. The child then wants to do sex-appropriate activities and so identifies with the same-sex parent to gather information about the sex-specific role details. This view suggests that children value the male role more highly because they see that men are bigger, stronger, and more prestigeful, and control more resources than women.

Our kindergarten data do not support this differential valuation of males and females by the child. Kindergarten children do not endow males with jobs which could be considered high status in terms of income, advancement, authority, control over wealth, mobility, or public fame. Rather, kindergarten girls before the intervention, and postintervention kindergarten boys, included significantly more high-status jobs for females than for males. These children did not automatically see the male role as superior in societal terms. Other kindergartners' responses to questions about real and ideal men and women suggested that children also did not immediately place a higher value on the male role and all its stereotypes. Rather, children were aware of the social and group evaluation of desirable characteristics, and chose to incorporate the characteristics that are generally valued, regardless of sex of the model. Both kindergarten boys and girls described themselves as slightly on the feminine side of a number of personal characteristics, indicating they valued such qualities as obedience, quietness, and neatness. On concrete variables like strength and beauty, *both* boys and girls emphasized an image of themselves as strong and good-looking. Kindergarten girls, for example, believed that they were quite "strong." Although the children stereotyped Most Girls (especially the boys) and Most Boys (especially the girls), they valued the desirable characteristics of both role stereotypes for themselves.

Cognitive developmentalists hold that children's cognitions of social and sex roles are best predicted by, and are correlated with, their stage of cognitive development. These invariant, sequential stages of cognitive restructuring prescribe what the child will believe about social roles. Children in the study were selected to represent three distinctive cognitive-developmental stages—preoperational (five-year-olds), operational (ten-year-olds), and formal-operational (fourteen-year-olds). At each age level, curriculum materials and the emphases and style of the intervention were chosen to be appropriate to the cognitive stage of the children.

Nevertheless, both the pre- and postintervention data on the children's sex-role concepts clearly showed that the stage of cognitive development had little predictive power.

Although we expected the ten-year-olds to be more conformist and to justify the established sex-role divisions, they were instead troubled about the justice of sex-role differences. The fifth graders clearly attempted to face and consider issues of justice and equality as they viewed sex-role differences in society. Frequently they were concerned about fairness for both sexes in employment, opportunities, and more subtle indices of sexism. They were nonconformist and unstereotyped about overt roles of power and passivity for both men and women in the workaday world. Stereotyping, when it did occur, appeared in their attitudes toward such unquestioned activities as spending of leisure time and daily routines.

Although the ninth graders were cognitively at a formal-operational level, the nature and content of their sex-role stereotyping was best explained by the social influences around them. We anticipated that the fourteen-year-olds would be able to handle abstract perspectives about many aspects of sex roles. Yet, they were not at all concerned with justice, equality, or even fairness in the arena of sex roles. They rigidly maintained that occupations were available to everyone, so long as women continued to provide the emotional and social support system for the family and men were the economic base of the family. After the intervention, the ninth grade boys moved even further toward stereotyping of sex roles. This movement was not a result of shifts in cognitive decisions about sex roles, but rather a response to increased conformity pressures from peers in the classroom. Their stereotyping was not rooted in the cognitive organization which they imposed on the world they see. Rather, it was a direct product of their external sociopsychological situation.

Summary

Results from this study indicated that an intervention program can be geared successfully to any age. The source of sex-role stereotypy lies in the general external contingencies exerted upon the child, through cultural expectations, peer groups, the dynamics of classroom achievement, the local social status systems, and media-induced sex-role stereotypes. Stereotypy is not a result of gender identity perceived and transmitted through a series of innate cognitive stages. Such a view tends to see stereotyping as a result of internal, unchangeable aspects of the child's development. This relatively pessimistic view of sex-role stereotyping was not supported by the findings of this study.

The findings, instead, support a sociopsychological view which emphasizes the environmental influences on the child through schools, peer groups, and the culture (e.g., TV). Sex-role stereotyping cannot be predicted from a detailed study of socializing agents in the primary group (e.g., time fathers spend with girls, mother's style of feeding babies, etc.) The data from this study indicate that stereotyping crosses socioeconomic lines. Maternal employment does not decrease children's sex-role stereotypy. Evidently, the particulars of a child's home situation do not accurately predict either the level or content of sex-role stereotyping. Children in upper-class homes with professional mothers can be as stereotyped in attitudes as lower-middle-class children with mothers at home. Rather, cultural attitudes, mediated by organized institutions such as schools, sex-role connected fads, sports activities, teaching and testing materials, social dating hierarchies, the legal system, employment outlooks, etc., define how the child will think about sex roles.

The findings of this intervention study point instead to the essential malleability of sex-role concepts, and the extent to which even brief attempts to expand them away from narrow cultural stereotypes can yield fruitful results for children of all ages.

This is an optimistic outcome because change is so possible. We can intervene by changing those group situations, e.g., classrooms, which provide the content of sex-role stereotypes. At any age, interventions can be successful. An intervention can work even if a child has grown up in a stereotypical setting. The critical factor is that the intervention be thorough, well-rounded, and intense. The enthusiasm and commitment of the teacher is the key variable. Apparently a small dose of new ideas about sex roles may produce an unfavorable reaction, as illustrated by some of the ninth grade boys. In early adolescence, a little intervention (for boys) may be worse than nothing, but a powerful intervention can have strong and positive effects.

Although gender identity may be early and irreversible, the content of sex roles and the child's definitions of masculinity and femininity are derived from external feed-back. In our society, the policies and systems which encourage sex-role differentiation are open to change. School interventions on children's sex-role attitudes can be used to point up the new possibilities and opportunities for crossing sex-stereotypical lines, and expanding job and human opportunities, at any age level.

References

Beaven, Mary. Responses of adolescents to feminine characters in literature. *Research in the Teaching of English,* Spring 1972, 48–68.

Bem, S. The measurement of psychological androgyny. *Journal of Consulting and Clinical Psychology,* 1974, *42,* 155–162.

Bem, S. Sex-role adaptability: one consequence of psychological androgyny. *Journal of Personality and Social Psychology,* 1975, in press.

Bem, S. L., and Bem, D. J. Case study of a nonconscious ideology: training the woman to know her place. In Bem, D. J. (Ed.). *Beliefs, attitudes, and human affairs.* Belmont, Calif.: Brooks/Cole, 1970.

Bement, S. Growing up male and female in America. In Johnson, L. O. (Ed.). *Nonsexist curricular materials for elementary schools.* Old Westbury, N.Y.: Feminist Press, 1974.

Bement, S., and Christian, B. Susan B. Anthony Day Kit. In Johnson, L. O. (Ed.). *Nonsexist curricular materials for elementary schools.* Old Westbury, N.Y.: Feminist Press, 1974.

Brandt, R. M. The accuracy of self-estimate: a measure of self-concept. *Genetic Psychology Monographs,* 1958, *58,* 55.

Brophy, J., and Good, T. Feminization of American elementary schools. *Phi Delta Kappan,* 1973, *54,* 564–566.

Broverman, D., et al. Sex-role stereotypes and clinical judgments of mental health. *Journal of Consulting and Clinical Psychology,* 1970, *34,* 1–7.

Broverman, D. et al. Sex-role stereotypes: a current appraisal. Unpublished manuscript, 1972.

Cherry, L. Pre-school teacher-child dyad: sex differences in verbal interaction. *Child Development,* 1975, *46,* 532–537.

Colloquy. November 1973, *6,* no 9: Poster pull-out, 22–23; Fact bombardment, 30–31.

Crandall, V. Sex differences in expectancy of intellectual and academic reinforcement. In Smith, C. P. *Achievement related motives in children*. New York: Russell Sage Foundation, 1969.

Donovan, V. Elementary schools teachers' sex-role attitudes and classroom behavior towards girls and boys. Unpublished manuscript, June, 1973.

D'Uren, M. The image of women in textbooks. In Gornick, V., and Moran, B. (Eds.). *Women in sexist society*. New York: Basic Books, 1971.

Eisner, E. Instructional and expressive educational objectives: their formulation and use in curriculum. In Popham, W. J., Eisner, E. W., Sullivan, H. J., and Tyler, L. L. (Eds.). *Instructional objectives*. AERA Monograph Series on Curriculum Evaluation. Chicago: Rand McNally, 1969.

Fagot, B., and Patterson, G. R. Analysis of reinforcing contingencies in sex-role behaviors in the pre-school child. *Developmental Psychology*, 1969, *1*, 563–568.

Felsenthal, H. Sex differences in teacher-pupil interaction in first grade reading instruction. Unpublished paper presented at American Educational Research Associates, Minneapolis, Minn., 1970.

Feminist Resources for Equal Education. P.O. Box 185, Saxonville Station, Framingham, Mass.

Feminists on Children's Media. *Little Miss Muffet fights back*. P.O. Box 4315, Grand Central Station, New York, N.Y.

Flanders, N. Interaction analysis in the classroom: a manual for observers. In Simon, A., and Boyer, E. G. *Mirrors for behavior, Vol. II*. Philadelphia: Research for Better Schools, 1967.

Fling, S., and Manosevitz, M. Sex typing in nursery school children's play interests. *Developmental Psychology*, 1972, *7*, 146–152.

Froschl, M. It's never too early: sex-role stereotyping in the pre-school years. *Colloquy*, 1973, *6*, 9.

Giller, P. *Books for liberating young readers*. Unpublished mineograph.

Good, T., Sikes, J. N., and Brophy, J. Effect of teacher sex and student sex on classroom interaction. *Journal of Educational Psychology*, 1973, *65*, 74–87.

Griffith, M. The class meeting. In Johnson, L. O. (Ed.). *Nonsexist curricular materials for elementary schools*. Old Westbury, N.Y.: Feminist Press, 1974.

Hoffman, A., and Hull, L. *Baby X*. Unpublished play adapted from Gould, L. X: a fabulous child. *Ms. Magazine*, December 1972.

Horner, M. Fail: bright women. *Psychology Today*, November 1969, *3*, 36–38.

Howe, F. Sex-role stereotypes start early. *Saturday Review*, October 1971, *16*, 78–82, 92–94.

Iglitzin, L. B. A child's eye view of sex roles. *Today's Education*, 1972.

Jackson, P. W. *Life in classrooms*. New York: Holt, 1968.

Jackson, P. W., and Getzels, J. W. Psychological health and classroom functioning: a study of dissatisfaction among adolescents. *Journal of Education Psychology*, 1959, *59*, 295–300.

Jackson, P. W., and Lahaderne, H. M. Inequalities of teacher-pupil contacts. *Psychology in the Schools*, 1967, *4*, 204–211.

Johnson, L. O. (Ed.). *Nonsexist curricular materials for elementary schools*. Old Westbury, N.Y.: Feminist Press, 1974.

Kagan, J. On the meaning of behavior: illustrations from the infant. *Child Development*, 1969, *40*, 1121–1134.

Karkau, K. Sexism in the fourth grade. *Know, Inc.*, August 1973, P.O. Box 86031, Pittsburgh, Pa.

Key, Mary R. The role of male and female in children's books—dispelling all doubt. *Wilson Library Bulletin*, October 1971, 167–176.

Kohlberg, L. A cognitive developmental analysis of children's sex-role concepts and attitudes. In Maccoby, E. (Ed.). *The Development of sex differences*. Palo Alto, Calif.: Stanford University Press, 1966.

Lansky, L. M. The family structure also affects the model: sex-role attitudes in parents of pre-school children. *Merrill-Palmer Quarterly*, 1967, *13*, 139–150.

Levitan, T. E., and Chananie, J. D. Responses of female primary teachers to sex-typed behavior in male and female children. *Child Development*, 1972, *43*, 1309–1316.

Maccoby, E. E. *The development of sex differences.* Palo Alto, Calif.: Stanford University Press, 1966.

Maccoby, E., and Jacklin, C. N. *The Psychology of sex differences.* Palo Alto, Calif.: Stanford University Press, 1974.

Martin, R. Student sex and behavior as determinants of the type and frequency of teacher-student contacts. *Journal of Social Psychology,* 1972, *10,* 339–344.

Meyer, W., and Thompson, G. Sex differences in the distribution of teacher approval and disapproval among sixth grade children. *Journal of Educational Psychology,* 1956, *47,* 385–396.

Mueller, E., and Cooper, B. The effect of preschool teacher's sex on children's cognitive growth and sexual identity. Final report to U.S. Department of Health, Education, and Welfare, Office of Education, August 1972.

Nilsen, A. P. Women in children's literature. *College English,* May 1971.

Ricks, F., and Pyke, S. Teacher perceptions and attitudes that foster or maintain sex-role differences. *Interchange,* 1973, *4,* 26–33.

Romney, Lenore. Men, women and politics. *Look Magazine,* April 6, 1971.

Rossi, A. S. Equality between the sexes: an immodest proposal. *Daedalus,* 1964, *93,* 607–652.

Serbin, L., O'Leary, K. D., Kent, R., and Tonick, I. A comparison of teacher response to the preacademic and problem behavior of boys and girls. *Child Development,* 1973, *44,* 796–804.

Sexism in education. Minneapolis, Minn.: Emma Willard Task Force on Education, 1973.

Shinedling, M., and Pederson, D. Effects of sex on teacher and student on children's gain in quantitative and verbal performance. *Journal of Psychology,* September 1970, *76,* 79–85.

Silvers, Patricia. Course materials for "Women in Society," Social Studies Department, Brookline High School, Brookline, Mass.

Spence, J., Helmreich, R., and Stapp, J. The personal attributes questionnaire: a measure of sex-role stereotypes and masculinity and femininity. *Journal of Personality and Social Psychology,* July 1975, *32,* 29–39.

Stein, A. The effect of sex-role standards for achievement and sex-role preference on three determinants of achievement motivation. *Developmental Psychology,* 1971, *4,* 219–231.

Stein, A. H. Sex role preference questionnaire. Mimeographed paper, Pennsylvania State University, 1973.

Stein, A. H., Pohly, S. R., and Muller, E. Sex typing of achievement areas as a determinant of children's efforts and achievement. Paper presented at Sex-Res Child Development, Santa Monica, Calif. March 1969.

Stein, A. H., and Smithells, J. Age and sex difference in children's sex-role standards about achievement. *Developmental Psychology,* 1969, *1,* 252.

Torrence, E. P. Changing reactions of preadolescent girls to tasks requiring creative scientific thinking. *Journal of Genetic Psychology,* 1963, *102,* 217–223.

Appendix: Protocol of Measures

DATA SHEET

5 and 9

SUBJECT I.D.   #_____

SEX OF CHILD   _____

TIME BEGUN   _____

TIME ENDED   _____

ASK CHILD:

1) NAME _____

2) AGE _____

3) WHO LIVES AT HOME?_____

_____

4) PARENTS' OCCUPATIONS _____

5) WERE YOUR GRANDPARENTS BORN IN THIS

COUNTRY?_____

IF NOT, DO YOU KNOW WHERE?_____

5 and 9
SUBJECT I.D. # _____

6) WERE YOUR PARENTS BORN IN THIS COUNTRY?___

IF NOT, DO YOU KNOW WHERE? _____

RECORD:

1. DATE   _____   4. SCHOOL   _____

2. TESTER   _____   5. GRADE   _____

3. TOWN   _____   6. TEACHER   _____

COMMENTS:

GENERAL INSTRUCTIONS

1. 10- and 15-year-olds should mark check list for themselves in the adjective check test. All other responses should be given orally, including the words for the opposite sex story test. You should write down these words on the lists.

2. Before giving the tests, talk to the child about what he likes best at school, his hobbies, etc., so that you and he feel comfortable talking to each other.

3. Tell the child about the tests. Tell him that these are not like tests in school, and that you just want to find out

5 and 9

SUBJECT I.D. # _____

some of his opinions. Tell him that there is a wide range of possible answers, that different kids give different answers, that there are no right answers and no wrong answers.

Assure the child that you just want him to say what he thinks.

PICTURE TEST

A. MALE PICTURES—MECHANIC OR TEACHER
THERE ARE 4 PICTURES—SHOW BOTH MECHANICS FIRST, THEN BOTH TEACHERS

- I'm going to show you a picture and I want you to tell me a story.

- This is a picture of a man at his job.

- Tell a story with a beginning, a middle and an end.

- Include what the person is doing, feeling, and thinking.

IF THE CHILD HAS TROUBLE MAKING UP A STORY:

1. Try to give him a clue
   a. Example—if he said that it's a mechanic, tell him to make up a story about a lady mechanic,
   b. try giving her a name and ask him to make up a story again.
2. If all else fails, ask the following separately:
   a. What is happening in the picture?
   b. What events led up to it?
   c. What will happen to the person in the picture?
   d. What is this person thinking and feeling?

5 and 9
SUBJECT I.D. # _____

PICTURE TEST

B. FEMALE PICTURES—MECHANIC OR TEACHER
THERE ARE 4 PICTURES—SHOW BOTH MECHAN-
ICS FIRST, THEN BOTH TEACHERS

- I'm going to show you a picture and I want you to tell me a story.

- This is a picture of a woman at her job.

- Tell a story with a beginning, a middle, and an end.

- Include what the person is doing, feeling, and thinking.

IF THE CHILD HAS TROUBLE MAKING UP A STORY:
1. Try to give him a clue
    a. Example—if he said that it's a mechanic, tell him to make up a story about a lady mechanic.
    b. Try giving her a name and ask him to make up a story again.
2. If all else fails, ask the following separately:
    a. What is happening in the picture?
    b. What events led up to it?
    c. What will happen to the person in the picture?
    d. What is this person thinking and feeling?

OPPOSITE SEX STORY TEST

A. WORD LISTS
  1. Jobs

- Now I want you to tell me what kinds of things a woman can do and what kinds of things a man can do.

- For example, what kinds of jobs can a woman have and what kinds of jobs can a man have?

---

5 and 9
SUBJECT I.D. #_____

OPPOSITE SEX STORY TEST

GIVE THE CHILD A PIECE OF PAPER—WRITE
DOWN THE WORDS THAT THE CHILD WRITES
DOWN HERE AS WELL

WOMEN   *MEN*

2. Descriptions

● Now I want you to tell me some other words.
  What words do you think describe most men and what
  words describe most women?

● This time tell me words which describe the men and
  women themselves.

● For example, tell me some words which describe the
  personalities of most women.

GIVE THE CHILD A PIECE OF PAPER—WRITE
DOWN THE WORDS THAT THE CHILD WRITES
DOWN HERE AS WELL
THE REST OF THIS TEST DEALS WITH THESE
WORDS.

WOMEN   *MEN*

B. MAN'S STORY (USING WOMAN'S LIST WORDS)

● Now let's play a game with these words.
  I want you to tell me a story about a man using (the
  woman's) this list of words

5 and 9
SUBJECT I.D. #_____

OPPOSITE SEX STORY TEST

- Use the words to describe the man in your story.

C. WOMAN'S STORY (USING MAN'S LIST WORDS)

- Now let's play a game with these words.
  I want you to tell me a story about a woman using this
  (the man's) list of words.

- Use the words to describe the woman in your story.

TYPICAL DAY TEST

A. SELF

- Tell me what you think a typical day in your life will be
  like when you grow up, when you are a man/woman.

- By typical day, I mean a typical weekday.

Add:

- Is this what you think it really will be like or is this what
  you want it to be like?

  IF IT IS WHAT HE WANTS IT TO BE LIKE, ASK
  "WHAT DO YOU THINK IT WILL REALLY BE
  LIKE?"

GENERAL PROBES:

- WOULD YOU (BARBARA, HAROLD) EVER
  DECIDE TO DO THE OPPOSITE?
  (I.e., would you/he/she ever decide to stay away from
  home all day or get a job instead of caring for the
  children?)

  WHAT WOULD HAPPEN?

5 and 9

SUBJECT I.D. #_____

TYPICAL DAY TEST

HOW WOULD YOUR/HIS/HER HUSBAND/WIFE FEEL (REACT)?

HOW WOULD YOUR/HIS/HER CHILDREN FEEL (REACT)?

WHAT WOULD YOUR/HIS/HER FRIENDS THINK?

- WHAT WOULD HAPPEN IF YOU (BARBARA. HAROLD) DID NOT WANT TO DO WHAT YOU/ SHE/HE NORMALLY WOULD DO?
(I.e., what if you/she/he didn't want to go to work any more or didn't want to fix dinner any more and refused to do so?)

WHAT WOULD HAPPEN?

HOW WOULD YOUR/HIS/HER HUSBAND/WIFE FEEL (REACT)?

HOW WOULD YOUR/HIS/HER CHILDREN FEEL (REACT)?

WHAT WOULD YOUR/HIS/HER FRIENDS THINK?

B. MAN

- Harold Wilson is a 30 year old man. Describe what you think would be a typical day in his life.

- By a typical day I mean a typical weekday.

GENERAL PROBES:

- WOULD YOU (BARBARA, HAROLD) EVER DECIDE TO DO THE OPPOSITE?

5 and 9

SUBJECT I.D. #_____

TYPICAL DAY TEST

(I.e., would you/he/she ever decide to stay away from home all day or get a job instead of caring for the children?)

WHAT WOULD HAPPEN?

HOW WOULD YOUR/HIS/HER HUSBAND/WIFE FEEL (REACT)?

HOW WOULD YOUR/HIS/HER CHILDREN FEEL (REACT)?

WHAT WOULD YOUR/HIS/HER FRIENDS THINK?

- WHAT WOULD HAPPEN IF YOU (BARBARA, HAROLD) DID NOT WANT TO DO WHAT YOU/ SHE/HE NORMALLY WOULD DO?
  (I.e., what if you/she/he didn't want to go to work any more or didn't want to fix dinner any more and refused to do so?)

WHAT WOULD HAPPEN?

HOW WOULD YOUR/HIS/HER HUSBAND/WIFE FEEL (REACT)?

HOW WOULD YOUR/HIS/HER CHILDREN FEEL (REACT)?

WHAT WOULD YOUR/HIS/HER FRIENDS THINK?

C. WOMAN

- Barbara Smith is a 30 year old woman. Describe what you think would be a typical day in her life.

5 and 9
SUBJECT I.D. # _____

TYPICAL DAY TEST

- By a typical day, I mean a typical weekday.

GENERAL PROBES:

- WOULD YOU (BARBARA, HAROLD) EVER DECIDE TO DO THE OPPOSITE?
(I.e., would you/he/she ever decide to stay away from home all day or get a job instead of caring for the children?)

WHAT WOULD HAPPEN?

HOW WOULD YOUR/HIS/HER HUSBAND/WIFE FEEL (REACT)?

HOW WOULD YOUR/HIS/HER CHILDREN FEEL (REACT)?

WHAT WOULD YOUR/HIS/HER FRIENDS THINK?

- WHAT WOULD HAPPEN IF YOU (BARBARA, HAROLD) DID NOT WANT TO DO WHAT YOU/SHE/HE NORMALLY WOULD DO?
(I.e., what if you/she/he didn't want to go to work any more or didn't want to fix dinner any more and refused to do so?)

WHAT WOULD HAPPEN?

HOW WOULD YOUR/HIS/HER HUSBAND/WIFE FEEL (REACT?)

HOW WOULD YOUR/HIS/HER CHILDREN FEEL (REACT?)

WHAT WOULD YOUR/HIS/HER FRIENDS THINK?

5 and 9
SUBJECT I.D. # _____

SEMANTIC DIFFERENTIAL TEST

A. SELF

FOR THIS TEST, LET THE 10 AND 15 YEAR OLDS
MARK THE SHEETS THEMSELVES

- This is a list of words which are approximate opposites.
  I want you to put an "X" where you think you best fit
  between each pair of words.

GO THROUGH THE MEANINGS OF THE WORDS
CAREFULLY

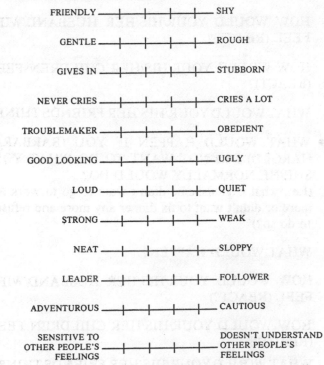

FRIENDLY ———|———|———|———|——— SHY

GENTLE ———|———|———|———|——— ROUGH

GIVES IN ———|———|———|———|——— STUBBORN

NEVER CRIES ———|———|———|———|——— CRIES A LOT

TROUBLEMAKER ———|———|———|———|——— OBEDIENT

GOOD LOOKING ———|———|———|———|——— UGLY

LOUD ———|———|———|———|——— QUIET

STRONG ———|———|———|———|——— WEAK

NEAT ———|———|———|———|——— SLOPPY

LEADER ———|———|———|———|——— FOLLOWER

ADVENTUROUS ———|———|———|———|——— CAUTIOUS

SENSITIVE TO OTHER PEOPLE'S FEELINGS ———|———|———|———|——— DOESN'T UNDERSTAND OTHER PEOPLE'S FEELINGS

5 and 9
SUBJECT I.D. # _____

SEMANTIC DIFFERENTIAL TEST

B. MOST BOYS
FOR THIS TEST, LET THE 10 and 15 YEAR OLDS
MARK THE SHEETS THEMSELVES

- This is a list of words which are approximate opposites.
  I want you to put an "X" where you think *most boys* fit
  best between each pair of words.

GO THROUGH THE MEANINGS OF THE WORDS
CAREFULLY

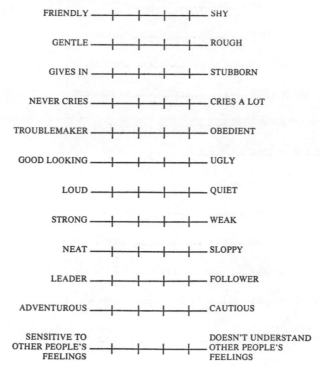

FRIENDLY	SHY
GENTLE	ROUGH
GIVES IN	STUBBORN
NEVER CRIES	CRIES A LOT
TROUBLEMAKER	OBEDIENT
GOOD LOOKING	UGLY
LOUD	QUIET
STRONG	WEAK
NEAT	SLOPPY
LEADER	FOLLOWER
ADVENTUROUS	CAUTIOUS
SENSITIVE TO OTHER PEOPLE'S FEELINGS	DOESN'T UNDERSTAND OTHER PEOPLE'S FEELINGS

5 and 9
SUBJECT I.D. # _____

SEMANTIC DIFFERENTIAL TEST

C. MOST GIRLS
FOR THIS TEST, LET THE 10 AND 15 YEAR OLDS
MARK THE SHEETS THEMSELVES

- This is a list of words which are approximate opposites.

- Here, I want you to put an "X" where you think *most girls* fit best between each pair of words.

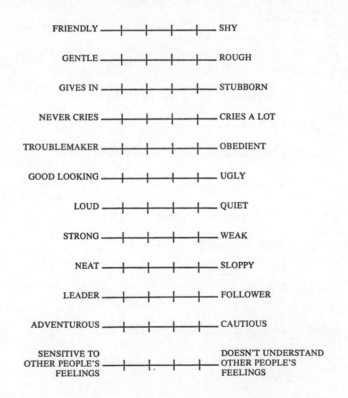

FRIENDLY	SHY
GENTLE	ROUGH
GIVES IN	STUBBORN
NEVER CRIES	CRIES A LOT
TROUBLEMAKER	OBEDIENT
GOOD LOOKING	UGLY
LOUD	QUIET
STRONG	WEAK
NEAT	SLOPPY
LEADER	FOLLOWER
ADVENTUROUS	CAUTIOUS
SENSITIVE TO OTHER PEOPLE'S FEELINGS	DOESN'T UNDERSTAND OTHER PEOPLE'S FEELINGS

5 and 9
SUBJECT I.D. #_____

SEMANTIC DIFFERENTIAL TEST

D. BOYS SHOULD BE
FOR THIS TEST, LET THE 10 AND 15 YEAR OLDS
MARK THE SHEETS THEMSELVES

- This is a list of words which are approximate opposites.

- Here, I want you to put an "X" where you think *most
  boys should* fit between each pair of words.

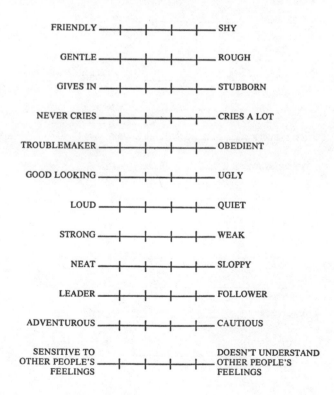

FRIENDLY ——|——|——|——|—— SHY

GENTLE ——|——|——|——|—— ROUGH

GIVES IN ——|——|——|——|—— STUBBORN

NEVER CRIES ——|——|——|——|—— CRIES A LOT

TROUBLEMAKER ——|——|——|——|—— OBEDIENT

GOOD LOOKING ——|——|——|——|—— UGLY

LOUD ——|——|——|——|—— QUIET

STRONG ——|——|——|——|—— WEAK

NEAT ——|——|——|——|—— SLOPPY

LEADER ——|——|——|——|—— FOLLOWER

ADVENTUROUS ——|——|——|——|—— CAUTIOUS

SENSITIVE TO
OTHER PEOPLE'S ——|——|——|——|—— DOESN'T UNDERSTAND
OTHER PEOPLE'S
FEELINGS   FEELINGS

5 and 9
SUBJECT I.D. #_____

SEMANTIC DIFFERENTIAL TEST

E. GIRLS SHOULD BE
FOR THIS TEST, LET THE 10 AND 15 YEAR OLDS MARK THE SHEETS THEMSELVES

- Here, I want you to put an "X" where you think *most girls should* fit between each pair of words.

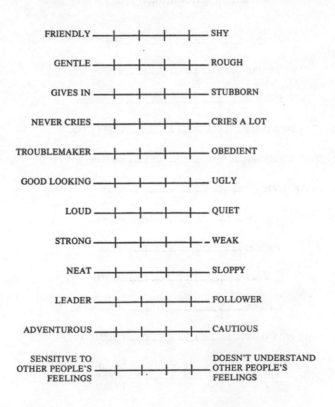

FRIENDLY —|——|——|——|— SHY

GENTLE —|——|——|——|— ROUGH

GIVES IN —|——|——|——|— STUBBORN

NEVER CRIES —|——|——|——|— CRIES A LOT

TROUBLEMAKER —|——|——|——|— OBEDIENT

GOOD LOOKING —|——|——|——|— UGLY

LOUD —|——|——|——|— QUIET

STRONG —|——|——|——|— WEAK

NEAT —|——|——|——|— SLOPPY

LEADER —|——|——|——|— FOLLOWER

ADVENTUROUS —|——|——|——|— CAUTIOUS

SENSITIVE TO OTHER PEOPLE'S FEELINGS —|——|——|——|— DOESN'T UNDERSTAND OTHER PEOPLE'S FEELINGS

5 and 9
Sub. I.D. #_____

• Now I want you to mark your answers to some more questions.

Beside each question are the numbers 1 to 5. You answer the question by circling the number that best says what you think. On each question you will be given what 1, 2, 3, 4, and 5 mean.

For example:

	very much	quite a bit	somewhat	a little bit	not at all
A. How much do you like apples?	5	4	3	2	1

5 means you like them very much.
4 means you like them quite a bit, but not as
   much as 5.
3 means you like them somewhat.
2 means you like them a little bit.
1 means you don't like them at all.

	almost always	often	some of the time	little of the time	hardly ever
B. How often do you like to watch TV?	5	4	3	2	1

5 means you like to watch almost always.
4 means you like to watch often.
3 means you like to watch some of the time.
2 means you only like to watch a little of the
   time.
1 means you hardly every like to watch.

5 and 9

SUBJECT I.D. #_____

Pick the number that you *think is the best answer for* you.
Remember, there are no right or wrong answers.

	very interesting	interesting	fairly interesting	little bit interesting	not interesting
1. How interesting do you think boys' books are?	5	4	3	2	1
2. How interesting do you think women's magazines are?	5	4	3	2	1
3. How interesting are women's occupations? (Jobs you get paid for.)	5	4	3	2	1
4. How interesting do you think men's magazines are?	5	4	3	2	1
5. How interesting do you think men's jobs are?	5	4	3	2	1
6. How interesting do you think girls' books are?	5	4	3	2	1
7. How interesting to play with do you think boys' toys are?	5	4	3	2	1

	very happy	happy	fairly happy	a little bit happy	not happy
8. How happy do you think most girls you know are?	5	4	3	2	1

	great fun	a lot of fun	some fun	a little fun	no fun
9. How much fun do you think girls' games are?	5	4	3	2	1

5 AND 9
SUBJECT I.D. #_____

	great fun	a lot of fun	some fun	a little fun	no fun
10. How much fun do you think boys' hobbies are?	5	4	3	2	1
11. How much fun do you think girls' hobbies are?	5	4	3	2	1
12. How much fun do you think boys' games are?	5	4	3	2	1

	very much	quite a bit	somewhat	a little bit	not at all
13. How much do you like women's clothes?	5	4	3	2	1
14. How much do you like men's TV shows?	5	4	3	2	1
15. If you could be born again, how much would you like to be a girl?	5	4	3	2	1
16. How much do you like girls' TV shows?	5	4	3	2	1
17. How much do you like girls' clothes?	5	4	3	2	1
18. How much do you like boys' clothes?	5	4	3	2	1
19. If you could be born again, how much would you like to be a boy?	5	4	3	2	1

	very much	quite a bit	somewhat	a little bit	not at all
20. How much do you like boys' TV shows?	5	4	3	2	1
21. How much do you like men's clothes?	5	4	3	2	1
22. How much do you like women's TV shows?	5	4	3	2	1

5 and 9
SUBJECT I.D. #_____

	dislike very much	dislike quite a bit	dislike somewhat	don't mind much	don't mind at all
23. How much do you dislike men's chores at home?	5	4	3	2	1
24. How much do you dislike girls' chores at home?	5	4	3	2	1

	almost always	often	some of the time	a little of the time	hardly ever
25. How often do you think it would be fun to be a man?	5	4	3	2	1

Index